"this grand supply"

The Samuel Hodgdon Letterbooks

1778-1784

Volume 1:
July 19, 1778-March 31, 1781

Joseph Lee Boyle

HERITAGE BOOKS
2011

HERITAGE BOOKS
AN IMPRINT OF HERITAGE BOOKS, INC.

Books, CDs, and more—Worldwide

For our listing of thousands of titles see our website
at
www.HeritageBooks.com

Published 2011 by
HERITAGE BOOKS, INC.
Publishing Division
100 Railroad Ave. #104
Westminster, Maryland 21157

Copyright © 2011 Joseph Lee Boyle

All rights reserved. No part of this book may be reproduced or transmitted in any form or by any means, electronic or mechanical, including photocopying, recording or by any information storage and retrieval system without written permission from the author, except for the inclusion of brief quotations in a review.

International Standard Book Numbers
Paperbound: 978-0-7884-5256-7
Clothbound: 978-0-7884-8601-2

CONTENTS

Introduction	vii
Editorial Procedure	xiii
The Documents	1
Document Chronology	304
Index	315

Introduction

In the holdings of the National Archives can be found Record Group 93, Microfilm Publication 853, Numbered Record Books Concerning Military Operations and Service, Pay and Settlement of Accounts, and Supplies in the War Department Collection of Revolutionary War Records. On Roll 33 are "Letters sent by Samuel Hodgdon, 07/1778-05/1784." This is somewhat of a misnomer, as the contents are letters Sent by Commissary General of Military Stores and Assistant Quartermaster Samuel Hodgdon, Commissary General of Military Stores Benjamin Flower, and Deputy Commissary of Military Stores Richard Frothingham, July 19, 1778-May 24, 1784.

These letters concern the procurement, shipment, repair and sale of military stores; estimates of stores needed and on hand; construction of ordnance installations; and payment and discharge of employees. Though authored by the three men, Samuel Hodgdon produced the majority of them in his various positions in the military stores operations of the Continental Army.

There are a large number of other records concerning the military stores department in this collection at the National Archives including: Volumes 77-81, 104-106. Receipt Books of Samuel Hodgdon, Commissary General of Military Stores and Assistant Quarter-Master General, Oct. 1778-Sept. 1779 and Mar. 1780-Nov. 1789; Volumes 100 and 144. Ledgers of Accounts with Officers, Other Persons, and States, 1778-92; Volume 114. Record of Receipts and Disbursements, Commissary General of Military Stores Department, Mar. 11, 1780-Oct. 7, 1781; Volume 117. Record of Disbursements by Samuel Hodgdon, Deputy Commissary General of Military Stores, Mar. 22, 1780-Mar. 8, 1781; Volume 152. Ledger of Samuel Hodgdon, 1777-98. The largely unpublished letters of

Henry Knox and Timothy Pickering also hold a great deal of information on the procurement, fabrication, repair and transportation functions, of the hundreds of items needed by the American military.

The Military Stores Department of the Continental Army has a complex history, which has not been fully researched. The best studies are: "A Most Intricate Department: The Commissary General of Military Stores or Ordnance Department under Benjamin Flower and Samuel Hodgdon, 1777-1782, Masters Thesis, University of Maryland, 1984, and Erna Risch, *Supplying Washington's Army* (Washington, D.C.: Government Printing Office, 1981). The latter only summarizes each staff department's history.

In July 1775, the Continental Congress authorized appointment of a Commissary of Military Stores, who was responsible for the receipt and issuance of military stores. George Washington was appointed to this post, but served only the main Continental Army besieging Boston. Other men were appointed to similar positions where there were significant American forces. Cheever served with the army until 1777, then assumed a post at the "Elaboratory" and magazine at Springfield, Massachusetts. None of these men had the wide authority and responsibility needed for the job.

Finally recognizing the need for an expansion in the supply of military stores in a prolonged war, Congress resolved October 1776, to establish cannon foundries, establish artillery artificer companies, and, as Henry Knox put it, attend to "a thousand other matters belonging to the Artillery." The Commissary General of Military Stores was formally established in 1777, under the command of Benjamin Flower, who received the rank of lieutenant colonel. Flower had been Commissary of Military Stores of the Flying Camp. As with all the supply departments, it was reorganized by Congress several times during the course of the war. This department was responsible for supplying the Continental Army with ammunition, arms, and accoutrements, and performing repairs as necessary.

In 1777 four companies of artillery artificers were raised and then a fifth, and put under Flower's command in February 1778 as the Regiment of Artillery Artificers. These men were distinct from artificers in the Quartermaster's department, whose artificer arrangement was formalized by Congress in November 1779 with the establishment of a Quartermaster Artificer Regiment of nine companies, in a unit commanded by Jeduthan Baldwin.

In February 1778, Flower was put under the direction of a Congressionally appointed Board of War. Flower was now to construct and manage armories, magazines and foundries to manufacture military stores, as well as to contract for, receive, and repair raw materials and stores. Working in this department were a variety of commissaries, deputy commissaries, clerks, wagon conductors, and clerks.

The artificer units were in the field or at work in manufacturing centers such as Carlisle, Pennsylvania, and Springfield, Massachusetts. To confuse things, artificers units in the field were under the command of a separate Board of Ordnance, headed by Brigadier General Henry Knox, while Flower was in direct charge of the others. It should be remembered that the term ordnance was defined in the eighteenth century to include all weapons, their ammunition, and accoutrements.

The importance of artificers to the army cannot be over-estimated. They produced cartridges and ammunition and repaired wagons used for transport as well as the harness. They repaired arms and artillery, shod horses, made and repaired tools and military accoutrements, and produced castings of all types. In 1779 Quartermaster General Nathanael Greene wrote a man "can as well feed himself without hands as an Army move without Artificers." In winter cantonments blacksmithing, gunsmithing, harness making, and woodworking shops would be established. Also a laboratory structure was built or taken over, where rifle and artillery cartridges were prepared.

An example of their productiveness is the winter encampment at Middlebrook, 1778-1779. In the Spring of 1779, about one quarter of the troops, were issued new or repaired arms. Of the 8,974 men, 2,173 new or repaired muskets were issued, 33% received new bayonets, 72% new cartridge boxes. And this was after Washington ordered Knox to send damaged weapons to Philadelphia for repair.

The separation of field and static ordnance operations created serious problems in the supply of military stores. Knox, as Washington's ordnance chief, was the man most familiar with the army's needs. However he had little control over what was produced at the manufacturing centers. Amazingly he found it impossible to obtain regular returns (lists) of supplies on hand or in production at the various centers, so that the army command was unclear what materiel it would have coming.

Knox therefore often had his field artificers duplicate the work of the artificers in the manufacturing centers, and the army was often hit with a critical supply shortage. This was aggravated by the immense difficulties in transportation. Carlisle, Pennsylvania, in the interior of that state was safe from enemy raids. But to supply Washington's army, the supplies had to come across several major unbridged rivers, subject to seasonal flooding or icejams.

By the fall of 1778 Knox was threatening to resign if the situation was not improved, and went to Congress in Philadelphia in January 1779, to plead his case. Knox obtained some relief. The Board of War was required to submit monthly returns to Washington, who passed these to Knox. Knox was also given control of a large field operation, at the head of which was the new position of Field Commissary of Military Stores. Samuel Hodgdon was appointed to this position, responsible for collecting and issuing all military stores in the field.

The men in the Military Stores organization were often given short shrift by the other departments who were tasked to supply the army with food and clothing. Hodgdon once wrote to Knox that had he not undertaken to feed his 200 or so men himself he would have fallen "a prey to their voracious Jaws." Shortages of clothing, food, and pay were epidemic problems in the Continental Army through the war.

By 1780 the "Regiment of Artillery and Artificers in the Department of the Commissary General of Military Stores" was on a fairly good footing and the magazines and supply operations at Carlisle, Philadelphia, and Springfield, seemed to be operating fairly well. There were seniority and organizational disputes, but these can be expected in any bureaucracy.

During this period the Continental Army operations in the Carolinas and Georgia were not matters of much concern for this department. In 1780, after the American disaster at Camden, some of the artificer units moved in Virginia. That state received much more attention as a result of the Yorktown campaign in 1781, and thereafter more attention was paid to Nathanael Greene's southern army.

Flower had been sickly since 1778, and finally died on April 28, 1781. On July 11, 1781, the Continental Congress appointed Hodgdon Commissary General of Military Stores, but did not give him Flower's military rank.

Samuel Hodgdon was born in Boston on September 3, 1745, but after the Revolution settled in Philadelphia, where he became well known as a public official and business man. During the war he had held various posts. In 1776 he was a Lieutenant in the Marines. In 1777, while occupying the post of Captain of Artillery, he was made principal Field Commissary of Military Stores. Hodgdon apparently carried out the duties of Field Commissary satisfactorily, for in 1780, upon the recommendation of the Board of War, the Continental Congress appointed him Deputy commissary general, and the next year promoted him to the post of Commissary General of Military Stores. As the war wound down, he also served as Assistant to the Quartermaster General, Timothy Pickering.

After 1781, and Cornwallis's surrender, there were no more major actions for Continental Army units. Hodgdon's letters now assumed a less frantic tone. By 1783, with peace a certainty, Hodgdon was well on his way towards dismantling his operations and disposing of its assets.

In the spring of 1783, when it became obvious that the war was finally drawing to a close and that both their departments faced eventual abolishment, Hodgdon and Pickering decided to enter business. The post of Commissary General of Military Stores was abolished July 20, 1785, and Hodgdon was out of public office, but only temporarily. His old friend Henry Knox, was named Secretary of War in 1785, and in 1788 Hodgdon was back on his old job, though this time under the lesser title of Commissary of Military Stores.

In 1785 Congress had also abolished the position of Quartermaster General. In 1791, after increasing problems with Indians on the frontier, Hodgdon was nominated for the position of Quartermaster General by President Washington and confirmed by the Senate, as Quartermaster of the army being raised for General St. Clair's expedition into the Western frontier.

In accepting his appointment, Hodgdon had promised to conduct the business of his office economically, and he did so, but unfortunately his economy in the procurement of supplies was at the expense of quality. Many of the items he forwarded were obtained from the surplus stock of the Revolutionary War and were urgently in need of repair. Not only quality but quantity was lacking in the supplies forwarded.

Hodgdon's lack of first-hand knowledge of the frontier was illustrated by the fact that the pack saddles he supplied from the East were too large to fit the smaller-sized horses of the western country. His inexperience with frontier conditions was further revealed by the fact that he procured fewer than a hundred axes, all of poor quality, and only one grindstone for an army proceeding into a wilderness where a road had to be cleared for the artillery and forts had to be erected.

On November 4, 1791, Arthur St. Clair suffered a devastating defeat to the Indians, at the Battle of the Wabash River, losing three times the number that Custer did at the Little Big Horn. General St. Clair held Hodgdon largely responsible for the entire fiasco. A Congressional committee appointed to investigate St Clair's defeat, reported on May 8, 1792, laid the burden of blame for failure of the expedition upon "the delays consequent upon the gross and various mismanagements and neglects in the Quartermaster's and contractor's departments," and exonerated completely the commander-in-chief.

Hodgdon served as Quartermaster General until April 19, 1792. Hodgdon was replaced by James O'Hara as Quartermaster General under the new arrangements made to retrieve the prestige of the army on the frontier. O'Hara respected Hodgdon's business ability, since he appointed him his deputy in charge of Quartermaster accounts at Philadelphia because of his industry and knowledge. Washington apparently did not lose faith in Hodgdon, as he reappointed him in 1794 under the new title of Superintendent of Military Stores, an office he held until Jefferson was elected President in 1800. Thereafter he pursued a successful business career, which culminated in his selection to the presidency of a trust and insurance firm, the Pennsylvania Company, in 1813. He died in Philadelphia on June 9, 1824, at the age of seventy-eight.

Editorial Procedure

These documents present a literal translation with spelling, punctuation and grammar remaining as they are found in the original. Each writer's abbreviations and contractions are also preserved as they are found in the manuscripts. Capital letters follow the text of the originals, although it is often a guess whether a letter is a capital or not. Brackets indicate questionable or illegible letters and words. *Sic* is used very sparingly as it would quickly detract from the text, given the numerous variants of spelling and oddities of expression.

Names are spelled a variety of ways in the letters. How James Gililand/Giliand/Gilliland and Joseph/Eayrs/Ayers/Eyres preferred their names to be spelled could be conjectural. In other cases such as Samuel Sarjant/Sarjent/Sargent, Sarjant is how the man signed his name. I have kept the names the way they appear in the text, but standardized them as much as possible in the index.

Letters are introduced by the names of the addresser and addressee. The dateline falls just below the heading, though the original document may have it at the bottom. The complimentary close is brought up flush with the last paragraph and the closing signature has been omitted. A note at the foot of each entry identifies the writer and recipient the first time each individual appears.

The index includes the names of all persons. However place names are selected, depending on relevance and frequency. Casual references to New York, for example, have been omitted. The letters contain so many references to materials and products, that it was not practicable to index every reference. For those seeking every mention of transportation problems, for example, the text itself will need to be reviewed.

To John Ruddock

Sir   Crotin Bridge [Croton Bridge, N.Y.] 19 July 1778
The great Consumption of Cannon Amunition in the late Battle at Menmoth Renders it Necessary that A Supply be sent With all posable despatch to Camp
   200 Six pound strap shott
   200 four pound Ditto
   100 three pounds Ditto is Much Wanted Also
   100 Good Arms & Accutrments—
I have sent by Mr Giles C^y M Stores five Load of Damaged Arms & Amunition who Will Conduct the above stores to Camp

Ruddock was a Deputy Commissary of Military Stores at Fish Kill, N.Y. This refers to the Battle of Monmouth, N.J., on June 28, 1778.

To William Butler

Sir,   Camp Crotin Bridge [Croton Bridge, N.Y.] 19th July 1778
The Numbers of Recruts that dayly Joine the Army Renders it Necessary that three hundred New Arms be forwarded to Camp with all posable dispatch You will apply to the Qr, Mr,r Genl at Morristown for waggons; and send them by Mr. Jones C M Stores who will Conduct them to Camp

Butler was Conductor of Military Stores at Morristown, New Jersey.

To Ezekiel Cheever

Sir,   White Plains [N.Y.] 27th July 1778
Inclosed You have an Invoice of sundries Stores immedatly wanted for service—Mr Giles Cr M Stores Who bring this Will Conduct them to Camp

On August 17, 1775 Washington appointed Cheever Commissary of Artillery Stores in the Continental Army and he served in that position until 1777. He then assumed the post of Commissary of Military Stores at Springfield, Massachusetts, until his retirement in the summer of 1781.

To John Ruddock

Sir   Camp White Plains [N.Y.] Augt. 4th 1778

By the bearer you will receive four hundred and thirty damaged Musquets fifty one Bayonets and fourteen thousand nine hundred damaged musquet Cartridges, which you will please to receive and give a receipt for—the whole of the waggons are to be loaded back with musquet Cartridges of sizes. you will please to send those that are in the most perfect order, as an oversight in this particular might prove fatal—

If you have any Tin Tubes on hand you will please to forward me a 1000 of sized carefully pack't to prevent damage—

I shall from time to time send all our damaged stores to your charge entreating your exertions to have them repaired that you may be able to answer any sudden demand, as the General as well as myself look up to you with great expectation

I am Sir with respect and esteem Your most obedient

NB if you have any spare Waggon covers you will forward me 6 or more—

To John Ruddock

Sir   White plains [N.Y.] 4th Augt 1778

I send by Mr: Alexr. Turner Waggon Condr
43[0] Damaged Musquits
50 Bayonits
14,900 Damaged Musquit Cartri[dges]

Mr Hodgdon D,C.G,M,S has Wrote for such Necessarys as are Wanted pleas to Give Receipts Received of Saml French Cy: M Stores for the Above Articles

To John Ruddock

Sir,   Camp White plains [N.Y.] Augt 5th 1778

This moment I received your favor and invoice by Mr Conductor Austin, and am much obliged by your dispatch you will please in addition to other favours send me fifty weight white lead, to paint the waggons and other service—and what lamblack you can procure, if

you can procure the stamps from Springfield by which their waggons are mark't and number'd you will oblidge me much as our painter is not used to makg letters in so eligant a manner as I could wish— pencils suitable for the above service are wanting, I should be glad you would give Capt Call of Colo Stevens Artificers, orders from him [sic] if arrived at Fish Kill to embark with his men without loss of time by the way of Tarry Town for this Camp, you will supply him to begin his work takg his receipt for what you deliver—In great haste I Remain your Oblidged I and very humble sert—
NB I should be glad you would forward the new waggons every time you send stores—Padlocks I want much 6 Dozen—

To John Ruddock

Sir   Camp White Plains [N.Y.] August 7 1778
    The great demand for drums has obliged me to write you again, and to beg of you, by some means another to forward me on two or three dozen immeadiately and a number of spare drumsticks the demand being very great. snares Cord Carridges Slings Cats and Fife Boxes are much wanted. if you have any cartridge Box
es or bayonet Belts being pressed hard for the above if your have enough of any or all of them to load one Waggon you will please to forward them without loss of time this for the present finishes my publick demand
    Your very huml Servant

To John Ruddock

                        Camp White Plains [N.Y.] Augt 9th 1778
    Capt Call of the Artillery Artificers will deliver you a considerable quantity of harness, an Invoice of which he has with him. as it is all out of repair, the Genl directs that you immediately have it repaired, put in compleat setts and sent to Camp, as it is much wanted—the drums and Cartouch boxes which I wrote you for I beg you will see forwarded, also 100 more fifes—With sentiments of esteem I Remain yrs
NB you are by no means to let the quarter Master or any one else have the harniss it being exceedingly wanted—

To Benjamin Flower

Sir— Camp White Plains [N.Y.] Augt. 17th 1778
    Though I have been a considerable time in the department under your charge, yet acting the whole time in the northern Army and receiving my supplies from the eastern States I have been prevented from an introduction either personal or epistolary to you, having been lately by the decission of the honl. Brigadier Genl Knox taken charge of all the Stores on the ground, in order to act as principal in the department I have avail['d] myself of this opportunity by Mr. French to present my compliments to you and request your Orders and Assistance to enable me to a right and faithful discharge of the duties on my Office—
    With respect and Esteem I subscribe myself Your very huml Servant

Flower was the Commissary General of Military Stores and Colonel of the Artillery Artificer Regiment.

To John Ruddock

Sir Camp White Plains [N.Y.] Augt. 19th 1778
    Being just going out of camp, have only time to acknowledge the receipt of your kind Favor inclosing an Invoice of Tea & Sugar, neither have as yet arrived as soon as we receive them the Colo. will remit the money. the bearer Mr Conductor Gililand waits on you with this. you will please to receive and receipt the Articles brought by him, and load the four waggon[s] with musquet Cartridges back to Camp
    In great haste I remain Your obliged Friend

To John Ruddock

Dear Sir Camp White Plains [N.Y.] Augt. 29th 1778
    Inclosed you have an Invoice of Stores wanted at this post a number of the Articles You will find on board the Ammunition Sloop you will be pleased to apply to Mr Gidley Conductor on board and take every article mentioned in the Invoice, that he has from that Magazine, as it is judged best that the oldest preparations should be

first used. you will give him a receipt for what you take and forward to me, and I will receipt the whole to the Person that comes on with the Stores which will prevent Mistake—

I am sensible that you have not the whole of what is sent for, having seen your late return what is wanting you will please to procure as quick as possible—

Being short off for teams and being informed by Colo. Hay, that you can have them by applying to his Office, I thought it best not to send them for fear a movement should take place before they could Return

The cash you sent to my care for Colo Stevens and General Knox is safe arrived and I have delivered their contents. Colo Stevens being gone to Stamford prevents the money being sent at this Time, it will come the next safe conveyance Yours &c

NB the blacksmiths Tools mentioned were left with Mr Gidley, you will send them by water to Tarry Town—

Invoice of sundry Stores

50 Ready Shott 24 pounders	50 Havresacks
50 do. 12 do	25 Gunners Horns
26 Shells 8 Inch Howitzer	22 Tube Boxes
4 setts & Malletts do	100 wt. white Lead
100 Flannel Cartridges do	1 spare Carriage 8 Inch Howitzer
4 Tenant Saws	
4 Chizzels	1 pr large Bellows
4 Rasps	1 Anvill
100 24 pound Tubes	2 sledges
100 12 ditto	2 hand Hammers
200 4 ditto	

To Jasper Maduit Gidley

Sir Camp White Plains [N.Y.] Augt 29th 1778

I have been for a considerable time expecting a return from you of the Stores under your charge none having arrived. I am obliged to apply for one, which I expect will be made out very exact and sent me by the Bearer Mr Cunningham Conductor. not having frequent Returns leaves me in a criminal State of Ignorance respecting the stores which to avoid, I must insist they be made to me by every convenient opportunity

I have wrote to Mr Ruddock for a number of Stores of which the inclosed is a copy. I have directed him to apply to you for what Articles you have on board, as I intend they shall be used first. you will let him know what part of the invoice you can supply him with, the Blacksmith tools mentioned you will assist Mr Ruddock in forwarding down to Tarry Town—

Relying on your care and strict attention to your important charge I conclude and remain Yours &c

NB you will inform Mr Ruddock that he can get the white Lead wrote for by applying to Colo Hay—

Gidley was a Conductor of Military Stores.

To Captain Langdon

Sir Camp White Plains [N.Y.] Augt. 31st 1778

Upon recollection since I saw you, I think it best that you call at Windsor, and get your Vessell properly ton'd and keept the certificate of the tunnage, untill you return from Albany as it will make but a few days difference to you in getting your pay, and as I find it more convenient to pay the Bills in my own departmen[t.] I hope you will be enabled to make this Cruize with out your pay. by the time your return, I expect to have the money on hand and your account shall be immediately discharged—

I would not have you carry old Jones if you can possibly get any one else to go with you as he is much wanted in his company. Mr. Spear has an Invoice of what things you are to bring from Albany—

To the Director of Hibernia Furnace

Sir Camp White Plains [N.Y.] Augt. 31st 1778

Inclosed you have an order from General Knox for one thousand six pound Shott and one hundred twelve pound ditto. if you have any nines it would be well to send on one hundred of then you will please to give him all the assistance in your power to forward them on without a moments loss of time I am Sir Yours

Hibernia Furnace was in Morris County, New Jersey. It was owned by William Alexander (Lord Stirling), and was operated around this time by Charles Hoff Jr.

To Philip Van Rensselaer

Sir   Camp White Plains [N.Y.] Augt. 31st 1778
 The bearer Mr Spear waits on you with a number of small Arms to be repaired an Invoice of which you have in his receipt. you will please to receive them and give him a receipt for the sam[e.] if you have any Arms repaired completely fitted with Bayonets you will send them on in charge of Mr. Spear. I have given him a memorandum of several Articles much wanted here which you will please to supply if in your power. should the Vessel not be filled with the articles which she is immediately sent for, you will much oblidge me in sending down a number of Boards as our workmen stand still for want of them. I should also be glad if you will send me the receipt for the Arms & Bayonets delivered you by Mr Lansingh, nothing new. in great haste I remain Your's &c

Philip Van Rensselaer was Keeper of Military Stores at Albany, New York.

To John Ruddock

Sir   Camp White Plains [N.Y.] Augt 31st. 1778
 In consequence of orders from Brig. General Knox, I have forwarded one hundred three pound shot four pounders we have none on the ground. I have directed Mr Spear the bearer of this to call at fish-Kill to inquire if they can be had from thence if they can he will take them on with him—
 Having Nothing further to add I remain with respect Yours

To John Ruddock

Sir   Camp White Plains [N.Y.] Septr 3d 1778
 By Mr French I have an opportunity to send the money, for the Articles which you lately forwarded to camp to my care, which you will please to give him a receipt for: I am also to desire you if you

have any Arms on hand to forward them immediately, as the demand is again become very pressing. so great that I obliged to send express to Springfeild to hurry a number from thence I have seen the Gentleman who is employed by you, making Cartridge Boxes, he has met with some difficulty in procuring raw hides which he says was part of his contract. I spoke to Colo. Hamilton the Generals Secretary upon the Subject. he informed me he believed there would be no difficulty if he produced a Certificate which I doubt not you will furnish him with.

The Waggon that comes on with Mr French['s] Baggage you will please to load back with Arms or Musquet Cartridges. I was a good deal surprized at not receiving a letter from you in answer to mine, by Mr Conductor Cunningham as I perceive that a numb[er] of the Articles send for are not forwarded, the 12 pound Ready Shott of which there was plenty on board the Sloop is wanted immediately as the Guns must remain a dead weight until some arrive[s] but a very small proportion of 24 pounders on hand—Mr Cunningham informes me the sloop is discharged I should be obliged to you if you would enquire and let me know by whose order and what is become of the Stores. on that Magazine I placed a great dependance as I have no Laboratory to give me any assistance nor is possible in Camp to form one for any considerable Services

I have nothing further to add but my fervent wishes for your prosperity. I am Dear Sir Yours &ca

To Jasper Maduit Gidley

Sir,   Camp White Plain [N.Y.] Septr. 3d 1778
When I wrote you last, you are sensible I did not know that the Sloop was discharged and you are sensible that my Information did not come from you at last. what I request from you now is, to let me know by whose order it was done and what is become of the Stores

To Ezekiel Cheever

Dear Colo.   Camp White Plains [N.Y.] Septr. 3d 1778
Inclosed you have an order from Genl. Knox for one thousand stand of Arms. the demand for them is again become very pressing

Mr. Conductor Douglas the bearer of this will take the immediate Care of them and any other Stores destined for this Army. we are exceedingly in want of Cartridge Boxes, by reason of which a vast deal of Ammunition is lost. if you have any on hand you will please to forward them by this conveyance. A number of Ready Shott 24 pounders twelves sixes & three's are much wanted, and a few Drums, this is all I shall trouble you about at this Time—
I have nothing particular in the News way, only the destruction of twenty six of our Indians, who were cut to pieces by the British Light Horse upon our Lines being on a Scout about two Days since—
my compliments to Mr Collins and regards to you, finishes this from Yours &c.

To Anthony Post

Sir   Camp White Plains [N.Y.] Septr. 5th 1778
Inclosed you have an order from Genl. Knox to forward Mr. Patten and Blacksmiths under his charge to this Place if it is in your Power to procure some Iron either from your own Stock or of the quarter Master Genl. at Fish Kills I should be very glad. as we are very scant here, and Smith work in great Demand an other Article axceedingly wanted here is white lead, as the Carriages are suffering for paint, and not one ounce to be had. the General would be glad if you could procure only one quarter of a Hundred and send with Mr. Patten. Oil we have plenty but being in great haste and nothing new to communicate I conclude & remain Sir Your very hum Servt.

Post was a Captain in the Second Continental Artillery Regiment.

To Stephen Buckland

Sir   Camp White Plains [N.Y.] Septr. 5th 1778
The painter being now out of employment for want of paints, and hearing that there was a large quantity of white Lead at West Point, the General has thought proper to order it brought to this place. you will please therefore to send it forward to Tarry Town with some trusty person, without delay as the carriages are suffering for want of it. when the person you send with it arrives at Tarry Town he is immediately to give information of it that no time may be lost. I

should have written to Colo. Malcom for the white Lead mentioned above but judging it to be in your immediate care, I thought the application to you would answer Genl Knox's design of having it forwarded without a moments loss of time. My compliments to the Gentlemen and congratulations to Mr. Ingersole concludes this while in the fervor of devotion I subscribe myself—Yours &c.

Buckland was a Captain in the Third Continental Artillery Regiment.

To Timothy Pickering Jr.

Sir Camp White Plains [N.Y.] Sept 14th. 1778
 Inclosed you have the return of all the military stores in this Camp, which you will please to present to your honble Board, assuring them that as it is my duty so it is my inclination to comply with every Resolution of their's respecting my Department, within the compass of my knowledge. if their should be any of a late date must beg your assistance for a sight of them as that is a circumstance on which the faithfull performance of my duty much depends—With respect I am Sir your very honble Servt

Pickering, from Massachusetts had been Adjutant General of the Continental Army at this time was a member of the Board of War and Ordnance. He became Quarter Master General on August 5, 1780.

To Jonathan Gostelowe

Dear Major Danbury [CT] Octr. 5th 1778
By Mr. Conductor Freeman I have an opportunity to acknowledge the receipt of your two very polite Letters. the one by Mr. Baker the other p[er] post, the last not received untill a considerable time after its Date, in this I was informed of a Number of Cartridge Boxes being sent to Eliza. Town to Genl. Maxwell, but not distributed untill the Generals pleasure should be signified by me. I in consequence waited on the General who informed me for various reasons, he did not chuse to have them retained, and I have by his orders sent on Mr. Freeman to bring them to Camp when arrived I understand they are not to be given out, but carefully stored, that if another Campaign should be

necessary the whole Army may be provided for in the Spring, it gives me sensible pleasure to hear you are likely to make a figure in the accoutrement way speedily as it will be a great saving to the continent and a grand addition to the Army in Military appearance which has a natural tendency to make it formidable. the musquetry you inform me is in your immediate charge, and request I would inform you what is most wanted in Camp[.] at present can only say that without something extraordinary turns up we have a plenty of Musquet Cartrid[ges.] as to Bayonet Scabbards and Belts we are incessantly haunted for them as well as Cartridge Boxes, but do not think it likely if these were at present on hand that the General would chuse to have them delivered untill the whole can be completely furnished; for which reason I have not sent for any, as they would be liable to waste and damage in the frequent removes we make in this our pilgrimage State. however must beg of you not to relax in the least having them ready to send when called for—

I have now to beg the favor of you to furnish me with a sett of Books of the same dimensions of Major French's, which he informs me are the same Size as those you use. your kind compliance in this Instance will serve me much and the favor shall be gratefully acknowledged—News I have none we every moment expect orders to move to the eastward but this depends altogether upon the enemies movements—

Major French is not yet returned from Boston but expect him in about a fortnight, the Gentlemen of the Department join me in complements to you, and the Gentlemen present with you

having nothing further to add at present I conclude and remain Your very Hum Servant

Gostelowe was a Major and Commissary of Military Stores.

To James Pearson

Dear Major   Danbury [CT] Octr. 5th 1778

By Mr. Conductor Freeman I have the pleasure of acknowledging the receipt of your kind Letter and Invoice by Mr Baker which I should have answered by him but that I was at Fredericksburgh when he arrived at Danbury. upon first sight of your Letter informing of the great want of Steel, I determined to return to Camp and see Colo. Petit the QMG and procure and forward as much as could possibly be spared[.] upon application he informed me that he know not exactly what quantity he had on hand but what there was I should have. the small quantity forwarded proved to be all. however he says he believes he has a quantity by this time at Fish Kill. when that arrives we may have the full demand, which I shall forward without any loss of time

At present I do not find it necessary for any more Stores to be forwarded, as soon as a prospect of more being wanted arrives I shall endeavo[ur] to give timely notice. what dependance I may place on the Laboratories to the eastward I have not as yet been able to ascertain but think its likely to be very considerable; should we still incline to the Eastward and find the Magazines well stored it will save a vast expence of transportation as well as prevent damage to the Stores—

Agreable to your direction I shall give orders for the return of all Ammunition Boxes that may be emptied in the several Brigades but have not much confidence in the orders having the desired effect as the frequent removes in a Country where the Roads are exceedingly rough is very unfriendly to Boxes composed of such heavy Articles as the several species of Ammunition nevertheless you may depend that is this & very other instance I shall exert myself to save expence to the publick—

With respect I remain Your Hum Servant

Pearson was a Major and Commissary of Military Stores at Philadelphia.

To Henry Knox

Honred Sir   Danbury [CT] Octr. 7th 1778

Agreable to your directions, I have procured a convenient place in New Milford to store such articles as are not immediately wanted to be delivered. Vizt the new Arms Cartridge boxes Pistols Carbines, a quantity of Musquet Cartridges &c &c upon the return of the waggons I loaded them up with a propotion of every species of stores on hand, and they are now paraded ready to march at a moments warning, every single box having been overhawld; those much damaged, of which there was considerable I have left in the Barn, where the Men are employed repairing ammunition, hope shortly to have the greatest part of it fit for use. for this purpose I must beg you would order Mr Kircher Colo Stevens tinman to come down for a day to two, to mend the straped shott a general return is making out as soon as finished shall forward it to you, by which you will be inform'd the true state of the stores under my charge and enabld to make a calculation what further supplies may be necessary—I have not wrote for any more thinking that as we are no encumbered with more than we can carry on, and nearer than Usual to our principal Larboratory it was unnessesary. to your supperiour judgement, I submit this in common with other matters, begging your directions with which, in full confidence that they are right and that it is my duty I shall Chearfully comply—

with Respect and Esteem I Remain Yours &

Mr. Cunningham the bearer of this relieves Mr Giles who I am informed you have given the liberty of furlough—

Brigadier General Knox commanded the artillery of the Continental Army

To Mr. Gililand

Sir   Danbury [CT] Octr. 8 1778

You are immediately to repair to Peeks Kill deliver the letters you has directed to Mr. Conductor Gray the purport of which is, an order to deliver all the Stores he has on hand to Mr. Ruddock which you will see done, and take Mr: Ruddocks receipt for the same. tis possible Mr. Ruddock may chuse they should remain where they are at present. tis best therefore you take Mr. Grays return, and carry to Mr. Ruddock take his receipt upon that; and let him order the matter as best suits him with regard to removal. if Mr. Gray has delivered any of the Stores you will take his vouchers to whom delivered.

Having finished this Business you will proceed to Fish Kill landing, and take charge of the Stores now remaining in charge of Jasper M. Gidley, giving him receipt for the same. after which you will deliver the whole to Mr. Ruddock and take his receipt for the same. if any thing should happen to prevent my coming up within two or three days, you will bring the receipts to me, in order to my making a settlement with said Gidley. Yours

Gililand was a Conductor of Military Stores.

To Mr. Gray

Sir Danbury [CT] Octr. 8 1778

This you will receive by Mr Gililand CMS upon the receipt of which you will make out a very exact return of all the Stores you have on hand belonging to me, to furnish Mr Gililand with, who is going to Fish Kill to Mr. Ruddock to deliver them up to him and take his receipt for the same[.] if you have delivered any of the Stores you will give Mr. Gililand the Vouchers to bring down

The above is in consequence of my not expecting to want, the articles you have on hand, and therefore think it best to deliver them up to Mr. Ruddock, as it is very possible I may remove with the Army farther Eastward Yours

Gray was a Conductor of Military Stores.

To John Ruddock

Dr. Sir Danbury [CT] Octr: 8 1778

By an intimation given me this day, from you by Mr. Giliiand, I have judged it best immediately to relieve Mr Gidley at the Landing. Mr Gililand is forwarded for that purpose. I have directed him to call at Peeks Kill and take an exact return of what Stores Mr Gray has in charge of mine, in order to deliver them to you. they are such Articles as I shall not want in Camp, you will please to receive them and receipt the same

Mr Gililand has instructions to take the stores from Gidley and give him a receipt for them to enable him to settle his accounts, after which he is also to deliver them to you. if I should want them afterwards, I can write you and as timely be supplied. I expect the pleasure of seeing you soon which will give real satisfaction to your Friend & Huml Servant

To Jasper Maduit Gidley

Sir   Danbury [CT] Octr. 8 1778
Having written to you repeatedly and know that my letters were delivered calling upon you to let me know what you was about, and by whose order in a particular manner you landed the Military Stores left under your charge on board the Magazine Sloop, and receiving no answer makes me conclude that it is quite time to take them out of your hands, for which purpose I have dispatched Mr Conductor Gilliland you will immediately upon receipt of this make out an exact return of what Stores you have on hand and deliver them to him taking his receipt for the same, after which you will come immediately and settle your accounts Yours

As later letters show, Gidley remained with the Department.

To Timothy Pickering Jr.

Sir   Danbury [CT] Octo 10th 1778
Inclosed you have a return of the military stores at present in Camp. by an overhawl of the stores of every species On hand since last return, I found a considerable quantity damaged, upon which I applied to General Knox for a party of me to repair them which was readily granted, and the men are now employed. these with the return, I trust will be sufficient for Camp for this Campaign. if any thing should occur to make me alter my oppinion I shall endeavour to communicate the same to your honble board, timely enough to receive the supplies necessary

A considerable quantity of new Armes and Cartouch boxes, you will perceive are on hand these I am informed the General does not intend to have delivered at present, determining to collect as many of those articles togather as is possible, that the whole may be supplied at the opening of next Campaign. to prevent these taking damage, I have deposited them in a temporary Magazine, at New Milford, having obtained Gen. Knox['s] consent for that purpose—My whole attention shall at all times be employed for the preservation of the stores under my immediate charge and if I may be so happy as to obtain your approbation the height of my Ambition is gratified in confidence of which I subscribe my self your honors most Obdt. humble. Sert.

To Benjamin Flower

Sir   Danbury [CT] Octo 10th 1778
    I am now to acknowledge the receipt of your favour of the 26th of Augt, which I should with pleasure have answered sooner but that I did not receive it untill the day Mr Conductor Baker left Camp, which was a month after its date—
    you begin by saying you are "ignorant upon what principal I superseeded Mr French but you presume with propriety," I think Sir it is proper you should know that I was appointed Commissary by General Knox in Boston February the first 1777 and in that Capacity I acted to the Northward under General Gates, untill he was pleased to appoint me DCG which appointment I shall continue to think valid until I am convinced that he had not as good a right to appoint me to the last Office as General Knox had to the first,—perhaps neither are valid. However I thank you for your generous conclusion that it was with propriety—Agreable to your instructions, I shall endeavour to make the resolution of Congress to which you refer me, and the advice of General Knox the rule of my Conduct while I continue to act, in doing which be happy to meet with your approbation—
    Major French has been gone to Boston about a month. Their [*sic*] is considerable sums due in the department, wheather he has sufficient on hand to discharge the same I am not able to say. if not I trust upon his arrival he will apply to you for further assistance, as I understand he is to pay the department—
    As to what supplies may be expected from the Eastward at present can only say that I expect I have enough on hand to finish the present campaign, before the opening on the Next doubt not a considerable quantity will be ready of this I shall write you more perticular after having been to the eastward which I propose in about a month to do if nothing material turns up—
    I am exceedingly oblidged by your kind declaration of corresponding with and Affording me all the Assistance in your power, in return for which you may depend I shall loose no opportunity of letting you know the true state of the stores in Camp and any other Matters usefull or entertaining—With esteem I remain your very humble Servant
    NB should be glad to know whether any particular item has been

ordered for the subsistence of the department, likewise with respect to riding expences at present by order of General Knox I pay the [ ]th Conductors 10 dollars p[er] month and riding expences as p[er] Acct. sworn to—

To William Maxwell

Sir   Danbury [CT] Oct. 12 1778
The bearer Mr. Freeman Conductor of Military Stores waits on you by Order of his Excellency General Washington to receive and conduct to Camp Five hundred and seventy eight new constructed Cartridge Boxes which were some time in September last forwarded to you, by Major Gostelowe Commy Military Stores at Philadelphia. Tis not his Excellencys intention to have any of those Boxes delivered untill a sufficien[t] quantity is procured, to supply the Army in General With Respect I am Sir Your very hum Servant

Brigadier General Maxwell commanded the New Jersey Brigade.

To Benjamin Freeman

Danbury [CT] Octo 12th 1778
Sir by order of his Excellency General Washington you are to proceed to New Jersey and deliver the Letter you have directed to Brig General Maxwell, the purport of which is to deliver you five hundred and seventy eight new constructed Cartrige boxes to be forward to this place you will apply for teems to bring them on. which they are procuring which will necessarily take some time you will proceed to Philadelphia and deliver the letters you are charged with as directed. if you should meet with any difficulties with regard to receiving the boxes you will take further instructions from Colo Flowers or Major Gostelow you will exert yourself to execute this business in as little time and with as little expence as possible— wishing you consumate happiness and satisfaction while on your journey I am Sir Yours

Freeman was a Conductor of Military Stores.

To Henry Knox

Honred Sir   Danbury [CT] Octo 26th 1778
 By Mr Giles you will receive this the consequence of which is to know your pleasure with regard to retaining the Ordnance Schooner Capt Langdon, who has been employed transporting stores the past summer between Albany and the several fortresses on North River. I have delivered all the stores at Fish and Peek's-Kill's to Mr. Ruddock and they are now landed. The Vessell at present unemployed and the Capt waiting for Orders—you will please to signify your pleasure about the Matter by Mr Cunningham who is to return here upon the arrival of Mr Giles—I have sent you the powder and lead you requested, and further commands shall be punctually and Cheerfully comply'd with, by your honors humble Servant

To John Ruddock

Sir   Danbury [CT] Octo 26th 1778
 The bearer Mr Gilliland CMS waits on you with a quantity of damaged stores as pr invoice which you will please to receive, and receipt him for—I have heard of your misfortune, and am heartily sorry for it, hope by this time you have for comfortable—Mr Gilliland is very desirous of being stationed at the landing. I have promised him I would write you and inquire if any Conductor was wanting, at that place, if their should as I have all reason to believe him an honest Man I would recommend him to you, if he cannot be usefull there, however, I might be disposed to oblidge any Gentleman, yet I would never do it at the expence of the Publick
 Yours

To Giles and Alexander Thompson

Instructions for Messrs Giles & Thompson
 Gentlemen you are to repair to Fredericksburgh and take charge of the Military stores deposited there, you will be very carefull in taking proper receipts, and making regular entries of all stores received, or deliverd and every Saturday either send by some trusty or bring yourself back and Vouchers in order to their being regularly entred in my books,—all Arms turned in unreparible in Camp and all

other damaged stores you will send off to Mr. Ruddock at fish-kill taking especial care that they are carefully transported deliverd and receipted—
Yours

Giles and Thompson were Conductors of Military Stores. Giles may be Aquila Giles.

To Captain Langdon

Dr Sir   Danbury [CT] Octr 28 1778

General Knox informs me that it is no ways likely your Schooner will be wanted any longer in the Service, justice to the publick therefore obliges me to dismiss her you will please to obtain a Certificate from Captn Winslow of the time he first took her into the Service and the circumstances which made it necessary. after which make out your account of the Vessells tonnage and the time he was employed and I will endeavour to have it settled immediately
Yours &c.

To Benjamin Flower

Sir   Danbury [CT] Novr: 8th 1778

By Mr Freeman Cr. MS I received yours of the 19th. Octr. for which & the kind sentiments there in expressed be pleased to accept my hearty thanks. Inclosed you have a return of all the Stores on hand, dated as directed on the first of the Month which I shall for the Futur make a standing rule. shall always take it kind to be informed of any particulars to make & Keep the business in the Several local situations to each other regular especially at the Fountain head—

Major French's not being returned and an hourly expectation of the evacuation of the City of New York has prevented my making any preparation to go to the eastward as I informed you in my last was my intention and the event may possibly justify my opinion with respect to that matter, for since I have been writing I have received a Letter from Genl Knox of which the following is an exact copy Vizt.—

Sir

The Park is under marching orders you will please to get every thing ready to move at a days notice. I mean of those Teams destined to follow the Army—this Sir I am sanguine enough to hope is to take possession of that long abused City but of this more hereafter—

I am Still of the opinion that I have stores enough on hand to last this campaign, the New constructed Carte Boxes, which I have received are all deposited in a temporary Magazine which I have at New Milford and are not to be delivered with a special Genl Order untill the opening of the next campaign by which time Genl Knox expects to have enough of those very usefull articles to supply the whole army, for which reason I should think it best to have them Stored untill sent for. am much obliged to you for the information respecting the expences of the Department and find myself happy in the reflection, that I have acted in concert with you in any instance—

You will excuse my not being more particular as I am confined to time in writing having considerable to do just before a March relying on your kind declarations of writing me as often as circumstances will permit and informing me of any new regulations or arrangements in the Department necessary for me to know—

I conclude and remain with respect & esteem Your very huml Servt.

To James Pearson

Dear Major   Danbury [CT] Nov. 8 1778
By the Post I have an opportunity of informing you that I received your two favors dated Octr 1st & 20th in the first of which you informed me you had forwarded several species of Stores which came safe to hand and that you expected to forward a Number more of sorts in a few Days these having not arrived I impute to my Letter informing I had enough to finish the present campaign. in this opinion I am confirmed by the seperation of the Army, one Division vizt. Genl Gates is at Hartford within 25 Miles of Springfeild of consequence may be easily supplied from that Magazine one division more of the Army is at New Milford there I have a Magazine. the other is in the Neighbourhood of Fish Kill, were [sic] they will winter at present is uncertain but I have 50 Waggons loaded ready to attend them—

You inform me that the honl Board of War & Ordnance have directed Colo. Flower to collect the Standards and other Trophies taken from

the enemy since the commencement of the War gladly would I contribute to So grand a Design but nothing of that kind graced the Triumph in the North the enemy having destroyed or secreted them all if any should appear you may depend it shall be duly noted—
The German Steel which you mention I am in hopes you received as soon as I did you Letter, as I procured an Order on the AQMG at Morris Town for half a Ton by Mr. Duff of this you will please to inform me in your next—
As to the Pistols you may depend I shall forward them by the first opportunity or any thing else in my power to Supply which you may want I am exceedingly happy to find to [sic] many of the requisites of a Military Character going on in Philadelphia, think you have made rapid progress since the time the enemy left your City. doubt not that by the unremitting attention of the Gentlemen who have the Care of the Several Branches we should soon be completely furnished—
Being under marching orders and in haste I must conclude after having presented my respects to you and the Gentlemen with you in the Department—Yours &c.
CMS

To Jonathan Gostelowe

Dear Major Danbury [CT] Novemr. 8 1778

Your two favours of the 30th Septr: & 20th Octr. came safe to hand and are now before me nothing but being in want of the means could have prevented my answering the 1st by Mr Duff being in Camp without Pen & Ink or paper to compleat all it was the 17th Octr. that he went away that, being the glorious anniversary of Burgoynes Captivity you may judge what a situation the Camp must be in especially as the Day was by Genl Orders to be celebrated. this much I hope may acquit me of Blame. the Articles which you have sent from time to time have arrived in good order as did them by Mr. Duff, and I am extreamely happy to find by your letter that we are likely to have a fully supply of the important articles of Cartouch Boxes and Bayonet Belts as I am confident that the saving the Ammunition by the invention of the New constructed Carte Boxes, will pay for the whole in one Year. At present I would not wish to have them forwarded, as there is a prospect of the whole Army being supplied early in the Spring, should our days of Trial make another Campaign necessary, I should think it would be best to pack them up 100 in a Box with Belts compleat, and Store them for the present upon the first call for them I shall give you notice

I do not recollect any particular articles immediately wanted in your way the winter coming on makes me carefull in sending for any thing that is not instantly upon its arrival to be given out, knowing that in the waggons they are subject to loss & Damages; after having been to the eastward which would have been before now, but for the dayly expectation of going into New York, from whence we hear repeatedly the mercenaries are taking Flight—

I shall be able to inform you have preparation[s] in your way will be necessary you mention my sending you Arms to repair, at present have none on hand having sent them to Mr Ruddock at Fish Kill—

I have had frequent applications from Mr. Van Rancelaer who has the care of a number of Armourers at Albany, and whilst we lay at the Plains I sent him a number on account of the easy transportation it being but 5 Miles land carriage[.] should our next situation make it convenient I shall send them on to you—

The Books have not yet arrive but I am exceedingly obliged by your information that they would be on shortly. I must beg one favour more of you, that is two or three quires large paper suitable for returns. by the next post I hope I shall be able to send you a New York Paper in return for your kindness in sending me two printed in the beautiful city of Philadelphia until which time with the utmost respect & determin'd Friendship I bid adieu Yours &c.

To Udny Hay

Dear Colo.   Danbury [CT] Novemr. 13th 1778

Yesterday I forwarded by Mr. Langdon One hundred and three dollars equal to forty one pounds four shillings New York Currency that being the sum which I borrowed of you as p[er] my receipt in your possession. I have now inclosed the Order which Genl. Gates gave on you for the payment of the money drew for the teemsters as p[er] the Vouchers in your hands. you may remember I gave you my receipt to produce the Order which receipt you will please to give to Major French also the receipt for the money if you have not destroyed it in consequence of my first letter—

No news can only add that any command you may have this way will be chearfully received by your determined friend and very humble Servant—

Hay had been appointed Assistant Deputy Quartermaster General with the rank of Lieutenant Colonel at Ticonderoga in January 1777. At this time he was a Deputy Quartermaster General at Fishkill, New York.

To Benjamin Flower

Dear Colo.   Danbury [CT] Novemr. 13th. 1778

By the last post I forwarded the General Return for the present month and several letters to Gentlemen in the department which I hope came safe to hand—

Nothing material has happened since I wrote. we are still under marching orders, which it is now said will be to Morris Town, for winter quarters, but the hourly expectation of the evacuation of York I believe has prevented our marching before this time and I still think will continue us, as it is very probable the final exit of the British Mercenaries may alter the intended disposition of our Army—The pistolls mentioned in Mr. Pearsons letter I have had no opportunity to forward but shall embrace the first that presents—

I am Sir with respect—

To Jonathan Gostelowe

Dear Major   Danbury [CT] Novemr. 13th, 1778

By the last Post I wrote you inclosed to Col Flower which I hope you have received. I have nothing perticular at this time to communicate, we still occupy the same ground as when I wrote you last and it is probable shall continue to do so untill with Jonah, we see what is to become of the City, (York) by the last Accounts only two ships of force remained in the East River and they ready to sail God grant they may find employment off this Continent—I wrote you in my last for some large paper suitable for returns which with the Books I should be exceeding oblidged to have forwarded in the first waggon—

My compliments to the Gentlemen with you in the department and determined friendship for you concludes this from your very humble Servt—

To James Pearson

Dear Major   Danbury [CT] Novemr. 13th 1778

Notwithstanding I has wrote you so latily as the last Post, yet I should by no means omit so good an opportunity as the present, not that I have any thing particular either in business or News way but on my part to keep up an agreable correspondence which perhaps may tend to mutual advantage and facilitate the publick business in which we are engaged—The Pistols which you mentioned in your last I have had no opportunity to send on as yet shall embrace the first that presents. had what you sent for Amounted to a load, I would have sent on a waggon immediately that not being the case must wait the return of one from your way—the steel I trust you have received long since—nothing new in haste I remain sir your very humble Sert.

To John Ruddock

Sir   Danbury [CT] Novr. 13th 1778

By Major French I have an Opportunity to acknowledge the receipt of Yours p[er] Mr. Gidley with his receipt for thirty dollars which shall be duly noticed upon his settlement, and remited you. The saddle also I will see returned—Mr Noyce brought the favour you gave in Charge to him, in which you say I may do as I will respecting or signing his Account for what Cartridge boxes he has delivered me fearing that me may have deceived you, I thought proper to inform you that he has never delivered me one box. nor have I any knowledge of any he has made he says he has delivered them as directed which concerns him to make appear—

I am Sir Your Most Obdt Servt

To Nathanael Greene

Sir   Danbury [CT] Novr. 23d 1778
    I received your favor of ye 20th Inst. the Waggons that you refer to were in number nine having just before received ten New Ammunition Waggons of Captn Post more suitable for my business I took the horses and harness that came from Pennsylvania and annexed them to these Waggons the Waggons that came are now at Fredericksburgh Town with my Magazine. This Sir, is the matter that has been represented to you as breaking up the Teams, and appropriating them to other uses as I receipted for the Waggons, I did not conceive myself under any obligation to inform Mr. Thompson how I disposed of them. had he furnished his Waggon Master with Harness for the new Waggons I should have been under no obligation to have made the substitute
    With much esteem I am Yours &c:

Major General Greene was then serving as Quartermaster General.

To Richard Frothingham

Dear Frothingham: Danbury [CT] Novemr. 24th 1778
    By the time this reaches you I hope You will be at rest and the Stores deposited in some safe receptacle, not to be moved again this winter. if in answer to this I find that to be the Case, I shall make my political exit to the Eastward without coming on to see you. I have wrote to Mr. French who I think will call at Pluckermin on his return to bring on with him the Gentlemen's Accounts of Pay and rations up to the first of November 1778, and their Expences accounts attested up to the present time in order to their being settled and paid before I go; for which purpose I shall send Mr. Boyer or Jones. you will please to see this Business completed with all convenient speed. I spoke to General Knox about your Expence Account, and he seems willing I should pay it this shall be finally determined before he goes away and then I will remit you the money—The remainder of this shall be your instructions untill I see you, and in the first place you will be sure to procure a Magazine for the Stores in such Order as to render them perfectly secure both from damage and Embezzlement you will be very exact in making entries both of receivals and Deliverys as on this

circumstance the Correctness of the books altogether depends you will repeatedly visit the Stores and have such as are damaged repaired, all your Waggons are to be paraded near the Magazine and be under charge of the same guard and you will see that they are all repaired. in any doubtfull Occurrence you will apply to General Knox for Direction who has kindly promised to Assist you—the Monthly returns will be made by Mr. or Boyer or Jones which ever I shall forward for that purpose, and at every return I shall expect you to make an Actual survey and oftener if you should find it Necessary, all other Matters I shall leave to your Management, expecting that you will write me by every Opportunity and let me know how things go on—

Having nothing further at this time I Conclude and Remain yours

Frothingham signed his Oath of Allegiance in March 1778 as "Conductor of Ordnance Stores." Hodgdon gives him the title of Commissary of Military Stores.

To Samuel French

Sir   Danbury [CT] Novr. 25th 1778

Finding that I shall be detained here some days, I have concluded to stay untill you come to this place. your books I have not sent away from here as yet, judging that we must refer to them, to see the last settlement made with the Gentlemen in the department, in order to see what sums are due to them untill the present time after settling and paying the several sums due. if Nothing material turns up I shall set out for Boston, without visiting that garden of America called Jersey in order to which must beg of you to desire the Gentlemen, to make out their Accounts of Pay and rations, due them to the first of Novemr. 1778 and their expence accounts up to the time you set out, and bring them on with you—

The General (I mean Knox) is very willing I should go from hence as it will save 200 Miles travel going and coming which is a consideration worthy of Notice in winter time.—the accounts you bring me of the situation of the stores and the Gentlemen who have them in charge will determine that Matter whether Boston or the beautifull regions of Jersey will be my first route—The stores at Fredericksburgh are to be sent to fish-kill. those at New Milford to remain where they are for the present. General Knox with the Park setts of next Thursday for Pluckermin the convention Burgoiners crosses the ri[ver] before the Park—I have Nothing further to add but that I am your determined friend and very humble Servt—

French was a Major and Commissary of Military Stores.

To John Lamb

Dear Colo   Danbury [CT] Novr 29 1778
   This morning I waited on Captn Starr the QMG at this Place in order to procure Waggons to carry the Stores from Fredericksburgh to Fish Kill. he at first told me it was impossible to think of getting them here on account of the demand made by the several Brigades just arrived in Town, but upon my representing the necessity of an immediate removal he agreed to furnish 6 Teams in case they could be shod, which I promised should be done. must beg the Favor of you to give orders to Captn Post to have the Shoes ready against the Oxen arrive which I suppose will be this evening I have also procured harness for the seven Waggons with our stores, hoping that you would be able to get Horses, and then they may go on with the Teams, that go from hence. the difficulty of getting teams on account of private people offering more than as much again, as the servants of the Public are allowed to give, makes me despair of getting any more this way but am informed you can get them from new Fairfield, tho' I suppose you will be under the disagreable necessity of pressing for the above mentioned reason. these that have come I have directed Mr. Thompson to load with the best of the Stores and forward without a moments loss of time, and if you should be able to procure horses, two trips will take the whole on
   With respect and esteem I am Sir Your very hum Servant

Lamb was Colonel of the Second Continental Artillery Regiment,

To Mr. Giles

Sir   Danbury [CT] Novr. 29th 1778
   I have forwarded six teams from this place to take on the Stores, that is all I could possibly procure. I have also sent on Harness for our

own Waggons, hoping that Colo. Lamb would be able to procure Horses that so they might go on with the ox Teams. whether this is the case or not, you will load up the Teams, and proceed with them yourself as Mr. Thompsons horse is so lame, as be utterly unfit at present. I have sent on coverings which you will see properly spread over the Ammunition and take every other possible method to prevent its taking damage. you will take an account of what each waggon has in and the Waggoners name that if any thing is lost we may know where to apply for compensation—Yours &c.

Giles was a Conductor of Military Stores.

To Alexander Thompson

Sir   Danbury Novr 29 1778
You will immediately proceed to Fredericksburgh and wait the arrival of Six Teams which are coming on to take loads of Military Stores to transport to Fish Kill. when arrived you will lend your assistance to Mr Giles to have them loaded taking particular care to have the stores well cove[red] with the oil Cloaths sent on from hence and keepg a Copy of the Invoice sent on; Mr Giles is to go on with the first party that goes off, and you are to be particularly attentive to those that remain—when teams are provided you will follow with the[m] and deliver them to the same person (Vizt Mr Ruddock) and in the same manner

Thompson was a Conductor of Military Stores.

Richard Frothingham to Benjamin Flower

Sir,   Pluckemin [N.J.] 1st Decr 1778
This is to Inform you the Military stores belonging to the Army Are Arrived hear from Danbury and Deposited in a safe store for the Winter—the Amunition was Much Damagd by Reason of bad roads which shall be Repaired soon as posable—As there as No place hear for the Armourers to work in I thought it proper to buld one which will be don in a fue days—Mr: Hodgdon Who has had the direction of the stores informs Me he shall go to Boston without Coming

Further—I am Ready to Receive with pleasure any Directions You have to give which shall Command My Greatest Attention—As soon as the stores are Examined and an Exact Account takein shall Mak Return—Genl Knox with the park of Artily: is Expected in five or six days

Addressed to Flower at Philadelphia.

To Benjamin Flower

Dear Colo.   Danbury [CT] Decr. 8th 1778

Time that is ever on the wing has revolv'd the Season for another monthly Return, inclination as well as Duty prompt me to obey its dictat[es] by the within you will perceive a considerable alteration in the disposition of the Stores since the last Return, those mentioned to be at Fredericksburgh, by the Generals order I am now moving to Fish Kill and shall deliver them to the charge of Mr Ruddock those at New Milford by the same order are to remain—

I am now waiting for the return of Major French, after which without further loss of time I shall retire to the eastward where I shall endeavour to get such information as may depended on with respect to the supplies that can be afforded to the Army from the several Repositories and Laboratories, and communicate the same to you[.] upon my return or by any sure conveyance that may present and I think it a matter of importance for you to know, to the perfecting your General Plans—

The Fifty pair Pistols wrote for by Major Peirson by your order, have had no opportunity as yet to send forward, but expect one in three or four Days which I shall imbrace for that purpose[.]

I have taken the liberty to inclose the returns for the Honl Board of War which you will please to have delivered.—The enemy have again made their appearance upon North River and a number of them, said to be about 5 or 6 thousand have landed near Croton, this side the River and are at their old Business robbing Hen roosts and spreading indiscriminate desolation. the Brigades at this Place have march'd to chastise their insolence which without their usual Flight prevent, I doubt not will be accomplished

Having nothing further worthy of your attention with all possible respect & esteem I remain Your very hum Servt

To Henry Knox

Honored Sir								Danbury [CT] Decemr. 8th 1778

Inclosed you have the General Return of the Stores under my charge, and an account in the Face of it where deposited. those at Fredericksburgh agreable to your direction, are now moving to Fish Kill. the difficulty of procuring teams has prevented there being removed sooner. I was obliged to get them in this Town none nearer could be obtained at any rate however I hope no damage will accrue by the unavoidable Delay—

The Arms & Accoutrements left by your order with General McDougall upon enquiring I find have by his order been delivered to the secon[d] Pensylvania Brigade. as I had nothing but a vague loose certificate from the Generals Son which specifies no number, I sent to desire him to furnish me with the receipt that he took from the Brigade, but find like the tale of a Tub, a copy of the same Certificate has served for the delivery. as it is proper that the Brigade that has them in use should stand charged with them, and as that is impossible at present, as the Generals son would not exchange the Certificate, must beg the favor of you to mention the matter to the Brigr Genl: of the second Peny Brige to give orders to the quarter Master of the Brigade to give a proper receipt specifiying the particular numbers of each article received. You will pardon my giving you this Trouble as it is a matter of importance which I am anxious to have set right, and am sensible you can procure the requisites quicker than any one else. the Articles delivered were as follows

    150 Muskets & Bayonets
    150 Bayonet Belts
    144 new constructed Cartd Boxes

With all possible esteem I am Your very huml Servt:

To Richard Frothingham

Dear Frothingham					Danbury [CT] Decemr. 8th 1778

By this conveyance you will receive the Monthly Returns inclosed and directed which you will cause to be delivered without a moments unnecessary Delay. I have not received one Line from you since you left me, of consequence am ignorant in what situation you or the Stores are. I have been expecting Mr. French for several Days but have heard nothing from him as yet. I have sent on the Stores that were at Fredericksburgh to Fish Kill those at New Milford are to remain having my Business here finished I am uneasy at the long Stay of Mr. French, as by him I expect to hear from you, and also to know whether I can effect a settlement with the Department without coming on to Jersey as I am determined not to retire home untill I see the Gentlemen who compose the Department made easy and happy in their winter quarters.

I cannot give you any further Instructions untill I know your circumstances. one thing I think proper to mention, that is, in case any of the Stores are detached to the Brigades or Divisions that you would be very particular in delivering the Stores to the Conductor that goes with them and take his receipt for the same. this is absolutely necessary to keep the Books correct

Mr: Giles and Richards I understand are ordered to join their Regiment immediately Mr. Jones is very ill at New Milford occasioned by making an unskillful use of Anguint[alln] Mr Downes and Lefebure are here waiting for the moving of the waters to travel Eastward. they all desire their compliments to you and all present, which with my own finishes this epistle

From your Friend and very huml Servt:
NB My particular compliments are due to the Gentlemen of the Department present with you—

Frothingham was serving as Deputy Commissary of Military Stores.

To John Lamb

Dear Colo.   Danbury [CT] Decemr 15th 1778

Your favour by your lad came safe to hand. the whether [sic] being uncommonly bad prevented my sending him with an answer on Sunday Monday Capt. Starr was out of town, and I thought best to retain him untill I could know what further assistance you might expect from hence. last night Mr. Thompson arrived with your other favour. him I shall detain untill I am able to inform you fully what more teems can be supplyed, and am in hopes to procure the number

wanted for which you may rest assured I shall strenuously press the other oil Cloaths I have inquired for and find they were so much damaged as to render them intirely useless, but if I am able to get the teems I can forward a number old tents which will answer for cover—
    I am with respect yours

To John Lamb

Dear Colo: Danbury [CT] Decr. 15th 1778
    Yesterday I was with Captn Starr on the business I wrote you last, and hope and trust, have fully accomplished it. seven Teems he says shall be with you to morrow and seven the next day following these I judge sufficient to take the whole of the Stores to Fish Kill with moderate loads. the whole remaining Oil Cloths will come on with them, and a number of old Tents to make up suitable covering for the whole. Captn. Starr informed me he gave written orders to the last Teems which went for Flour to call and take the Stores & in consequence supposed they were all gone untill my application made him sensible to the contrary—
    Inclosed you have a copy of the return of Military Stores, which I informed the General were at Danbury. as they are mostly useless untill repaired I would advise to have them sent to Fish Kill, but I suppose it impossible to procure teems here at present to carry them on. if you should think it best to remove them a line from you to Colo Hay requesting the favor of him to order the returning Teems; which I doubt not he is every day forwarding to Danbury with Flour for the Army might with ease expedition & safety effect it. if they are not repaired immediately perhaps it may be as well to continue them where they are at present deposited. this you will determine & act accordingly
    I am Sir with all possible respect & esteem Yours &c.
NB the Military Stores mentioned in the Return are in charge of Doctr Wood formerly DQMGenl in Danbury

Richard Frothingham to Samuel Hodgdon

Sir   Pluckimin [N.J.] 16th Decr 1778
    I Received You [sic] faver of the 24th Novr: by Mr Butler also

that of the 8th of this instend Whare by I larn you intend to Shape your Corse Eastward—I shuld have Wrote before but No opportunity presented=Our March from Danbury to his place was attended with Much difficulty Occasioned by Exceding bad Rhods and Waggons bracking Continuly but by the spirited Exertion of the Gentleman Conductors we proformed the Journey with Great Safty—I have the Stores Deposited in a Very Safe place Secure from the weather and other Accidents—On Examination I found Considerable Amunition Damaged Which shall be Repaired soon as posable

Major French Arrived from Philadelphia Yesterday Who informs Me the Expence Accounts will Not be paid Untill settled by Congress: for which purpose a Committee is allrady Choicen=On Our Way to this place we Met with stores bound for head Quarters Which we Received & Gave Receipt

I am sorry for Mr. Jones Mis-fortin it is allways dangerous handleing Edg Tools

Addressed to Hodgdon as Deputy Commissary General of Military Stores at Danbury, Connecticut.

To Henry Knox

Dear Genl   Danbury [CT] Decr: 20th 1778

With a mixture of grief & shame I address a Letter of this date to you from this place my only consolation is that it was Fates determined decree of consequence no fault of mine. the unnacountable delay of Mr French who has now been gone about five weeks to Philadephia to bring money to defray the expences of the Department while at this place, and the many disappointments made by the Quarter Masters in procuring teams to forward the Stores from Fredericksburg to Fish Kill after the most positive and solemn promises made has suspended me like the Body of Mahome[d] between earth & heaven, and kept my mind in a continual pertubation, and at this moment remains so, as neither of the above causes are removed. the disress of that part of the Army stationed to the eastward of this Town for Flour which is all drawn from Fish kill has employed every Waggon & Team in this Vicinity the whole of which on account of the Badness of the roads have scarcely been able to transport enough to keep the Army in consequence about 12 loads of Stores remain at Fredericksburgh these I am in hopes will be forwarded in two or three Days, as we have fresh assurances from the Quarter Master. after which without waiting long for Mr French I shall set out for Boston this is become absolutely necessary as I am almost naked and no cloathing of any kind to be had here—

Inclosed you have a return of the Stores which I informed you were in the charge of Doctr Woodford formerly DQMG at this Place, a Copy of which I have sent Colo Lamb with my advice as they are damaged to send them to Fish Kill when Teams can be had.—I have also forwarded a Hat Box & two small Casks directed to you, which I happen'd to see at the Quartermaster Stores. these Mr Gidley who accompanies the Waggons will Deliver—

Mr Conductor Jones I shall leave in charge of the Stores at New Milford and forward my Clk Mr Boyer to make monthly returns & to keep the business regular in all its Branches untill my return, which I intend shall be with all convenient Speed. I have nothing further to add but to offer my Services to your commands while in Boston. any of which I shall be happy to receive which I can no better convince you off [sic] than by the manner they are performed

I am Sir With Respect Yours &c.

I have this moment an account that the Teams were arrived and that the last of the Stores at Fredericksburg would be forwarded Thursday—

To Jasper Maduit Gidley

Sir,   Danbury [CT] Decembr. 20th 1778

You are to go on with the Stores and baggage in the two Waggons drive by Guinup & Mc.Knight which setts of to morrow morning you will proceed with them to Fredericksburg and take in the baggage belonging to M Giles, Thompson & Richards after which with all possible speed you are to see them on to Pluckermin in the Jerseys taking Special care that Nothing is damaged or lost. upon your arrival you will wait on Mr. Frothingham, who in consequence of what orders I have sent him will shew you a proper place to Deposit them and your Quarters. you will immediately upon your being settled if the books have come on from Philadelphia take out the Ledger and open it as I have already given you verbal Directions you are to be Carefull to keep your Journal up and Carry the whole into the Ledger as fast as possible. you are to Assist Mr Boyer in making the Monthly Returns and any other service in the Clerk way, as on him and you I depend to have the books in perfect order and every part of the business in the writing way properly and in time accomplished—for any other Assistance Necessary to carry these orders to full effect you apply to Mr Frothingham DCMS who is to act as principal in the Department untill my return. so wishing you a pleasant and prosperous Journey I Remain Yours—

Richard Frothingham to Benjamin Flower

Sir   Pluckimin [N.J.] 20th. Decr: 1778
     I wrote you Under the 1st Instent informing of My Arrival with the store[s] at this place Which I hope You Recd;—the following Articals Are Much Wanted at Camp, pleas to Order them On Soon as posable—

Viz 20 Drums	20 sheep skeens
200 Drum Cores	1 bbl Sweet Oil
50 Pr Drum stocks	10 pounds Chalk

To Richard Frothingham

Dear Richard   Danbury [CT] Decemr. 21st. 1778
     Nothing could have surprised me more than your neglecting to inform me the situation of the Stores; for so long time and that too when I am informed by Mr Edmunds who lately passed thro' this town on his way home that the whole department knew of his coming. sure I am that you must suppose me anxious to hear before my departure for Boston, of consequence I take it very unkind. three weeks I have been detained waiting for Mr. French whose conduct I think very extraordinary, as he knew the miserable state of the Department with respect to money occasioned by his long stay at Boston whether he makes himself thus easy, thinking I have found a way to make money or the department to do without it I am at a loss to determine. having waited thus long and not a word or information of Money or Stores, and having tired my money out and almost my Credit I have determined to send on the Books and Baggage and set

out myself for Boston without further Delay as I am sure the Department will acquit me of Blame for any inconveniences they may experience my patience being entirely exhausted—Mr Gidley is forwarded in charge of the Waggons who I have directed to apply to you for a suitable place to deposit their Contents in, and for his quarters, which you will furnish him with. Mr Boyer and Thompson will set out in a few days and probably may arrive with you as soon as the Waggons. Mr Boyer I have left in full charge of the Books to make the month returns, and when the money arrives receive it & settle with the department. in doing which I have directed him to apply to you for assistance as principal in the department untill I return thus as it is your duty so I know it will be your inclination chearfully to gran[t.] the Hat Box and two kegs directed to Genl. Knox you will please to see delivered. the Case of one hundred pistolsyou will forward by the first opportunity to Colo. Flower at Philadelphia[.] As it is probable I may write you again by Mr. Boyer, I shall conclude this after desiring my Compliments to the Gentlemen present with you—With esteem I remain Yours &c.

To Thomas Jones

Dear Jones   Danbury [CT] Decemr 22d 1778
My patience being entirely exhausted and no news arriving of Mr French, and having settled my matters here and forwarded the Stores from Fredericksburg to Fish Kill I have sent off the Waggons with the Baggage under the charge of Mr Gidley to Pluckermin, and given orders for Mr Boyer and Thompson to follow them on Thursday next. on which day I purpose in company with Mr Downes to set out for Boston. Mr Lefebure I have ordered to Fish Kill to wait the arrival of Mr. French & bring on my Letters and other necessaries but before any of these matters took effect my word to give you information assistance and instructions occurred, and this will make you sensible that though out of sight you are not out of mind. the information being above, and the assistance inclosed. now comes Instructions Vizt. You are to continue in charge of the Stores at New Milford and deliver any of them upon an order of a Brigr. Genl: except Musquets and new constructed Cartouch Boxes, these you are not to deliver but upon an order from the commanding Officers of the Divisions this side the River Vizt. Genl. Putnam or Mc.Dougall you will know what

authority from the other side the River have a right to Draw and will act accordingly—you must forward a Monthly Return every Month time enough to be inserted in the General Return the first of which you will be carefull to forward by the last of January indeed it will not be amiss to forward one with your Vouchers by every opportunity. you will be carefull to write me as often as possible which I shall with pleasure answer, and give any further directions. all other matters shall leave for your good sense & sound judgement to determine, not doubting but you will aim solely at the publick good. I have inclosed you 60 Dolls, that being the utmost that I could spare at present. With my best wishes for the restoration and establishment of your health and the possession of every enjoyment—I bid adieu for a short time—and remain with affection Yours &c

Jones was appointed a Deputy Field Commissary of Military Stores on June 15, 1779. In June 1781, he was ordered to join the Southern Army. At the time of this letter he was probably a Conductor of Military Stores.

To Mr. Lefabure

Sir,   Danbury [CT] Decr 23d

You are to proceed to New Milford and deliver the letter you have as directed to Mr. Jones. after which you are to go to Fish Kills and if Major French is there deliver him the Letter you have in charge for him if not remain there untill he arrives. if he is coming to Boston you will naturally accompany him, if he is not you will take charge of any Papers, Letters or sum of money he may have to forward to me and proceed without delay to Boston for which place I am now setting out if any thing particular should detain Mr French in Philadelphia or the Jersies, Mr Boyer is directed to give you immediate notice and at the same time forward to your charge what you are to bring to me—

I am Sir Yours &c.

Lefabure was referred to as a "CMS" – either a Conductor or Commissary Military Stores.

Richard Frothingham to Benjamin Flower

Sir,   Pluckimin [N.J.] 10th Jany: 1779

With this you will Receive a Return of the Military stores with the Army for the Month of December—

the General has Ordered that the troops be furnished with forty rounds Cartridgs Pr Man, we have Not Sufficient for that purpose—pleas to Order on the Musquet Cartridgs & Other Articals Mintioned in the Invoice Which I have Inclosed—

General Knox Desires the Small Articals Come on in the first Waggons

Since the Return has been Made three Brigades has take in 100,000 Cartridgs to Compleat them Agreeable to Orders—

Addressed to Flower at Philadelphia.

Richard Frothingham to Samuel Hodgdon

Sir, Pluckimin [N.J.] 11th Jany: 1779

I Received your faver by Mr: Gidley Also that by Mr: Boyer—I am sorry you shuld have any Reason to Conclude I Neglected to Give you the Earlyest inteligence of My Arrival at this place and the situation of the stores—I left word at Each Tavern and inquired of such Gentlemen as Was like to Convay a letter to You this without success—

Mr Edmonds Who You Mentioned I knew Not of his going that way or I shuld wrote by him—General Knox informs Me the stores are to be Removed to the park Whare a place is prepairing for the Reception of them

I am at a loss to know the Reason of Majr Frenches long tarry at Philada: The Department being in so Great Want of Monney—this day I Sent Mr Freeman to Philadelphia for 200,000 Musquet Cartridgs As we Are like to be in want as the Orders is the troops to be furnished with forty rounds pr Man

I Send You a Return of the Mil Stores for the Month of December, Since the Return was Made three Brigades has takeing 100,000 Musqt. Cartridgs to Compleat them Agreeable to Order

Addressed to Hodgdon at Boston.

Richard Frothingham to Alexander Scammell

Sir,   Pluckimin [N.J.] 13th Jany 1779
 Inclosed you have Account of the Musquit Cartridges delivered from this store Also the Damaged Received from the several Brigades Agreeable to Your Request—As part of the troops passed through Fish Kill I am Not Able to Determin the Quantity that has been Received or Delivered there to Any of thoes Brigades—
at head quarters, Bound Brook

Scammell was the Adjutant General of Washington's Army.

Richard Frothingham to James Pearson

Sir,   Pluckimin [N.J.] Jany 15th. 1779
 Your faver pr Mr Freeman I have Received; And Note the Contents; As the General is very Anxious to have a Number of the Articals Which are Most Wanted forwarded without a Moments loss of time has Directed Me to send a parson [sic] to See them On And for that purpose have Despatched Mr Cuningham Condr M Stores by Whom You will pleas to forward the inclosed Memorandum with out any Delay—As the signing of the Invoice Was intirly a Fault of the Mind: shall endeavor for the futer to proceed in the Way You point'd Out—Your information Concarning the time we May Expect Majr French is Very Acceptable as the Money that was left with us is almost Exhasted

Richard Frothingham to James Pearson

Sir,   Pluckimin [N.J.] 23d Jany. 1779
 I Received Yours by Mr Cuningham and the Contents as Pr Invoice—the tin will Answer the purpos but Not so well As we Culd Wish—we have Not Amuniti[on] Boxes suffisent to pack What Cartridgs We have in store—I have Sent by John Wilty Waggoner twenty pounds Red Lead With Some Other Stores for Majr Gostilowe—If you will Send Some Cotton it will Answer in the Lue of Quick Match

Richard Frothingham to Jonathan Gostelowe

Sir,   Pluckimin [N.J.] 24th Jany: 1779
I have Sent by John Wilty Waggoner thirty two Damaged Musquits Ninety Eight pistols twenty pounds Red Lead the pistols & Red Lead Ware wrote for by Majr Parsons [sic] being in great haste Must be the Excuse for the Shortness of this Letter—

Richard Frothingham to Samuel Hodgdon

Sir,   Pluckimin [N.J.] 24th Jany 1779
I Wrote you by Mr Morriss Which I hope You Received—In Which I Neglected to inform you I have procured a Recept for the Musquits and Accutrements delivered to the 2nd Pensa. Brigade— Business of late has been plenty in prepairing for the Anivarecry of Aliance with France on the 8th [sic] of Next Month: Which time is to be Exhibited the Grandest Vue of fire work Even Seen in America
Genl Knox has been sent for to Philadelphia by the Board of War supposed to be on Some settlement in the Ordnance Department

This was addressed to Hodgdon at Boston.

Richard Frothingham to Alexander McDougall

Sir,   Pluckimin [N.J.] 3d Jany. [February] 1779
In Concequence of a letter Directed to Lieut Coll. Stevens dated 25 Desiring a Return of the Arms & Accoutrements Deliver'd to Coll Poors & Woods Regiments of Militia, I would inform you that we have No Charge against Either of those Regiments, As we Make No Charge Only to Brigades, the Matter Must be Determined by the Q Master of the Brigade thay are Annext to
I Am Your Obt

McDougall was a Major General from New York.

Richard Frothingham to Samuel Hodgdon

Sir   Pluckimin [N.J.] 6th Feby 1779
    By this You will Receive the Return for the Month of Jany:—by Capt Barr from Philadelphia I larn Coll: Flower is Drawing his last Change—
Genl Knox is Expected to Morrow from Philada:—Nothing Since My last of the 24 Jany: has transpired Worthey Notice in our Department
    I am Yours &C

PS I shall Esteem it as a perticular faver if You will procure for Me any Privlige that May be Granted to the officers of the Massachusetts State

Despite what Captain Barr reported, Flower did not draw "his last Change" until April 28, 1781.

Richard Frothingham to James Pearson

Sir,   Pluckimin [N.J.] 10th Feby 1779
    General Knox being Desirous that Nothing shuld be Wanting to Compleat the Grand Exhibition of fire Works on the 18th of this Instent has Directed Me to Send Some parson [sic] Express for the following Articals for the purpose I have Sent Mr Boyer Condr M Stors Who will bring them to Camp

Viz 6 lb Quick Match
    6 lb fine binding Wire Brass or Iron
    1 Galln. Spirits Turpentine

Festivities were planned for February 18, 1779, to celebrate the first anniversary of the signing of the treaties of alliance and commerce with France.

Richard Frothingham to Benjamin Flower

Sir,   Pluckemin [N.J.] 19th Feby 1779
    I Recd: Yours by Mr Geo: Parks and the Articles Agreeable to Invoice I shall Apply to the Qr, Mr, Genl for the Germin Steel You

Mentiond & send it on if posable to procure any, I have sent You a Return for Jany: by Mr; Baker; the Returns has been sent Regular by the post on the first of Each Month for the Month past—

Richard Frothingham to William Stevens

Sir,   Pluckimin [N.J.] 26th Feby 1779
    Mr. Gidly Cr My Stors the bearer of this Letter is sent to Receive from You the remaining packages of Military [*sic*] in Your possesion beg You will Assist him in forwarding them to this place

Stevens was a Deputy Quartermaster General.

To William Richards

Sir   Pluckermin [N.J.] April 12th 1779
    You are immediately to repair to New Milford to take charge of a number of Military Stores at present under the charge of Mr. Jones CMS. as you are to receipt him for them, you will be carefull in examining to see that they agree with the Inventory you receipt upon. you are to forward a return to me of every species of Store receiv[ed] issued & remaining on hand on or before the last day of every Month, and by every opportunity make me acquainted with the State of the Stores under your charge and the requisitions of any part of the Army near your Post. your fidelity and integrity on this command shall be duly noticed by your Friend & very huml Servt.

Richards was appointed Deputy Field Commissary of Military Stores on June 15, 1779. He was probably a Conductor of Military Stores at the time of this letter.

To Benjamin Flower

Dear Colo.   Pluckermin [N.J.] Apr 14th 1779
    I embrace this first opportunity, although I have but an hours Notice to inform you of my return to Camp. at the same time to simpathize with you on the long and tedious illness with which I am informed you have been visited and which still confines you, happy

should I be to be informed in answer to this that you have the prospect of a confirmed state of heal[th] speedily—

I find since my absence the Ordnance department has been under the consideration of the honble Congress and Board of War and I have been favour'd with part of their resolve thereon. by them I perceive that a field Commissary I and unconected with you is to be appointed. whether I shall have the appointment or indeed any other I am not able to say. I understand however through the unmerited favour of General Knox I am recommended to the honble Board time will at last determine what part I am to act—

I am settling the department up to the 18th Feby agreeable to your request in a letter to Mr Frothingham and shall shortly have it I. any new orders or requiets [sic] from you will be received and executed with chearfullness by him who has made himself happy during the connection and still remains your oblidg'd friend and very humble Sert

NB you will please to present my compliments to Major Pierson and the Gentlemen present with you

To James Lovell

Sir Pluckermin[N.J.] April 14th 1779

By Mr Howe Brigade Q Master of Artillery you will receive two letters, which I received of the honble Major General Gates a few days since at Boston, and I was then under expectations of coming immediately to Philadelphia I promised the General to deliver them with my own hand, as indeed it was proper I should as I have some reason to believe a Matter of mine was recommended to your patronage. upon my arrival at Camp I find my department has been under consideration of Congress and some regulations made which it is probable may prevent the Necessity of an application I meant to make; it will at least for the present; I have taken the liberty to inclose some letters for Mr Adams which with my regards you will please to deliver—This conveyance I know to be safe as Mr Howe is my perticular friend and is to return to Camp again immediately—I have nothing further but that I am with respect and Esteem Yours

Lovell was a Delegate to Congress from Massachusetts.

To James Pearson

Dr Major   Pluckemin[N.J.] April 20th 1779

To day I received part of the Indent sent you sometime since with a Letter address'd to Mr Frothingham by which I perceive that the remainder with some few exceptions will follow soon, am much oblig[ed] by those already forwarded, and doubt not but the rest will soon arrive. I am particularly happy to hear, that your Infant Manufactories, afford a prospect of a supply of those Articles which are necessary to secure Freedom & I to the rising States of America. in addition to which I hope & trust your City will be filled [by] Commerce with any requisites not immediately to be furnished thro' want of material[s.]

Should be glad you would forward with the next Stores a suitable proportion of Black Paint, Yellow Oker, Venetian Red & white Lead ground, to paint our Feild Waggons as they are now suffering. agreable to your request, I have returned all the Casks forwarded with Drums and in them sent on a number of Carte Boxes, which were past repair in Camp, Number you will see by the receipt. with respect to the Steel, you may rest assured, I shall use my utmost endeavor, to procure & forward it by the retu[rn] of the next Waggons. Mr. Frothingham says that the DQMGenl. at Sussex inform'd him that you might be supplied with any Quantity, at Easton. this however true shall not prevent my application to the QMGenl. here to insure a fully supply

I have nothing further to add but my particular respects to Colo. Flower who I am rejoiced to hear, is gitting abroad and my compliments, to the Gentlemen who composes the Department—

With esteem I am Sir Your very Hum Servt

PS. I did expect upon my arrival in camp to have visited Philadelphia and to have made Col Flower acquainted with the circumstances of the Artificers at Springfield but business at present prevents

To George Washington

May it please your Excellency   Pluckemin [N.J.] April 28 1779

Captn: Winder calls on me with a Letter from Mr Henry inclosing an Invoice and receipt for sundry Military Stores delivered Captn. Winder for the use of the First Maryland Brigade, and requests that I would take the Brigade Quarter Masters receipts & charge them to the Brige. and forward him my rect. to Cancel Captn. Winders. as this mode is entirely new, and for several reasons exceptionable, I did not chuse to make a precident. I therefore waited on General Knox for advice and direction he was of opinion that I ought not to do it with a positive order from your Excellency these are the reasons Sir, that gave Birth to the reference

With respect and esteem I am Yours &c

To James Lovell

Sir   Pluckemin [N.J.] May 7, 1779

Your favor of the 20th of April in answer to mine by Mr. Howe came safe to hand for which and the kind expressions therein contain'd be pleased to except my hearty thanks—

That I am your Townsman is my greatest glory, and to raise & support the character of a Bostonian has ever been my endeavor in the humble sphere in which I was consign'd to act since the folly of Britain first promp'd them to subjugate America. in this I find to my great satisfaction, I have not been wholly disapointed by the notice you inform me, General Gates has taken of me in his Letter to you. with this intrepid Gentleman I served in the Office of Comy of Military Stores in the Campaigns of seventy seven & seventy eight to the Northward, after the reduction of Genl Burgoynes Army, which ended the War in that Quarter. In May following we moved down the North River to form a junction with the Main Army at white Plains, halting occasionally at the sever[al] Fortresses on the River all which the G[eneral] was indefatigable in his endeavors to have put in the best posture for defence. that at West Point was found to be of the most importance which being fully supply'd with Cannon the General was ever attentive the great Business he had undertaken, called for a General Return of Military Stores. these being in the hands of Conductors who had no connection with each other, convinced the General of the necessity of Issuing an Order to the whole to bring in their Returns to one person, that the whole might be brought into one General Return at the same time he was pleas'd to appoint me unsolicited to be Depy Comy Genl M Stores and require this last service of my hand. this was done in such a manner as to give satisfaction and the appointment operated without being called in

Question untill the junction of the two Armies at White Plains in July. with the Grand Army was a Mr. French Comy Mility Stores, he supposing himself principal, called my right into Question. after looking into each others pretensions, we agreed to leave the matter to the decision of General Knox and Col Harri[son] who after examining our pretences confirm'd me as the principal, to which Mr French like a Gentleman acquiesced, and immediately delivered me all the Stores he had on hand & all was again quiet. Mr French was now employed as a pay master to supply the departments the other Side the River quite to Boston, but finding this not so agreable, & have reason to think he employed some Friend (perhaps Colo Flower CGMS with whom he was intimate) to suggest the impropriety of my appointment, to the Board of War & get them to call Genl Gates's right in question. This has been done and a resolve past that I should be considered only as Comy Mility Stores thereby declaring that he had no right. This I was determined & by the General have been ordered never to give up, and this was the matter on which I tho't to solicit your powerful assistance. but on my return to Camp from a Furlough I found the Department had been revised by Congress on the Board of War's order and a New Officer by the name of I Commy appointed Independent of all others except the Board of War & Genl Knox the appointm[ent] being left with Genl Knox he has determin'd it for me before my arrival, not having determin'd when I wrote you what part [ ] was the reason of my saying that the necessity of an application I meant to make was for the present prevented—

Thus, Sir, I have trespassed upon your time and patience with a long and very tedious epistle to give you some knowledge of the matter that had been recommended to Your attention. This I thought my duty and although I must fervently solicit your Candor upon my imperfections which you read yet I flatter myself the perusal may be of service to me should I be obliged to trouble you further on the Subject, to secure the General's right to give me my appointment which the Board of War without hearing me have annihilated and consequently secure my pay while acting which at present remains unsettled—

With all possible respect I am Sir Yours &c.

To Benjamin Flower

Dear Colo.   Pluckemin [N.J.] May 7th 1779

Inclosed you have the return for the Month of April. Nothing remarkable in Camp, Major French not yet arrived but dayly expect him. by him I hope to be able to transmit to you my Account of Money expended in the department and make a settlement of all Cash in full drawn from you—wishing the restoration and Establishment of your health I Remain Yours

With Esteem I am yours

To Jonathan Gostelowe

Dear Sir,   Pluckemin [N.J.] May 13th 1779

By the return of Mr: Leaver I have an opportunity to acknowledge the Rect. of your's of the 6th. Instant, together with the Invoice of Stores immediately under his charge the whole of which came safe to hand a seasonable supply I do assure you, for which I think the publick may thank your exertions—

I am exceeding glad the time's and aspects, promises the very agreable satisfaction of your renewed and profitable correspondence rest assured Sir, while I have life & health to write it shall be kept up on my Side—When the wheels of time shall waft me to the beautiful regions of Pennsylvania I shall be happy in partaking of the Provi[ ] of a Friend I value like you—

I find it necessary to have one hundred Drums more forwarded as soon as convenient, for which purpose I have returned the Casks lately sent to Camp when these come I must renewedly beg you would send on the Ledger which I wrote you for some time since. the one I have bei[ng] so small as to occasion threefold more trouble than is needful, the dimensions Mr Leaver will inform you, this & two or three quires of Paper suitable for Returns will very much oblige me. one hundred Dutch Quills and two or three Papers of Ink Powder and a small quantity of sealing wax at the same time will lay me under great obligations which shall be returned with as large a proportion of Interest as paper money has depreciated below Silver, within this Year past, whenever in my Power—

Major French is not yet arrived, dayly expect him. I shall make a point of sending back the Arms, with damag'd Musquets and other damaged Stores by every opportunity—
With esteem I am Your's &c

To Udny Hay

Dear Colo.   Pluckermin [N.J.] May 14th 1779

The bearer Mr. Thornton Taylor CMS waits on you with an order inclosed from General Greene For two tons German Steel, which I have procured to be sent to Colo. Flower Comy M Stores Philadelphia. the demand there being Great I have forwarded teems to prevent Loss of time in getting it on and Shou'd take it kind if you wou'd lend your assistance to forward my endeavours—

I have nothing matariel to Communicate, every thing at present Very Still. my best Compliments accompanies this to Mrs. Hay who I hope enjoys her Health better than when I had the pleasure of Seeing her last—

To Thornton Taylor

Sir

Immediately upon the receipt of this you will proceed to Fish Kill, with three Waggons which will be given you in charge upon your arrival you will wait on Colo. Hay DQMGenl. and deliver the letter you have for him the purport of which is to deliver you two Tons of German Steel which after having received you will see that the Teems are properly supply'd with Forage (if to be had which[h] You may know and procure by the Friendship of Colo Hay) and return by the nearest route to Philadelphia if forage is not to be had you will either procure it of the keepers of the Magazines on the Road or by purchase upon the best terms you can get it you wi[ll] make all possible dispatch to prevent any unnecessary expence as at lest [sic] it will be considerable wishing you success I am
Your Friend &c
NB You will enquire of Colo. Hay whether it will forward you to go the upper Road without coming to Camp if so you will take that

course and upon your arrival at Philadelphia deliver the Steel to Colo Flower CGMS or his order and take receipt for the same—

Taylor was appointed a Conductor of Military Stores on March 10, 1779.

To James Pearson

Dear Sir   Pluckemin [N.J.] May 14th 1779
    By the return of Mr Leaver, I have an opportunity to acknowledge the receipt of your's of the 6th instant, and the invoice of stores all which came safe to hand, as you will see pr my receipt—I am exceedingly pleased with this grand supply.—some little articles of importance still remain, which with some additional articles such as four B. Clarinets a small box of Cane sutiable for reeds of bassoons and Clarinets two french horns Concert and twelve D. Concert fifes. thease are sent for by the perticular desire of General Knox, the inspector of musick having informed him that the band which is now a grand addition to the brigade of Artillery, Must cease their Martial and Animating sounds for want of instruments. Mr Clumberg inform's me the horns may be had at the QM Gens store at Philadelphia, and English Clarinets at the Musick shop, which he can inform. if this should not be the case, the Musick Master says they may be had, very good of Mr Anthony. your perticular attention and speedy information of this mater will very Much oblige the General and your friend also—the files Anvils and Vices wrote for are exceedingly wanted, to fix out the different brigades with travelling forges, which cannot be done untill they arrive which I hope will be soon—a quantity of Musqt. Cartridges will be Necessary, each brigade is to be furnish'd with 20,000 these you have in the last indent—four setts of Copper Powder Measures, Vizt One pound one quarter pound one Ounce and one quarter of an ounce, you will please to send on. these are some of the most Material Articles that I at present recollect and these I am sure will engage your Attention—
Agreeable to my promise in my last I waited on General Green QM Genl and from him obtained an order on Col Hay DQMG at fish-kill for two tons German steel. upon the Arrival of the teems I stoped one brigade, three of which I sent to fish-kill under the direction of Mr Taylor CMS to receive the above steel and see it on by the shortest route to Philadelphia. This tis probable will be with you in a few days

and I hope will prove a present supply. if the Articles I have wrote for can be obtained you can send them on by Mr Taylor—the other part of the teems comes on with damage stores and empty Casks—if you have any proper holster Pistols on hand, should be much obliged by a pair for my own use this closes my Numberless requests and with it my tedious letter—

I am Sir you obliged I and very humble Servt

To Thomas Jones

Sir   Pluckemin [N.J.] May 15 1779
Your will take charge of a waggon now waiting for you, and see it loaded with one Barrell of damag'd Powder, which is at the Laboratory and what more may be in the Stores, and as many empty barrel as it can take, and proceed to Morris Town and deliver the whole to Majr Lindley the Superintendant at the Powder Mill and take his rect. for the same. after which you will present the order which you have to Major Lindley who will deliver You half a Ton of Powder, five hundred weight of each, which you will receipt for, see properly loaded to prevent damage or accident, and in charge of the same proceed with all possible dispatch to this Place—

Yours &c.

To Benjamin Flower

Dear Colo.   Pluckemin [N.J.] May 28th 1779
By Major French you will receive my General account with its Vouchers for the moneys expended in my Department all which he has examined and passed. but a settlement is prevented, on account of his not thinking himself at Liberty to allow what I have charged for my Pay & Subsist. from my Commission compared with the Resolve of Congress I am at no loss to determine what is my due—The Commissi[on] I have shewn Mr: French and if you think it necessary, upon advice I will send a Copy for your perusal, which I doubt not will convince you that I have not deviated from the strictest Rules of justice in what I have charged I should be happy to be order'd to Philadelphia to make the Settlement, should you suppose yourself so confin'd by any act of the Boa[rd] of War from settling the acct. in its

present form—This would secure my expences and at the same time give me an opportunity of paying my personal respects to the honorable Board, to you & the other Gentlemen who have corresponded with me, and perhaps remove some prejudices which a partial representation may have made to my disadvantage. This I know I aim at nothing but what the nicest Rules of honour & justice will warrant, and ignorance must be my excuse in any Breach of either—

If your should order the account to be settled I am ready to account to you[r] order for the Cash on hand

I am Sir With respect Yours &c.

To Henry Brower

Sir   Pluckemin [N.J.] June 3 1779

You are immediately to go to Morris Town and present the order you have to Major Lindlcy who in consequence of it will deliver you all the powder belonging to the publick which he has under his charge in the Mill—

You will apply to Colo Abeel DQM Genl: for Teems to bring to whole to this place, and to the Officer Commanding at Morris Town, for a proper I to assist you to bring it on in safety. you are to bring an Invoice of the number & contents of each Barrell particularly noting the tare. You will keep with the Teems & see that none of the Drivers smoak as it will be dangerous[.] You must set out time enough in the Day to arrive here before night. As it is a matter of importance you have in hand I shall expect your greatest care & attention

To Major Lindley

Sir   Pluckemin [N.J.] June 3d 1779

The General has directed me to order all the powder which you have in charge to be brought to this place, Mr. Henry Brower CMS waits on you to receive & forward it. You will please to deliver it to him, together with an Invoice of the number & weight of each Cask & its Tare the Teems to employed [*sic*] in the removal are to be had of Colo Abeel DQMG and the I from that stationed in the Town as it is an affair of importance to the publick, to have it come on in safety, I

must beg you to assist Mr Brower in procuring and properly loading the teem[s] and like wise to obtain a proper Gaurd
    I am Sir Your very huml Servt

To James Abeel

Sir   Pluckemin [N.J.] June 3 1779
    The General having ordered all the powder in the Mill at Morris Town to be brought to this place, I have forwarded Mr Henry Brower CrMS to take it in charge & see it on. You will please to furnish him with the number of Teems necessary to effect this purpose as none can be supplyed at present from here. As it is a matter of importance to have it moved immediately, your particular attention to it will very much oblige
    Your very huml Servt

<small>Abeel was a Deputy Quartermaster General.</small>

To Benjamin Flower

Dear Colo.   Pluckemin [N.J.] June 3d 1779
    By Mr Jones who comes express for Stores you will receive the General Return for the Month May: inclosed also you have an Invocie of several speicies of Stores due upon former Indents these you'll please to observe are not included in the present demand of consequence will be sent in addition
    The musquet Cartridges are immediately wanted as the compleating the Army to their full compliment take nearly all I have on hand. This circumstance will convince you of the necessity of their being forwarded without a moments loss of time. the six pound strap Shot is another article of the last [*sic*] importance to be forwarded as you will see by the Return I have none on hand and am much press'd for them. The Steel sent for is not equal in quantity only twenty six hundred weight being on hand, this I have forwarded this day. Mr Jones will see to the Delivery and you will please to rect. him for it. The General Invoice of Stores now sent for you will receive from the Honl Board of War and from former experience I have reason to I the whole will speedily come to hand

We are all upon the move the Park marches tomorrow the rout I understand to be towards North River where it is conjectured the Enemy mean to open the Campaign: and its with heart felt satisfaction that I now can inform you our Army are well accoutred and in high Spirits. I absolutely anticipate the Glory of the Day that we come up with the invaders—

My compliments are due to Major French and the Gentlemen in the Department—

I am Sir your very huml Servt

I am requested to desire you to send on all the Sappers Musqts and accourtrements which General DuPortail left an indent for lately

To Thomas Jones

Sir   Pluckemin [N.J.] June 3d 1779

Upon receipt of this you are immediately to set out for Philadelphia and deliver the Several Letters with which you are charged according to their directions, the purport of them being to obtain Stores with which you are to be charg[ed.] you will with all possible dispatch see them to Camp the Musquet Cartrids and 6 pd Strapt Shot in particular.

The 2600 lbs German Steel forwarded this day to Philadelphia you will see delivered and take receipt—

The command being of importance you were Selected to execute is this [sic] I am sure will be a sufficient incitement to your performing it with accuracy and dispatch. as the charge of traveling runs high I expect you will be frugal

Yours &c

To Cain and Blair

Gentlemen   Pluckemin [N.J.] June 8th 1779

Being detained at this place upon business at the removal of the Artillery General Knox requested that I would take charge of the Artificers and guards, and sign all provision returns and order'd Mr Strach[in] the Issuing Comy of Provision to deposit as much provision in charge of Col McDonnald as he could spare— accordingly a small potion [sic] was left, which will be nearly issued this day and serves for three to come—several guards upon the out post's have applied and been supply'd that we knew Nothing off [*sic*] I have given Col McDonnald the Assistance of my Clerk, who was somewhat acquainted with the business but must request you to send on such a quantity of provisions as you think proper for the supply of 200 Men a few days, and some person to Issue it as the Col declines any further service in the Issuing way—or impower him to appoint some sutiable person to do it—

I am Gen Yours

They were Commissaries in charge of food stores at Raritan, New Jersey.

To James Thompson

Sir   Pluckemin [N.J.] June 9th 1779

Last evening twenty six waggons loaded with Ammunition arrived from Philadelphia. these Teems. I am informed by Mr Jones were coming to Camp for the direction of Genl Green and from several circumstances I am induced to think the General ordered them on for the express purpose of transporting the spare ammunition of the several Brigades, but if that should not be the case I must beg the Favor of you to let them go on to Camp, with their present loads as our Waggons are in not situation to risque their Contents and that at a Time when its very possible they may be wanted before they arrive. I shall send you back the remaining part of the Brigade of Waggons of which the five that are at Mr. Weiss are a part, and I should be oblidged to you to send the one that came with those five that belongs to a Brigade here. by this means you will have ten of the number that came on; and I shall for the present have the remainder. the Waggons that are at present in the Park as fast as they are repaired, are at your service in lieu of those going on until General Green's pleasure respecting them is declared—

I am Sir Your's &c.

Thompson was Waggon Master General.

To Thomas Jones

Sir,   June 12th 1779

You are immediately to proceed to Camp with the Waggons loaded with Military Stores Given you in charge, by the road of Morris Town at your arrival there you will wait on Major Lindley and present him the Orders which you have on him for fifty Barrils Cannon Powder and twenty Barrils Musket ditto. these you are to see properly loaded in the four Empty Waggons Which Accompanies you, after which you Are to apply to the Authority in Command whether Civil or Military was a suitable guard to insure your very important loading to Camp. if Obtained you will send back the Artillery guard which goes on with you from hence if not take them on with you proceeding by the way of pumpton and from thence the same rout the park of Artillery took to Smiths Clove Whare it is probable the Army is at present and you will get further instructions. the Teams loaded with Powder you are to see on to New Windsor, whare you will halt them and give Col Lamb notice of there Arrival Who will give Orders for their destination; the Musket Cartridge paper goes on also to Windsor With the Powder—you will wait on Genl. Knox if present and deliver him the letter Directed for him if not forward it—You Will upon your arrival at Camp Issue the Stores you have by a proper Order to the several Brigade Conductors taking There receipts as usual—if you find any particular Spiecis wanting You will forward a letter & teems to this place to be supply'd. I have nothing further to add but my Compliments to the General and other Gentlemen in the park—

To Henry Knox

Dear General   Pluckemin [N.J.] June 12th 1779

I have the pleasure by Mr Jones to acknowledge the receipt of yours 9th Instant and at the same time to inform you that I have comply'd with its Contents[.] the night before last the teams from Philadelphia arrived with the Stores as pr Invoice inclosed, the Teams being ordered to return to Trenton and our horses not being arrived perplexed me much however I forcibly detain'd twelve, and this morning procured Horses for sixteen Waggons which I had repaired twelve of these I loaded, and the other four sent empty to Morriss to take on the Powder that their might not any time be lost. I have inclosed you an Invoice of what Stores I have forwarded and I have taken particular care to sort them to the wants of the Army

    I expect another Brigade of teems in from Philadelphia to morrow or next day. these I shall forward without unloading. I have applied for Horses to take on the remainder of the Waggons and hope to have them ready to come on with those expected from Philadelphia after which I shall leave a Conductor to take care of the remaining Stores in the Magazine and come immediately to Camp—My command here if it may be called one, has been as difficult as ever I experienced, no Commissary of Provisions left nor scarce any Provisions and at least 200 Mouths to Feed the whole of which applied to me and had I not immediately exerted my self have reason to believe I should have been made a prey to their voracious Jaws I sent to the Magazine and obtain'd an order for what Provisions I wanted but not person could be found to Issue it out when here this I remedied by doing it myself untill I wrote to the Commissary and had Mr Collis appointed since which all goes on smooth in that Department—

    My next trouble was the Gaurd was insufficient the Inhabitants were breaking open all the Barracks and the QM Genls. stores were exposed this I put a stop to by taking a Corporals gaurd out of the Laborat[ory] which put an end to that. upon sending off the Stores a fresh Difficulty came in view, how to get a Gaurd to go on with them it being in my opinion unsafe to send then without any upon the whole I concluded to send a Corporal and four from the Magazine Gaurd two of the Artificers and send a Chest of Arms for the use of the Waggoners, and ordered Mr Jones to endeavor to procure a full gaurd at Morris Town and send them back if that could not be done take them on to Camp but its time to cease the relation of my troubles, e'er long I hope to enjoy the pleasure of seeing you which will give instant relief to Your obliged friend & very huml Servt.

To James Thompson

Sir   Pluckemin [N.J.] June 13th 1778

    being detained here still for want of Waggons and horses to take the remaining stores on hand, I yesterday applied, both to Col Berry and Mr howe DQM. they each informed me you had got a number on hand which had just arrived, and that you expected they would be wanted here—if that is the case that you have any that you can possibly spare, I should be greatly obliged if you would order one brigade of about ten or twelve here to load to Camp, as I must be detained untill some are procured—

I have about six more waggons of my own which have no horses if these could be supply'd it would take on the whole which I wish to carry—

I am Sir

NB Please to send an answer by the bearer—

To James Thompson

Sir   Pluckemin [N.J.] June 15th 1778

I am exceedingly obliged to your endeavors to serve me, and am loath to give your further trouble, but if it were possible to persuade the men that drives the Brigade of nine covered Waggo[ns] which you mention to take them on to Camp it would effectually answer my end as I have Waggoners there who woul[d] immediately relieve them. this I will promise them on my Honour shall be done, if they will not consent I think it would be best, to load them with your Flour and send them to Morris, and I should be glad you would write a line to the Q Mr. to reserve them for my use, and I will go to Camp and send the Waggoners to Morris to receive the Waggons and come to this place and load my Store[s] for Camp—

I am Sir Yours &c.

To Cornelius Austin

Sir   June 15th 1779

You being to remain here untill further orders from General Knox you will carefully attend to the Men in the Ammory and see that they diligently improve the proper hours of work and faithfully perform the repairs necessary to make the muskets compleat the arms as fast as got in order are to be Boxed up and mark'd while Boxes can be had afterwards carried to the church, now improved as a Magazine and pil'd up as you are taut on the ground you will collect the unrepair'd Waggons and every species of stores that you get knowledge of into one place to prevent loss to the publick—should you not be ordered on to Camp, by forwarding your pay Abstracts they shall be paid as usual

Austin is listed as a Captain, apparently serving in the Military Stores Department.

To James Abeel

Dear Colo.   Chester [N.Y.] June 21th 1779

    Mr. Brower CMS waits on you to receive the nine new Ammunition Waggons lately sent to you charge loaden with Flour from Mr. Thompson W M Genl. he wrote me word he would send a line to you to request the Waggons might be kept and the Horses put in good pasture untill I should send Waggoners from Camp to take them on. these accompanies Mr. Brower for that purpose and you will very much oblige me and serve the Army—(as a march is soon expected) in furnishing the Horses that came with the Waggons if in order, if not, such as is
    With esteem I am Yours &c.

To Henry Brower

Sir   Chester [N.Y.] June 21st 1779

    You are immediately to repair to Morriss and deliver the Letter which you have for Colo. Abeel DQM Genl: there, the purport of which is to deliver you Nine new covered Ammunition Waggons, upon receipt of which you deliver one to each of the Waggoners you have in charge. five of them you will sent to Pluckemin to load with Case Shot of 3, 4, 6 & 12 pd: the other four Waggons in the mean time you are to take and proceed to Mendon with & load each with twelve hundred weight of Powder, mostly cannon or at least a proportion of two thirds. these you will take down to Morriss, if you can put them under a proper I untill you proceed to Pluckemin load and bring on the other five, and with the whole proceed to Camp with the utmost expedition provided the Camp remains where it now is or in case upon enquiry you find it the nearest rout and as safe to go by way of mendon to Fish Kill you will leave the Waggons loaded with powder in charge of the I at that place, and bring up those from

Pluckemin and come that way[.] the powder is intended to be left at Fish Kill with Mr Ruddock DCMS and the other Stores to be brought to the Army should we alter our situation before you arrive you will use your best judgement that both these intentions are answered.
   Your's

To Nicholas Ricketts

Sir   Chester [N.Y.] June 21st 1779
   At present it is impossible to procure teams to take the whole of the Stores but hope it will do done shortly. all the Teams I could procure accompanies Mr Brower for Stores you will please to furnish a Corporal and three men to come on with them as I think it not safe to have them come without a I—
   Yours &c

Ricketts was a Lieutenant in the Regiment of Artillery Artificers.

To Christian Holmes

Sir   Chester [N.Y.] June 21 1779
   The General directs you to order the person in whose care the powder is lately sent to Mendon to deliver forty eight hundred weight to the Bearer Mr. Wm. Brower CMS to be brought to this place
   I am Sir Yours &c.
Commanding the Artillery at Mendon   Major

Holmes was Major of the First Continental Artillery.

To William Davies

Sir   Chester [N.Y.] June 23d 1779
   Your Billet of this day's date I have received and am much surprized at its contents. Had Colo. Butler made a regular application for Ammunition inclination as well as Duty would have produc'd an instant supply the regular mode of application is by a return of the articles wanted sign'd by the commandant of the Brigade and then

presented to General Knox whose order is a proper Voucher for the delivery had this been done I am sure there would have been no cause of complaint

For my own part I know not of any application having been made to any person, the Stores we have on hand ready to be delivered the instant the return comes properly qualified—

I am Sir Your most obedt Servt.

Davies was Colonel of the Tenth Virginia Regiment.

To Henry Knox

Dear Genl. Chester [N.Y.] June 29 1779

By the return of Mr. Frothingham I am informed of your wanting a Conductor to go to Philadelphia supposing his Business to carry dispatches, and being short of Conductors have forwarded Mr Clumburg (this moment arrived from Philadelphia and returning tomorrow morning) to receive your commands the Invoice of Stores arrived you have inclosed. if he will not answer your end I expect one in every minute which will be sent to you, at present have none with me having sent one Yesterday to supply Mr. Cunninghams place who has resign'd—

I am Sir Yours &c.

Mr Frothingham will wait on you Thursday morning to receive your Commands to Boston—

To Nathanael Greene

Sir Chester [N.Y.] June 29th 1779

Mr Howe BQM has this moment informed me that you have ordered him to send on a Brigade of Waggons, left with me the day before yesterday, the Circumstances of which I beg leave to relate. a waggon Master Call'd on me at my lodgings & informed me he had a Brigade of twelve Waggons which he was directed to leave with me after delivering their contents which was Flour, I told him I was happy to receive them as the came very opportunely, I being distrest for want, after which he drove to the Commissaries and unloaded and

then came and paraded them with mine Mr. Turner DWMG appeared at the same Time and receited for them. this I supposed was to be the regular mode of supply, and am exceedingly sorry that any uneasiness should arise on accot. of its being done without a special order from you. this day another Brigade of teems arrived from Philadelphia with stores, which were unloaded into the twelve refered to besides which I have not more than twelve fit to move—I flatter myself when the General is made acquainted with the Circumstances of there being brought and the Great Necessity of their being Kept to their present use, he will order it to be done—if any further receipts are Necessary I will see that they are procoured as directed—
    I am Sir with Esteem Yours—

To James Pearson

Dear Sir   Chester [N.Y.] June 30th 1779
By the return of Mr Clumburg I have an opportunity of acknowledging the receipt of the Stores as p[er] Invoice & the twenty two Cannon Havresacks not mentioned, for all which he has a receipt
    I have heard nothing as yet from Mr Cook, the Army in great of want of the Cartridges he has in charge, which I hope will be principally 19 to the Pound more than two thirds of the Armies call for the Size, and except what is in the hand of the Brigade Conductors we have none of them. youll please to attend to this matter in what you forward in future—Our next greatest distress is the Armourers tools which if possible please to send on immediately, Vices & Anvills in particular—The inspector of Musick impatiently waits the Return to the request for Musical Instruments, please to inform me what he may expect—No particlar news in Camp, daily expectation of the enemies advance to the Fort at West Point but at present they are quite still—
    Inclosed you have the return for the Month June by which you will perceive a considerable quantity of damaged Stores, which will be forwarded to you to be repaired by the first opportunity. they are deposited in the Magazine at Pluckemin under the charge of a Conductor who is left there for purpose of seeing them on—
    I am Yours &c.

To Jonathan Gostelowe

Dear Sir   Chester [N.Y.] June 30 1779
By the return of Mr Clumburg I have an opportunity of acknowledging the receipt of your kind Favor by him[.] we have near a thousand Damaged Muskets on hand waiting for some returning Waggons to take them on and likewise several other Species of damaged Stores. they are left at Pluckemin under charge of a Conductor for that purpose, and hope you will receive them soon.—I am happy to hear the news from the Southward gains credit hope it will turn out equal to our most sanguine expectations—Nothing worthy of notice has taken place as yet in this Quarter, daily expect there will
           Yours &c

To Samuel French

sir   Chester [N.Y.] June 30th 1779
    By Mr Clumburg I have the agreable opportunity to present you with a scrawl as the entering wedge to our future correspondence having nothing particular new to communicate. Mr. Clumburg being short of money I have supplied him with Fifty Dollars and taken his receipt to account with you for the same you will please to place this to my account of Credit hope shortly the whole will be settled to your and my Satisfaction
    I am Sir Yours &c:

To Nathanael Greene

Honored Sir   Chester [N.Y.] July 1 1779
    Your's of this Days date I have received I am exceedingly obliged by its contents. I am fully convinced of the propriety and necessity of confining every part of the Business of the Army to its own proper Department. from this conviction shall see that the teems mentioned, pass through the Department to which they belong in such a manner as to insure their being regularly returned, and convinced of your ready disposition to give every assistan[ce] (consistent with Duty) to my Department shall for the future rest assured of being

supplied by a regular application & shall admit none but such as are obtain'd in that way.—

With respect I am Yours

To Thomas Jones

Sir   Chester [N.Y.] July 1st 1779

You are to take charge of the four teems loaded with Powder and proceed with all convenient speed to Fish Kill and deliver it [to] John Ruddock DCMS and take his receipt for the same—then order the Teems back to this place immediately

You will then proceed to New Milford and procure a Return in the Form order'd from Mr. Richards, overhaul the Stores and see that they agree with the Return now made and formerly. you will desire Mr Richards to send on the Box of Duck in his possession as quick as possible, if no opportunity presents to send it immediately to me he will send it properly directly to the Care of Mr. Ruddock at Fish Kill to be forwarded. you have leave of absence for one week—

To William Richards

Sir   Chester [N.Y.] July 1st 1779

Nothing could have surprized me more or warp'd my confidence in you than to find you absent from your charge for three Days at such a Time of expectation as the present. the consequence has been the General Return is gone to Congress without any reference to the Stores at New Milford, though an Officer was sent on purpose to obtain the return

Money left for you without any regular receipt and you may be oblig'd to the Gentleman who did it for you as it would have been returnd had not he undertook. I am not disposed to be captious, but must seriously recommend it to you not to give the same occasion in future   Yours

To Cornelius Austin

Sir   Chester [N.Y.] July 6 1779

   The General on account of the great number of Muskets daily brought for repair, has thought best to order you with your men, Forges, & Tools, to come immediately to Camp. what muskets you have repaired, you will deliver to Mr. Shineman C M S to be forwarded to me by the Return of the Waggons, under the charge of Mr. Brower, with these it is best for you to come on, as they have a Waggon Master with these which may be of Service to you. the Damag'd Arms which you have must also be delivered to Mr. Sheineman. Colonel Berry will give you any assistance in his Power you may need
   I am Sir Yours &c.

To Christian Henry Sheineman

Sir   Chester [N.Y.] July 6 1779

   Mr. Brower is sent in charge of eight Teems to receive all the repair'd Muskets, you have on hand. you will apply to Captn. Austin for what he has on hand, and forward them at the same time, as the demand had again become very pressing; You are also to forward seven or eight hundred New Constructed Carte Boxes, the machine for drawing Fuzes, all the spare Bayonets, and scabbards all the Drums & Fifes, and if these should not fill the Waggons, (which depends on the number of Arms you have on hand) you will forward such other Articles as you suppose most wanting in Camp. I hope before this you have had an opportunity to forward more Damag'd Muskets and Carte Boxes to Philadelphia as they are almost out of employ, and have wrote for these to keep the men at work—For want of Waggons I am not able to remove all the Stores from Pluckemin at present and indeed the enemies motions are so very uncertain, as makes me doubt whether it would be best. perhaps the next news we have from them may be from some part of Jersey in which case the Stores would be best where they are. Damaged Arms coming in very fast, Mr. Austin with his men is sent for to come on immediately. the remainder of the Muskets which he has unrepaired you will take into your charge to be forwarded with the rest to Philadelphia. As you will have a considerable number of Stores still on hand it seems best to

continue to Guard, as Captn. Austin's men will be sufficient I to come on with those forwarded tis probable the remainder of the Stores will be a few days be removed to Mendon. should that be the Case the remainder of the I with Lieut. Ricketts will be ordered to join the Park of this more hereafter—My particular compliments to Mr Teeple and all his good Family, tell them I am very agreably situated but sometimes wish for some of their Sallet & Milk Punch nothing new in Camp
    Yours—

Christian Henry Sheineman, who also appears as Henry Christian Schenemann, was appointed a Conductor of Military Stores on April 7, 1779, and resigned on December 25, 1775.

To William Brower

Sir   Chester [N.Y.] July 6th 1779
    You are to repair to Pluckemin and apply to Mr. Sheineman CMS who I have ordered to deliver all the repaired Muskets he has on hand. likewise the new Constd. Carte Boxes all the Flints the Machine for drawing Fuzes, and whatever other articles you may judge most wanted in Camp to fill the eight Waggons you have in charge. the Drums & Fifes are to be particularly brought on, and all the Spare Bayonets and Scabbards after having loaded them in the best manner you will proceed to this place with all possible dispatch
    Yours &c

William Brower served as a Conductor of Military Stores until August 30, 1780.

To John Ruddock

Dear Sir   Chester [N.Y.] July 6 1779
    The bearer Mr. Jona Bradford has in charge an engine for Drawing Fuzes which General Knox requested me to send to the Fort at West Point, thinking it most likely to arrive safe I have forwarded it to you and must beg that you would immediately forward it to the Point.
    I am much press'd for Tools to furnish the Travelling Forges orders to the Brigades, must beg the favor of you to endeavor to procure some Anvills, Bench & hand Vices and Files Sorts suitable

for Armourers if to be had on any Terms. None to be had from Philadelphia you will be kind enough to give me the most early information if you have any prospect of obtaining them—
Yours &c.

To James Pearson

D^r. Sir　　　　　　　　　　　　　　　　Chester [N.Y.] July 6 1779
By the return of Mr. Schultz I have an opportunity of acknowledging the receipt of yours of ye 22d June inclosing the Invoice of Stores sent by him the whole of which I received except sixty six Tin & Iron C Boxes. these I suppose were inserted wrong in the Invoice as the Box. No. 1 is said to contain 576 whereas the parchment on the Box is mark'd only 510. the Contents I have not examined shall be particular in counting them when I have leisure—

The other Stores are a very timely supply and for the present will be enough the [three lines illegible] both the draw one for small peices, and those with a Flap for the large. you will please to have them made accordingly—With respect to the Carte Boxes I am utterly unable to [s]ay any thing at present hope they will answer some valuable purpose, but am inclined to think they will not answer since the army is well supply[ed] with Leather which upon all occasions are judg'd the best. must beg you not to forward any more untill you hear how these are disposed of—

The Armourers still press me hard for Files, Anvills & Vices of this I wrote you be Mr Clumburg. am happy to hear of a prospect of a full supply of Files—As to the Musket Carts. I am exceedingly sorry to find them all 17 to the lb. as I have a considerable number of that Size on hand—none of 19 & but very few of any other Size—should those coming in charge of Mr Cook be of the 17 I shall be perplex'd beyond measure I shall immediately endeavor to have a quantity of Lead forwarded from Springfeild if any in Store and must beg that a quantity of Carts. 19 be made & forwarded immediately, as more than 2/3d of the Army have French Musketts nothing new in Camp our Army still keep the old position the enemies said to have retire to York except about one thousand who remain at the redoubts near Kings ferry. my complims. to Colo Flower if present and the other Gentlemen in the Department—

　　　with esteem I remain Yours &c.
I have forwarded the Wag[gons]

To Jonathan Gostelowe

Dear Sir   Chester [N.Y.] July 6th 1779
I am exceedingly oblidged by your frequent epistles, and am determined not to fall in debt. The Tin & Iron Cartridge Boxes came to hand except sixty six which I suppose to be a mistake in the Invoice Box No. 1 aid to contain 576 is marked only 510, from thence arises the mistake

Having never heard of the intention of ordering on these Boxes, cannot pretend to judge of their Utility but hope their Design may be fully answered, but having had a full supply of the new Constructed Leather Boxes which are universally admired I am afraid these will lye on my hands for which reason beg you would not forward any more untill I have informed you of the Disposition of these—I still hope & believe the present Campaign will be the last that the Genius of Britain in an evil hour has deserted her, that France and United America will rise the wonder of the world and that these western climes will be an asylum for the oppressed, till time shall be no more. Nothing further at this Time only my compliments to Major French in return for his and my unalterable affection for my personally unknown Friend—

Yours &c

NB Nothing new the face of affairs with us much as when I wrote last the waggons not being suitable for the I I have ordered them to Pluckemin to load with Damaged Musketts & Stores and return with all convenient speed to Philadelphia—

To Christian Henry Sheineman

Sir   Chester [N.Y.] July 6 1779
The Bearer Mr. Schultz CMS waits on you with a number of empty Waggons to be loaded with Damag'd Stores for Philadelphia. as these opportunities does not often present and as I am very desirous to have those Stores go on, I hope you will attend and see the Waggons loaded to the best advantage and if possible send of [*sic*] every Damag'd Musket you have and likewise Cartridge Box. this being accomplish'd will insure you a release from your present confinement shortly, as I shall come myself or send Mr. Boyer to get the good Stores on to Mendon (that are not wanted in the I)—Once

more I say get away as much of the Damag'd Stores as possible and take two Receipts of the Conductor for the whole amount and what you send agreable to the Form inclosed, one of which he will take along with him the other you will send me—

You will dispatch the waggons under Care of Mr. Browner if not already come on, as their contents are much wanted here—Mr. Boyer says he would have renewed his Correspondence and sent another epistle, but that he finds or hears you can not read english, and he cannot read Dutch. he desires however to be remembered to you and through you to every [ ] in Pluckemin—

Yours &c

To James Thompson

Sir Chester [N.Y.] July 7th 1779

I have this moment been favour'd with a sight of your favour to Mr James Currey WC must inform you that it appearing that too [sic] of the waggoners were inlisted by Mr Turner They and their waggons are detained—the horses which were unfit for any service are order'd to be delivered to Colonel Broderick—the waggons are in my service you will please to return them accordingly—the other teems are partly loaded with damaged stores from here and sent to be fully loaded at Pluckemin

Nothing could have happened more timly as I have Near a thousand damaged Musketts their [sic] waiting for an Opportunity to be forwarded to Philadelphia to be repair[ed.]

I am Sir Yours

To James Pearson

Dear Sir Chester [N.Y.] July 7th 1779

Since writing the Letter which accompanies this, I have unloaded the Waggons and examined the Stores, and am much surprized to find in what situation the Cannon Ammunition has been Issued from the Magazine or Laboratory. never a Cap or Cylinder on any of the 12 pd. Ammunition, whi[ch] is indeed the preservative of the Life & elastic Force of the Powder besides agrea[ble] advantage in keeping it in order when travelling—I mention the matter that you may put a stop to any more being sent in the same manner—

I have supply'd Mr. Schultz CMS with one hundred Dollars to enable him to return. inclosed you have the Duplicate receipt, wherein he promis[es] to account with you for that Sum—We can determine in some future Day the best mode of settling this and any other Sums which may occasionally be advanc[ed] CMS or any other persons employed by us in the public Business—

Yours &c.

To Nathanael Greene

Honored Sir   Chester [N.Y.] July 10 1779

Last evening the Bearer arrived in Camp in charge of Eleven Teams loaded with Ammunition from Lebanon, these are continental property, and the Drivers inlisted for one Year, their Waggons of the open Sort with Covers loose over. As I have no place to Deposit the Stores in, and the Waggons mentioned above unsuitable for the transportation of any Stores—I am constrain'd to solicit the favor of an exchange of these for the Same number of close covered ones if possibly they can be spared, and an order to retain the Men and have them annex'd to the Spare Ammunition. if this is granted I am in hopes it will prevent my troubling the General with any more applications of this Sort during the Campaign as I have several of my old ones repairing[.] the whole number of waggons employed in my Department at present is forty one which is considerably short of what we had last Year and falls short of the calculation made by General Knox & myself at the opening of the Campaign Fifty nine being the number supposed necessary to keep the Army fully supplyed with Military Stores

With respect I am Sir Yours &c.

To Thomas Jones

Sir   Chester [N.Y.] July 16 1779

You are immediately to proceed to Fish Kill with the eight hundred & three new constructed Carte Boxes and 1115 Bayone[t] Belts given you in charge and deliver them to Jno. Ruddock Esqr.

DCMS at that place together with the Letter which you have for him—After having them properly receipted you will order The Teems immediately to return to this place—On your return you will call on Mr. Kemper DCG and request the Favor of him to deliver you the Shirts mention'd in a Return of cloathing left with him sometime s[ince.] if he has any suitable for the Gentlem[en] belonging to the Department endeavor to ascertain the price of the cloathing already drawn, and of the Shirts if obtain[ed] likewise informing yourself what other specie[s] of cloathing is in Store
Yours

To John Ruddock

Sir Chester [N.Y.] July 16 1779
Mr. Jones waits on you with eight hundred & three new constructed C Boxes eleven hundred & fifteen Bayonet Belts to compleat the eastern Brigades you will please to receive them and give the Conductors annexed to those Brigades notice of their arrival, that they may be supplied without loss of time—

I have sent more than the return of wanting brought me by Mr. Frothingham supposing it likely more men may have join'd since that return was made—You will please to let me know as soon as possible whether these will answer the whole demand. If not I can furnish more
I am Sir Yours &c.

To William Cook

Sir Chester [N.Y.] July 17th 1779
You are immediately to repair [to] New Windsor with the Stores given you in charge, and if possible you are to fin[d] Colo Carrington and leave the 24 & 12 pd. Am[m]unition with him taking his rect. for [the] same. if he should be gone you will wait on General Knox and take his orders resp[ec]ting the propriety of following him; the 18 pd. Shot and Shells are intended for West Point and you will take the Generals ord[ers] whether to deliver them at Fish Kill as the readiest conveyance, or proceed on wi[th] them on this Side yourself in either case you will procure proper receipts of their Delivery. having

accomplished this Bu[si]ness you will return with the two Waggons to this place, without a mome[nts] unnessary Delay should the Wagg[ons] on any pretence be detain'd, the Waggoners are to return to their Brigades [with] you
    Yours &c.

Cook was a Conductor of Military Stores.

To John Glover

Sir   Chester [N.Y.] July 19th 1779
    Mr. Wm. Cook Conductor Military Stores, waits on you with his Instructions by which you will perceive that he is annexed to your Brigade, agreable to General Orders. you will please to direct the QMr. to furnish him with the Teems necessary to comply with his orders two may possibly do, but three much better. you will also please to order the Brigade returns to be given in to Mr. Cook of every Article wanted to compleat, after which you may be assur'd they shall be supplied as quick as possible with every thing on hand or that can be procured
    With respect I am Yours

Glover was a Brigadier General from Massachusetts.

To Henry Knox

Sir   Chester [N.Y.] July 21 1779
    Yours of yesterday by Mr. Brower came to hand, and is now before me, shall now endeavor to give you the reasons that gave birth to my supposition, that those Boxes already sent would answer ther prese[nt] purpose. When the new Cartridge Boxes arrived, you inform'd me it was your intention to supply the Continental troops intirely with new, and desired me to keep as many of the best which were return'd in, as would supply any Bodies of Militia that might occasionally join us. this was done, but on account of our movement they were ordere[d] to Philadelphia; The same orders I conclude[d] had been given on the order side the River, had that been the case surely when the whole as supply'd, there must have been a very great

number of the old on hand, perhaps sufficient for the new Levies. this I thought would fully answer every purpose, and keep the remaining New ones on hand, for the use of such as may have join'd the several Brigades since their first returns were answered. Agreable to your request, I shall send off this day for the whole of the Boxes and Belts remaining at Pluckemin; in the meantime must inform you, that I have 1110 on hand here, waiting your order for distribution;—I am exceedingly sorry to hear, that Mr. Ruddock's conduct renders it necessary to remove him, should that finally be determined on, [must] recommend Mr. Thomas Frothingham [at] present the oldest Conductor in that De[part]ment to the appointment, being as I am [ ] well qualified to discharge the duties of it, and having acted for a long time at that Post to the satisfaction of all concern'd;—Mr. Jones with your approbation I shall send to West Point. should you think proper to commission the above Gentlemen, by a Line informing me of it, I will order them to wait on you immediately, and take their orders.

I mention'd to Mr. Jones the matter of not calling on you on his return. he says in defence, that after leaving you he proceeded to deliver the Powder, after which ageable to his Instructions from me, he went to New Milford to view the Stores and bring a return. on his arrival found the Stores were removed to Litchfield, to which he immediately proceeded, did his Business, and on his return call'd at your Quarters, where he was inform'd you was gone to Pluckemin. this relation he hopes will free hi[m] from the charge of remissness, and account to you for his conduct;—To day I shall forwar[d] on 900 Iron Ball 18 pds. to the Fort, and should [be] glad to be inform'd, whether any twelves are wanting, as I have some which I could sen[d.] Mr Cook CMS delivered 634 18 pd. Shot at the Fort yesterday, and return'd last night.—

I should be happy to have your orders as often as possible, being fully sensible, that my knowledge of the movements of the Army is by no means sufficient to determine what is best to be done, should they not be executed rationally ignorance must be my excuse, for in point of attention & zeal I will yeild to no one.

With Esteem I am Yours &

To Christian Henry Sheineman

Sir   Chester [N.Y.] July 22d 1779

Mr. Quailly Waggon Master waits on you with five empty Teems to receive all the New Cartridge Boxes and all the Bayonet Belt[s] you have on hand. after these are loaded up, if there is any room left on the Waggons, you may send on some of those Spunges & Ladles that stand in the Corner of the Stores, the Box with the small Paints in it, and any other Articles you may think we need. if Mr. Kerker the Tinman has finish'd his work, as I suppose he must long before this time, you must send him on with the Teems, as he is much wanted here. send a few sheets Tin with him. As I have no Conductor I could send Mr. Quaily has promised to take charge of the Stores, and bring them on. I forgot to mention he has a few Damag'd Stores as you will see by the Inclosed Invoice
    Yours &c.
N.B You will send on by Mr: Quailey all you Papers of receivals and deliveries and a return of all the Stores you have on hand without this I shall not be able to make my General Returns

To Mr. Quaily

Sir   July 22d 1779

You will immediately proceed to Pluckemin with the five Teams under you charge an deliver the damage stores and the Letter you have to Mr. Christian Henry Scheineman Conductor Military Stores or in his absence to Lieut. Ricketts, or such other person as he may have left in charge of the Stores. he or they will load your Waggons with new Cartridge Box[es] Bayonet Belts and some other small Stores agreable to Directions in the Letter. Having received & loaded them up carefully you will make all possible dispatch in returning to this Place—
    I am Sir Yours &c.

Quaily was a Wagonmaster. The preceding letter spells the name "Quailey" and "Quailly" so the correct spelling is uncertain.

To William Cook

Sir   July 22d 1779

You are to proceed to New Windsor with the shott you have in charge, there unload and discharge the teems. from thence you are to proceed to the fort at West Point by water and deliver them to Mr John Banks Conductor M Stores, take his receipt for them and return immediately to this place—the water carriage you will obtain by an Application to the Quarter Master at the Landing

you will call on General Knox and deliver the letter you have for him by which you will know whether he has any Orders that you can execute at the fort and like wise call upon him on your return and inquire is he has any commands to me

Yours

To Thomas Jones

Sir   Chester [N.Y.] July 23d 1779

In consequence of orders from Genl. Knox you are immediately to proceed to West Point to receive and take charge of the Military Stores at that place now under the care of Mr. John Banks Condr. M Stores who is to continue there are act under you. you will carefully examine the state of the Stores delivered you, and without loss of time have them put in proper order for delivery. should you find any deficiency in any particular species of Stores you will make a Return thereof to me, that nothing possible to obtain may be wanting for the defence of the Fort. You will obtain the number & size of every peice Ordnance on the ground noting which are Iron and which Brass and send me an account by some trusty hand as quick as is convenient after your arrival this will enable me to determine what further supplies are necessary after receiving your Return of Stores which you must send me by the last day of this Month, and continue so to do while you remain at the Post—You will furnish yourself with Books, to make a regular entry on what Stores you receive from Mr. Banks at your first arrival and what you receive, and deliver from, or to and other person afterwards, in which you will open and keep your accounts, Regimentally. all orders for deliveries must be sign'd by the Commanding Officer of the Garrison or Artillery—

These may suffice for the outlines of your conduct, at first entering on you Comman[d,] any further Instructions necessary, may be [co]mmunicated from time to time, as your circumstances and my acquaintance therewi[th] may render usefull and proper. in any immediate difficult case, you will take the best advice you can obtain and act accordingly

I am Yours &c

To John Banks

Sir,   Chester [N.Y.] July 23d 1779

Mr. Thomas Jones DFCM Stores waits on you by order Genl Knox to receive and take Command of the Military Stores now under your charge. this is not occasioned by any complaint against you, but from a conviction that the number of Stores deposited in the Fort, demands more assistance and is thought a command of importance enoug[h] for the management of a DFComy. you are to be continued with the Stores and act under Mr. Jones, who is a gentleman of such a disposition, that I am sure you may make yourself very happy in your connections with him—

I am Sir Your's &c.

Banks had been appointed a Conductor of Military Stores on April 12, 1777.

To Mr. Pennington

Sir   July 24, 1779

You will proceed with the Teams given you in charge, loaded with 249 eight Inch Shells & 282 5 ½ Inch ditto to New Windsor. there unload & discharge the Teams, after which you will obtain a water Carriage and proceed with the Shells to West Point and deliver them to Mr. Thos. Jones DFCM Stores at that place and take his receipt for the same. you will then return to New Windsor, and releive Mr. Douglass Condr. M Stores and receive & receipt him for the Stores he may deliver you and join yourself in his stead to the first Pennsylvania Brigade & their continue to act agreable to Instructions given to him, untill further orders

Yours

Pennington was a Conductor of Military Stores.

To William Cook

Sir   Chester [N.Y.] July 29th 1779
   You will take charge of two Teams and their contents, going to New Windsor upon your arrival, you will deliver eighty one New Cartridge Boxes, three hundred Flints and one hundred & sixty two Dozen M Cartridges to Captn. Belding of Colo Sheldons Regt: of Dragoon[s.] if he should not be there you will deliver Mr. Eayrs or Copeland to take the charge of them untill he calls for them—The sett of Drag Ropes six sheepskins, and one Havresack, you will deliver to the order of Colo Carrington after having informed them that you have brough[t] them, down these articles are already receipted for. you will then proceed to West Point and deliver the nine hundred & fifty seven Tin & Iron Carte. Boxes to Mr. Jones DFCMS and take his receipt for them, unless you shou[ld] meet Mr. Pennington CrMS with the return for Genl. Wayne's Brigade in this case, you will deliver them to him, and let him go on with them and immediately supply the Brigade and take the proper receipts. the overplus if any he will deliver to Mr Jones
   Having finish'd this business you will proceed to Ridgefield, and execute your other Instructions—
   Yours &c.

To Edward Carrington

Dr Sir,   Chester [N.Y.] July 29 1779
   Yours pr. Captn. Lillie I have received and to day have forwarded as many of the articles wrote for as I had on hand Vizt six sheepskins one sett Drag Ropes and one Havresack. the Paper Cartridges and Spunge Tacks you may get by applying to Mr. Jones at West Point. the Paint I shall endeavor to forward as soon as I know what colour will answer
   Pray write me as often as possible & let me into the arcana as I am naturally impatient. Nothing new in this quarter—
   With esteem I am Your's

Carrington was Lieutenant Colonel of the First Continental Artillery.

To Mr. Pennington

Sir   Chester [N.Y.] July 30 1779
You are to take charge of the Waggons containing four hundred Tin Carte Boxes & Belts one Case qt. eleven setts trail Ropes & six setts of Drag Ropes, one Cask qt. two Drums, Carriages & Sticks, and proceed to New Windsor. when arrived, you will inform yourself whether the Boxes, that went on yesterday are forwarded to West Point. if so you will immediately follow with the Stores you now have, except the Drums which you are to leave with Mr. Eayrs or Copeland and deliver the Case of ropes to Mr. Jones. take in the Tin Cannisters that went on first, and go on to Fort Montgomery and deliver them to the several Regiments agreable to the return you have with you taking each commanding Officers receipt for them after which you will find Mr. Douglass and receive the Stores he has belonging to the first Pena Brigade & continue to do duty in the Brigade as CMS untill further orders. you will sent what Rects. you have on by him
      Yours &c.

To Timothy Pickering Jr.

Honored Sir   Chester [N.Y.] Augt. 1st. 1779
Excess of business must be my apology for not acknowledging the receipt of your kind Favor of June 4th, and thanking you for it contents. I am happy to hear that the Honble. Board have acceded to my appointment, and shall endeavor to justify by my future conduct the favorable impressions that have been made on the minds of the Board respecting me in gratitude to the author who is at present unknown—
With respect to the charge in my account of expences to Boston to which there is an objection made, I believe I may appeal to the Board when I say that not an account from the principal of any department can be produced, for the whole of last Year, so moderate as mine. howev[er] as it is the judgement of the Board, that it ought not to be allowed I shall settle it according to their direction—
I must now request to be informed on what foundation I and my department stand and under what description we act, not a Commission (or if that may not be expected), or Warrant to be found

among us. I mean under the new regulations, of consequence, as some of the Department are with every Garrison or Brigade should the fate of War put them in possession of the enemy, they must expect no other usage than the private Centinel. this and the miserable pittance they receive for their services, join'd to our being precluded the benefit of all Stores both State and Continental, has occasioned many resignations and unless something is immediately done, the department must sink into contempt. for my own part notwithstanding my determined frugality I am every day growing poor, and nothing but my zeal for the sacred cause, could induce me to continue the present Campaign—

I mention our situation, not from any piqu[e] or resentment at our being neglected, but purely for the publick good. having nothing on hand or in reversion to offer, I find it already very difficult to get persons suitably qualified to fill the several Offices in the Department which is very essential to proper supply of the Army, and the preservation of the Stores—

Inclosed you have the General Return of Stores immediately under my charge at Chester & Pluckemin—Having by the Generals direction forwarded Mr Jones DFCMS to take charge of the Stores at West Point, I at the same time instructed him to make Returns agreable to the last Regulations, but coming too late to be inserted in mine, I contented myself with sending it inclosed hoping by the time the next become[s] due, I shall have it in my power to comply with the Letter of the resolve by a full insertion of all the Stores at the different posts in the vicinity of the main army being determined to make timely requisitions for that purpose—I have nothing further to add but my most respectfull compliments to the honl. Board assuring them that I am unfeignedly their & the publicks—Huml Servant

To James Pearson

Sir   Chester [N.Y.] Augt: 2d 1779

By Captn. Austin I have an opportunity to forward the General Return for July. he waits on you pr. order General Knox to endeavor to procure several articles in the Armourers Branch which as they are much wanted I hope you will be able to supply I could wish to have a quantity of Musket Cartridges forwarded of nineteens to the pound as quick as possible, as they will be most wanted and I have the least proportion of them on hand. also a quantity of spunge Tacks, Hammers & Pinchers and a number more rounds of 12 pd. fix'd Shot. a particular circumstance which ought to be mentioned, makes us in want of a number more six pound fix'd Shot. the last that came were so out of size that very few of them would enter the Calibre of the six pound Ordnance, and after delivery have been return'd. you will attend to this to prevent any more coming untill they are proved, a mistake of this nature in the day of Battle would be fatal two hundred will be a present supply of either—

It is now a considerable time since I heard from you, should be exceeding glad to be informed in your next that Colonel Flower had recovered his Health if present you will please to present my regards to him. pray inform me also whether Congress has done any thing for the Ordnance Department and what if any thing

Nothing new in haste I am Yours

To the Board of War and Ordnance

Gentleman   Chester [N.Y.] Augt: 2d 1779

The Bearer Captn. Cornelius Austin is forwarded by order General Knox to procure if possible a number of Articles wanting to compleat the Armourers annex'd to the different Brigades. as it is of importance that they should be immediately supplied, I doubt not that you will give him every Assistance to enable him to accomplish the Business he has on hand

Captn. Austin informs me he intends to solicit the Board for the indulgence of an order on the cloathing Store to furnish himself with some necessary Articles of Cloathing to forward which, he supposes it necessary to have a recommendation from the head of the Department under which he has immediately acted. as that falls upon me shall only say that he has faithfully perform'd his Duty in every instance within the Compass of my knowledge and being equally exposed in Camp to the loss and destruction of cloathing, am inclined to think the Board will consider hi[m] as an Officer, and give him such assistance as they shall think proper and necessary to enable him to appear decently in character

With respect & esteem I am Gentlemen Your very huml Servt.

To Henry Knox

Sir   Chester [N.Y.] Augt. 4th. 1779

Before my return to Chester from the Poin[t] the waggons had return's from Pluckemin with the Cartridge Boxes & Bayonet Belts. I have now on hand nine hundred new Carte Boxes and eighteen hundred Bayt. Belts ready to deliver to your order. I have about 300 Boxes still remaining at Pluckemin and between two & three thousand Bayt. Belts which if you think best, upon advice I will immediately send for—

I have seen Mr. Collins who informs me that he has brought on one thousand new Musk[ets] & thirty seven Drums, a judicious distribution of these will I am sure amply supply the Army with those articles for the present Campaign, and being at your dispose [sic] I am confident that will be the case. I have taken the liberty to inclose for your perusal a Copy of the Letter which I wrote to the Board of War by Captn. Austin hoping as you was kind enough to furnish me with the outlines the drapery will meet with your approbation. I am sensible of its defects; but they will understand (as Mr. Hi[rvi]ll says) what I mean—This moment I receiv'd your Directio[ns] to send the Teems for the Shot, and intend to have them all under way early to morrow morning and shall forward them to the Point without a moments loss of Time in order to facilitate the Business shall send Mr. Boyer who is every way equal to the charge. indeed I have no one else to send Mr. Pennington having by order of Colo Lamb join'd his company this day untill he returns I must be Comy. Clk and Condr. of course you will suppose me confin'd to my post—

With esteem I am Your very huml Servt.

To James Boyer

Sir   Chester [N.Y.] Augt: 6 1779

You are immediately to proceed to Mr. Faesh's at the furnace in Mount Hope and deliver him the order you have in charge for a quantity of round & Grape Shot of different Sizes as many of each sort to the amount of the order as you can procure, you will see loaded up and immediately forwarded to this place—

Should you have more Teems than you can get loaded with shot you will order them on to Pluckemin to fetch the remaining Carte.

Boxes, Bayonet Belts, and other articles which you know are most wanting here sufficient to load them properly; those loaded with Shot you are to send on under the care of the Wagn. Master and come on with the other yourself if you find that the Carpenters an Tinman [*sic*] at Pluckemin can be spared you will bring them on with you. while you are at Pluckemin you will wait on Colo: Berry to know if it is not possible to get Teams to carry off the Damag'd Stores at that place to Philadelphia or only to Trenton, if this can be done Mr. Sheineman will go on with them immediately. if they go on to Trenton by applying to the Quarter Master he may procure other Teems or water Carriage which will answer quite as well you will give him any further instructions according as you find the circumstances—

You will present my most respectful compliments to Colo McDonalds family Mr Teeples & all enquiring Friends

As the Business is of importance you will make all possible Dispatch and be frugal as the charge of travelling is at best enormous. I wish you success in your business and a pleasant journey—

Yours &c

To John Jacob Faesh

Sir Chester [N.Y.] Augt. 6 1779

By order Brigadier Genl Knox I have forwarded Mr James Boyer Clk to my Department with a suitable number of Teems to receive from you the followg Articles—

Vizt. 2600 12 pd: Shot
 1000 3 pd   do:
 500 4 pd   do:

and five Tons Grape shot of 4 & 8 oz Weight you will please to furnish the whole if on hand if not as many of each as you have you will be kind enough to give Mr Boyer the nearest & best rout for the waggons to return—

With esteem I am Sir Yours &c:

Faesh was one of the leading ironmasters of the time. He owned Mount Hope Furnace in New Jersey which produced cannon and shot as well as other ironwork for the army. A native of Switzerland, he originally spelled his name Faesch.

To Henry Knox

Sir   Chester [N.Y.] Augt 7th 1779

Yesterday I rescived from Philadelphia in 6 Cases—66 Muskets 66 black belts 66 Cartridge boxes and 12 prs. horse pistoles Directed for Majr. Lees Dragoons—they were intended immediately for the regt. but from whome adrest or in whose perticular charge does not ap[pear] the waggoners horses tireing was the Reason of their being Left with me—you will please to inform Majr Lee whear the articles are or give such other orders respecting them as you shall think best.—

The waggons went off for the shot Yesterday—
Yours—

To Charles Harrison

Sir   Chester [N.Y.] Augt. 11 1779

This morning I received a Billet from Captn. Doughty inclosing an order from you for one of the Tumbrills that came to me yesterday from Windsor, with Horses Geers and Drivers the last in the Billet in return to him I inform'd were return'd to New Windsor the Tumbrells being ordered up by Genl Knox and I not knowing for what reason, I likewise inform'd him, I did not consider them at my dispose to any order except the Generals—this has occasion'd a second Billet or Letter in which disappointment at a suppos[ed] insult at calling in question your order has broke out into rancour and scurrullity—As I cannot take it as coming from you who I am sure uncapable of such composition on a real insult, much less what was never intended as such, but an act of Duty. "and being inform'd that you wait for my answer to know what steps to take" unawed by menaces shall repeat that they were sent to me by the Genl. without and orders as is common when any thing comes. however if you suppose them under these circumstances, under your Direction, they are at your dispose—
Yours—

Harrison, from Virginia, was Colonel of the First Continental Artillery Regiment.

To William Stephenson

Sir   Chester [N.Y.] Augt. 12th 1779

You are to proceed to New Windsor and take charge of the above Invoice of Shot and see them safely landed at West Point under the charge of Mr. Thomas Jones DFCMS and take his receipt for the same, after which will wait on General Knox to know if he has any commands and return with all convenient speed. you will call at the Post Office and enquire if there is any Letters belonging to the Department—

Yours &c

Stephenson was appointed a Conductor of Military Stores on July 20, 1779, and resigned on May 7, 1780.

To Henry Knox

Dear General   Chester [N.Y.] Augt. 12 1779

Mr. Stephenson CrMS waits on you in charge of some portion of the Stores lately sent for to Mount Hope Furnace, the intolerable badness of the road and the disappointment of the Teams promised to go from the Park has prevented the whole's coming on. these I hope will answer for a present supply as the Horses by continual going are so emaciated as to be scarcely able to draw the empty Waggon. the last seven that I received was a great imposition not one of them being fit to go one Mile[.] this the Waggon Master says he told Mr. Thompson WM Genl: before he brought them from him they are now repairing. to day Mr. Cook calls on me by your order for two Waggons to go to General Glovers Brigade. I shall supply them, but must again remind you to prevent blame, let the occasion be never so pressing, I shall be unable to remove the Stores. however as you are acquainted with the circumstance I doubt not of receiving timely and effectual assistance—

         Yours

NB. one waggon with 60 Rd Shot 12 pds. is broke and left in the mountains. these I shall forward in addition to the Invoice. No 4 pd Shot at Mr Faeshs but plenty of them at Hibernia—

To Friedrich Wilhelm Augustus, Baron de Steuben

Hond. Sir   Chester [N.Y.] Augt: 16 1779

Inclos'd you have a Letter and by Mr. Stephenson CrMS you will receive a Box which were sent to me by the Honl. Board of War, to be forwarded. this with pleasure I readily undertook and have given such directions, as I flatter myself will bring them speedily to hand, and I hope in good order—

With respect & Esteem I am Sir Your very huml Servt.

To Henry Knox

Hond. Sir   Chester [N.Y.] Augt: 16th 1779

Mr. Stephenson again waits on you with a number of peices of Ordnance & some carriages as pr. Invoice inclosed the other articles I have on hand waiting your orders. I understand that there is one more 18 pdr with its carriage and one Travelling Forge still on the Road, these I shall forward as soon as they arrive. a number more twelves were preparing when these came away, which I suppose to be daily expected—At the foot of the Invoice you will see the number of articles delivered Mr: Cook for Genl Glovers Brigade, this I thought necessary that you may know from time to time what Stores remain on hand—

Yours &c.

To Daniel Kemper

Sir   Chester [N.Y.] Augt: 16th 1779

Yesterday a number of Stores arrived from Philadelphia, among them a number of Boxes address'd to Daniel Kemper Esqr. DCG said to contain Brass Buckles for the Army as pr: Invoice these I should have gladly forwarded immediately but a number of the Horses being unable to proceed prevented me. must beg the favor of you to send on[e] of your waggons to this place for them immediately

Yours

Kemper was Deputy Cloathier General.

To William Stephenson

Sir   Chester [N.Y.] Augt: 16th 1779

You are immediately to set out for New Windsor to receive and transport a number of Cannon their Carriages and other Stores as pr Invoice to West Point and deliver them to Mr. Thos: Jones DFCMS at that Garrison and take his receipt for them. The Letter and Box which you have in charge you will deliver as directed to Baron Steuben. the Box I have receipted for, you will therefore request his receipt at the Delivery You will upon your arrival wait on General Knox and deliver the Letter you have for him the other Letter which you have directed to Daniel Kemper Esqr. you will proceed on your arrival to New Windsor request the Favor of Mr. Copeland or Eayrs to see immediately delivered. you will also request them to endeavor to find some Vessell going to Albany, and inform you the Captns name upon your return, as I have seve[ral] articles of importance to forward immediately

Having finish'd this Business you will return with all convenient speed to this place
                Yours &c.

To James Pearson

Sir   Augt 17th 1779

Inclos'd you have a receipt for the stores sent by Mr Baker—the boxes Mark't PVR I shall immediately forward to Albany with the Letter to Mr Philip Van Rensalear agreeable to their direction—The shoe Buckells to Daniel Kemper Esqr whose store is near at hand—am obliged by the Portfires though not immediately sent for—The Musket Cartridges are a very timely supply, should be glad to have the next of the same size—the files sent will give a present supply to the Brigade Armourers many of which were in great want. am glad to find a number going to the Armourers at Albany as there is a fine company of men their in that branch, to whowm on account of the easy and cheap transportation I have send a considerable number of arms to repair—Mr Austin I suppose will bring what other Necessaries are requisite to complete the Armourers in the field, as that made part of his bussiness to Philadelphia—As to the powder made at [writer's blank] I have forwarded most of what I received intire can only say that what has been made use of in Camp, both of Cannon and Musket has been generally approv'd off [sic] both for the size of the grain and strength of the powder and on al[l] accounts as good as any made among us—I have observ'd, whether on account of the coal not being made of proper wood or what other reason can't assign that the powder Manufactur'd among us is not equally clean with that imported consequently I should think not so strong. this I do not undertake to determine but as you are about contracting I thought it not amiss to mention it—possibly some improvement may be made with regard to that perticular—Mr Cook is long since arrived a large proportion of the Cartridges brought by him were seventeen's to the pound.—the sums of mony by him received he has accounted to me for, and I have past them to your Account of Credit ready to be settled, when opportunity and business will permit—I am fully satisfied with your account of the mistake in sending the twelve pound Ammunition, and here give me leave to say without being suspected of flattery that the whole of the stores sent to Camp under your direction, mark the attention of the faithfull Officer join'd to a perfect knowledge of the bussiness—

We have Nothing New in Camp the Army still occupy their old ground waiting the movement of the enemy—having Nothing perticular to send for at this time with a kind remembrance to those to whom I am so happy as to be known I conclude And Remain Yours

To Daniel Kemper

Sir,   Chester [N.Y.] Augt. 19th 1779

By the bearer you will received the Buckles sent to my care. I have forwarded four boxes mark'd PVR with a letter which I must beg to the favor of you to put on Board the Sloop that goes from Newburgh to Albany every Tuesday. Your complyance will very much oblidge—Yours &c.

NB Mr. Ranselaer will pay any charges that may arise from transportation

To Philip Van Rensselaer

Sir   Chester [N.Y.] Augt. 19th 1779

By the Packet that sails between Newburgh and Albany I have sent four Boxes mark'd PVR and a Letter inclosed which I have just received from the Comy. Genl: M Stores Philadelphia which upon receipt you will please to give me credit for and forward a receipt to me as soon as possible the articles contain'd in the Boxes were inserted in my Invoice and I have a receipt for the number of Boxes said to contain, as pr: Invoice this is all I request of you, nothing new in Camp, we are waiting the motions of the enemy. you will please to present my compliments to Mrs. Renselaer, Mr. Lansing & family and Captn. Lamb. In haste I am Yours &c.

To Henry Knox

Dear General   Chester [N.Y.] Augt. 28 1779

Your kind favor of yesterday pr. Major Shaw I have received for which, and the information there contain'd thus early communicated respecting my department be pleased as a small but just tribute to accept of my gratefull thanks—

I would suppose that the order for commen[ce]ment of additional pay has by some mistake been ordered to take place from the first of this instant as I have been inform'd from Philadelphia that the Com[y]. Genls: department has received it since the first July should be under fresh obligations to the General, to have this matter ascertain'd, as I am about settling m[y] General accts. as the resolve has been construed to exten[d] to all, in its true spirit time as well as substance w[ill] apply—Agreable to request I shall immediately inform Mr. Ruddock that he is considered by the honl. Board as a Depy. Feild Comy. and shall call on him for his returns, and the State of his Department and shall give him to understand that the resolve of February last is to govern his whole conduct. and you may rely on it that I shall look with Candor on his future management, making gracious allowances, at the same time, that I endeavor that the Bussiness in that part of my Department be so regulated as to annihilate any further complaints—

As soon as tis possible after receiving the several Returns which are to compose mine I shall forward mine for the present Month, by which at one view, you will see the state of the whole stores with the army after which I shall wait on you and make my personal acknowledgements.

With esteem I am your's &c.

NB this moment I have you order for 60 Carte Boxes for Genl Glovers Brigade

To John Ruddock

Sir   Chester [N.Y.] Augt: 28th 1779
I have it in charge to inform you that the Honl Board of War and Ordnance have thought proper to arrange you as Depy. Feild Comy. and annex you to my department and at the same time to inform you that your Pay and those Gentlemen serving with you still continuing in the Service will be double from the 1st. Instant the regulation of the Feild Comy M Stores department, you will fully understand by perusing the Resolve respecting it of 18 Feby last. by this you will please to regulate yourself in your more General conduct and you may rest assured of my most friendly assistance in any particular cases which may occur You will please to forward me a return of what Stores you have on hand, and a list of the number and commencement of their engagements in the publick Service under you by the 1st day next Month as a general arrangement is to take place, which will establish the department and make it I have reason to hope far from being the most contemptible in the army—

With compliments to the Gentlemen present with you belonging to the Department—
I am Yours

To Henry Knox

Dear General   Chester [N.Y.] Septr. 2d. 1779
By Captn. Nichols you will receive this inclosing an Invoice of sundry Stores, just arrived from Philadelphia the 18 pounder with its apparatus I have forwarded to the Point and must beg your direction with respect to the 100 Barrels of Powder already arrived and the other hundred which will be in to morrow or the next day on many

accounts I should suppose it improper to be deposited here such as having no proper stor[e] nor sufficiency of waggons and only a Corporals gaurd in charge of the whole. as I heard nothing of its coming, I did not chuse to forward any of it untill I heard from you its destination. some Portion of ye 12 pd: Pound Shot fix'd and the whole of ye: 9 pd: Grape, I judge you will order to the Fort as we have no 9 pd: Cannon in the Feild inclosed you have a minute of the further supply given to Genl: Glovers Brigade. the time having elaps'd for receiving my General Returns, you will excuse as I am entirely waiting for Mr Ruddock the moment that come to hand, shall insert it in its proper place and send it to you. if that does not come to day shall finish mine without it—

You will be kind enough to send me particular direction pr: Captn: Nichols what is best to be done with the Powder should you order it to be forwarded I will send on the other waggons without unloading—

I am Sir Yours &c.

To Thomas Jones

Sir   Chester [N.Y.] Septr. 3d 1779

I received yours by Mr: Douglass, am glad to hear that their [*sic*] is Officers cloathing to be had shall endeavour to get my part. with regard to the last part, Letter had it been conveyed by an unknown Hand from the Moon I should have understood it as well. "Mr: Clark is return'd to his Brigade." I never knew he had left it, "not having Teams to bring on his Stores from you." pray what are become of his Teams what stores was he to bring on from me, "be pleas'd to forward a note to me, and his Stores." as soon as I can divine what Stores he wants. I think Mr. Clark should have let me know his difficulties when this is done shall give in my best advice—

Yours &:

To James Pearson

Sir   Chester [N.Y.] Septr. 3 1779

Inclos'd you have a receipt for the Stores received by the hand of Mr. Isaac Warner Condr. M Stores also for those originally committed to the care of Mr. Mc:Fee. also an account of Shot & Shells received by the way of Trenton, conducted by the QM General the powder and stores brought by Mr: Warner I have had no time to overhawl, but am much afraid I shall find them in poor order, from the appearance of the Casks (some of which were stove and the excessive rains while on the road, with miserable waggon covers, must have sensibly affected some of them. Mr: Warners attention to his charge, I am inform'd & beleive has been great but the clement [*sic*] I fear has in some measure baffled his exertions—

Have agreable to your request sent on one Box of six pound strapt Shot, the other I hope to make answer for the French sixes at the Fort. I have likewise sent you a shot Gauge taken with Burgoine which perhaps may be of service in some of your works. I have another for my use of the same kind

As to the Grape it is for the present out of use altogether, those sent I shall forward to the Fort. you will be kind enough to forbear sending any more without they are particularly wrote for—Captn. Austin has arrived. the Stores among which, are those for the Armourers, he left some distance behind—observe by the Invoice he brought a sufficient supply for the present[.]

Am exceeding happy to hear there is a hopeful prospect of Colonel Flowers recovery to health and return to his usefullness in the City, you will please to present him with my best regards—

Mr. Sheineman's application may be warrantable from the circumstance of having a number of Men with him repairing the Stores but by no means to be persisted in as it is altogether irregular and done without my knowledge. I shall always endeavor to have all Business relative to the Department pass thro' its proper channell

I could wish the Honl: Board of War would fall upon some mode to encourage Gentlemen of Abilities to engage in the Military Stores Department the temporary order of double Pay from ye: 1st: July give but little satisfaction, but we still live by faith and hope for better Times

I should have forwarded some damaged Muskets & Stores with the Box of 6 pd: Strapt Shot mentioned the other side, but the Teems ordered to take them in, being private property, refus'd to have any thing to do with them & have return'd to Philadelphia empty perhaps it may be proper to mention the matter to Colo: Mitchell DQM General—

The inspector General of Musick renews his applications to me, to obtain 2 B clarinets. I have before wrote you on the subject but never receiv'd any answer, must request the favor of you to purchase them and send them on with the Bill, for which I will give you credit or immediately remit the money, as shall pr advice find most agreeable—

Nothing new in Camp only a general expectation of the enemies paying us a visit at West Point. am very sorry to hear you was unwell when you wrote, shall be very happy to hear by your next that you are perfectly restored to health—

Yours

NB must beg the favor of you to fall upon some method to have the Shells intended for Camp prov'd at the place where they are cast. no less than 154 8 Inch & 116 5 ½ of those sent already have upon trial been condemned, this after the great expence and trouble of transportation together with the disappointment of the number, is worth of the greatest attention—

To William Stephenson

Sir   Chester [N.Y.] Septr. 9th 1779

You are with the Teems under your charge to proceed to New Windsor, when there arrived you will procure some suitable Vessel to take the Stores you have in care, immediately down to West Point. you will on no pretence suffer and fire to be made in the Vessell untill the Stores are landed, when this is done you will deliver the whole to Mr: Jones DFCMS take his rect. for them and return will all convenient speed to this place. you will leave word with Mr Eayrs or Copeland, if any Stores should be forwarded while you are gone to the Fort to take charge of them, get them safely loaded and either of them that can be best spared to proceed to the Point and deliver them to you, or should they miss you to Mr: Jones. you will still inform them that I shall esteem the service from them as a very particular favor—   Yours

To Henry Knox

Sir Chester [N.Y.] Septr. 9 1779

By Mr. Stephenson who is forwarded in charge of a Quantity of Stores as pr Invoice inclosed, I have an opportunity to forward my General Retur[n] for the Month August. you will readily perceive I have altered my usual form, and perhaps be ready to call for an abridgement, but my motive was to collect the whole of the Stores in such a manner in one Return, that at one view, you might see what was in every Magazine, and then by casting your eye on the lower Line see the sum Total[.] this I thought best to be in one strait Line, which makes it very long but quite as portable as the other way. however if you had rather have them one sheet the next shall come in that form—

I wrote to Mr: Ruddock (agreable to your request) informing him of the order of the Honl. Board of War and requesting in as delicate a manner as I know how his returns for insertion, as the first step to his complyance with the resolve of Feby. to which I was desired to refer him, as the standard of his future action. to this I have neither received Return nor answer of consequence you receive the present Return, deficient in that singular particular. I am heartily disposed to treat Mr. Ruddock with tenderness, but if he is to be connected with me and I am amendable for his conduct, he shall abide by my directions in every instance or take to consequences. the orders of my Superiors I mean to obey and those acting under me shall be brought to the same temper. if it is not of importance to the Service I want no connection with him more than usual as I have nothing to act upon, but the extract in you Letter I feel at a loss, and shall for present move no further in the matter—

The other powder which I menton'd in my last in not yet arrived but I expect it every moment shall immediately forward it—

With esteem I am Sir Yours &c:

To James Pearson

Sir Chester [N.Y.] Septr. 10 1779

Inclos'd with this you have the General Return for the Month August including the Stores at West Point & Litchfeild—yesterday I received your Favor dated Augt: 18 its contents respecting the Shot &

Shells sent by the way Trenton. in my last you had a minute of what I received, for which I gave the waggon masters receipts in the name of Mr Peter Gordon DQM Genl. from whom they were address'd shall always forward rects. for any Stores that I know comes directed from your Office—you will please to forward 50 Drums 50 Drumheads and 5000 Brushes & Wires as soon as is convenient, the demand for them is pressing. should be glad you would also send on half a Barrell Linseed Oil by the next conveyance. This moment we have a report that the enemy have embark'd 7000 men at New York their destination the west Indies were [sic] the same report says De Estaing has beaten their fle[et] in a second rencounter, is sacking their Island without molestation. should this be true a total evacuation is at no great Distance which God grant. In haste just setting out for west Point must conclude—
 Yours &c

NB the Teems with the Armourers Tools not yet arrived—

To Philip Van Rensselaer

Sir   Chester [N.Y.] Septr. 20th 1779
 By Captn. Barr I have an opportunity to forward six Dozen wood Screws to you from Philadelphia to my charge since those sent you by the Packet. your Letter inclosing the receipt came safe to hand. must request the favor of you to forward a receipt for those by the return of Captn. Barr—
 with esteem I am Yours &c.

To Henry Knox

Sir   Chester [N.Y.] Septr. 23d 1779
 Mr. Stephenson is again forwarded with two hundred & eighty Barrells of Powder, fifty seven of which are Cannon, the remainder Musket. one hundred Barrells more were on the road from Carlisle the whole Cannon Powder it set out about ye: 8th. or 10 instant consequently may be hourly expected—
 Eleven peices of Ordnance 12 pds. set out for Camp at ye: same time with the above. these cannot be far distant, when arriv'd here shall be sent on immediately—

If you have any commands they will be che[er]fully received and executed with all possible dispatch by—Your huml Servt

To William Stephenson

Sir

You are immediately to go on for New Windsor, when there arrived procure a suitable Vessell to transport 280 Barrells of Powder to West Point, which you will see properly loaded conveyed down, safely landed and delivered to Mr. Thomas Frothingham DFCM Stores and by him receipted in behalf of Mr. Jones. tis needless I trust to renew the repeated orders for care on this occasion. your own preservation join'd to your natural disposition to preserve the publick Stores which I have often experienced forces this conclusion—

Having executed your Business, you will return with all convenient speed to this Place—

Yours &c.
Condr M Stores

To Messers John Eayres or Asa Copeland

Sir　　　　　　　　　　　　　　Chester [N.Y.] Septr: 23d. 1779
I must again trouble you with three Boxes buckles for the Clothier General at Newburgh containing as pr. Invoice 1420 pair— these I shall be obliged to you to notify Mr. King are in your possession if you have no opportunity to send them to him you will be kind enough to take a receipt in the name of the person you deliver them to—

If you carry them to him you will enquire what cloathing he has on hand and acquaint me therewith as soon as possible that I may provide for the Department—

They were Conductors of Military Stores. John Eayrs/Ayers/Eyres/Eayres is the same individual. Eayres was appointed a Conductor of Military Stores on April 21, 1779, and was "deranged," as they sometimes referred to someone whose employment had been terminated, on October 1, 1782. Copeland had been appointed a Conductor of Military Stores on April 21, 1779.

To Timothy Pickering Jr.

Honored Sir   Chester [N.Y.] Septr. 25th 1779
Notwithstanding my last remains unnoticed, a circumstance upon settling my accounts has made it necessary for me to address you again—In the regulation of ye. 18 Feby. it is ordered "that all monies necessary for the Department shall be drawn by a warrant from the Commander in cheif from the Military Chest, and the expenditures adjusted & settled with the Auditors." in conformity to which on the 27th April I drew 10,000 Dollars which sum notwithstanding the lamentable Depreciation, has been sufficient to Defray the expences of the Department near four months. the whole being expended I apply'd as directed for Settlement, not chusing to draw again untill this was done. having done my duty you will judge of my surprize when the Auditors told me that had no orders to settle such account[s.] I immediately produced the resolve mentioned above upon sight of which they said they were put to the Blush by having resolves produced, by Gentlemen who came upon Business of which they had never before heard. they were then clear to make a settlement but after examining the Vouchers which they said were clear and fair, a difficulty arose in their minds, respecting the expences of the Conductors, as they had never allowed more than three Dollars pr Day. I told them I had a warrant for my mode of paying which w[as] after solemn attestation that the accounts exhibited were just, to pay them this, upon application I obtained from Colo. Flower when acting under him and had settled my accounts accordingly, but whether this was a resolve of Congress, or an ordinance of the Honble. Board of War I could not determine. this they replied "was sufficient for me but not for them" I then went to his Excellency, shewed him my acc[ts.] & stated the difficulties made by the Auditors, at the same time presented him with a certificate from General Knox that this had been the invariable mode of Settlement and requested to be informed whether the usage as founded on a positive resolved this he said he could not determine, but as the matt[er] was new, to give satisfaction to the Auditors. he advised me to take another warrant for what sum I wanted and then write to the Honl Board of War for an order for Settlement in the usual way this I have done, but as I am very desirous to have the matter settled, must beg it as a particular favor of the Honl. Board to be furnished with the means as soon as convenient. as

I detest long Settlements I shall still continue to pay the accounts as usual, if any other mode has been fallen upon, the Board will be kind enough to give me early notice—

With all possible respect I am Yours &c:

To Jonathan Gostelowe

Dear Sir, Chester [N.Y.] Septr. 25 1779
Your favor by Mr: Lucas I have received & now lies before me, and beleive me I feel affected and diverted at mix'd fortune of our Friend Major French as this is I beleive his first adventure at sea, it seems really discouraging. am happy however to hear that he has rose superior to his Difficulties and is return'd in Health & Safety to his Friends as I shall not have time to write him by this conveyance, you will please to present my regards to him

I am exceedingly oblidged by the inclosed news Paper, should take it kind if you would forward them by every convenient opportunity. the accounts therein contained, of the valuable prizes affords agreeable reflections, that at some period our money will appreciate, surely when every other article is as plenty they will be as cheap. am very sorry to hear of the confusion & distress in your City on account of the exertions of those noble Souls to compass this happy purpose, surely the People must be mad who endeavor to frustrate this laudable undertaking what reason they can urge for their Conduct I am at a loss to conceive—

We are still as it were at anchor waiting for a wind, and as much at a loss to know where we shall go next, as what Quarter the wind will Blow from—continual reports of the arriv[al] of the French Fleet, but this I fear is rather to be hoped than expected. with 10 Sail of the Line at this time properly disposed I am led to believe, we might enjoy a glorious peace by the captivity of every British Ship & Solder in America perhaps you may think me Sanguine and prehaps that may be the Case, but I assure I endeavor to think & judge rationally, but prehaps I may be mistaken. I heartily wish the event may determine it a sudden opportunity for an exertion I am convinced wou'd be best for us under present Circumstance only cast your Eye on our Army and behold the Time of the engagement of more than half of them expiring the first Day of the coming Year their last engagements so partially complyed with, and the families of a great many of them so shamefully neglected that scarce one of them will renew their engagements at any Rate. the horrid Depreciation of our paper Medium the Source of the above & all other Disagreable prospects, but not to dwell too long on the dark side of the Question. may not the People at large as well the Army be call'd to one powerfull exertion and these evills be done away I think with the greatest propriety, and I will indulge the thought that the sickly Virtue of America has constitution enough left to do this, then shall Health spring forth Speedily and the salvation of American go forth like Brightness, the Envy & dread of admiring Kingdoms, the Olive Branch of Peace shall deck her Temples, and these happy shores be crouded with emigrants from under either pole. but whither am I transported my fancy I find is on the wing I check myself. I am sure you will think it time to write a Volume was not my intention, but the dictates of Friendship has carried me too far. I will trespass no longer on your patience, than just to request the favor of you to inform me what you can procure a genteel pair of Boots for at Philadelphia. perhaps in your connections you can furnish a Continental Devil (as we are call'd by some) with a pair at something of a moderate rate—

My compliments to all Friends and determined Friendship for you finishes this from Yours &c.

To the Clothier General With the Army

Sir   Chester[N.Y.] Septr. 27th 1779

Inclosed you have the Invoice of all the Buckells which I have received and forwarded to your Store. you will please to examine and see whether they have all come to hand if so send by the Bearer Mr: Jas. Boyer my Clk a receipt for the whole

Having miss'd Mr: Wm. Cook Condr M Stores in the list I drew upon, when at your Store drawing for the Department, as you will see by examining the List Mr: Boyer has with him, must request the Favor of you to Issue it in such articles as he has a minute of with him for which & the Balance of my acct. he will settle—

Yours &c.

The Continental Congress had appointed James Wilkinson Clothier General on July 25, 1779. This letter may have been sent to him.

To Henry Knox

Dear General   Septr 27th 1779

Inclosed you have a return of the Department made out I trust agreeable to your wish

As it is probable this will be forwarded immediately I think it best to inform you, th[at] it is my expectation, and that of the whole Department, founded as we trust on solid reasons, that Commissions, with suitable rank, be given to us all, and as I know it is best to be explicit, I will inform you what is expected by the Gentlemen (my own expectations wave) the DFCMS expect Captn. of Artillery's and the Conductors, Subalterns rank which will of course entitle them to the same advantages, both now & hereafter. to you I submit these claims, this I take to be my Duty, and I am sure if they appear to you reasonable and for the good of the Service they will find a powerful advocate. this I earnestly request may be made a part of your conversation with his Excellency, when the subject is debated being fully sensible, that what you jointly recommend will be immediately adopted by the Board of War—for my own part I want nothing for the Department, inconsistent with the unnerring [*sic*] Rule of Right, or the publick goo[d] but as the matter is coming under consideration I wish to have it fully discuss'd and settled that we may all know what we have a right to expect. After which I promise no applications shall be made not strictly adhering thereto—

With respect I am Yours &c.

To John Ruddock

Sir   Chester [N.Y.] Septr. 27 1779

By this you will be inform'd that I have received a small proportion of cloathing for the use of my Department which I have only to lament is not better suited to their wants, however their will be a shirt apiece and some Articles to the amount of twenty one dollars and a third to each man at a very moderate rate—These I shall immediately divide as equally as possibly I can—After which if you will inform me who of the Gentlemen is present with you I will forward your and their parts to the Care of Mr Eayrs or Copeland at New Windsor at which place you may Apply and receive them giving a receipt for the above sum—

The return you will have forwarded by the first day of the ensuing month—at which time you will please to send a perticular Return of all the stores delivered each Brigade since the last Return as I am Order'd to make a Return of that Nature to head quarters every Month besides the General Return. you will therefore consider this as a standing order and let it accompany your General Returns Accordingly—
Yours

To William Richards

Sir   Chester [N.Y.] Sept 28th 1779
    I have the Pleasure to acknowledge the receipt of your favor inclosing the General Return wich by a transient view the only one I had time for, as the Gentleman staid but a few minuits I beleave to be perticular and perfectly right I am Glad you took the same Method with this as the Last, if you found no prospect of sending it free which you will always endeavor to do as the expence of the Department is already enormous
    I have forwarded three hundred Dollars by Mr Baldwin and taken his receipt for the same this I shall place to your account—
    I have just obtained an order for the purchase of a few articles of Cloathing but was only able to procure one shirt a peice one pair of elegant Shoes and several other small articles to the value of eight pounds Pena Currency pr man which I shall shortly destribute and if you think proper to order it, will deliver your par[t] to Mr. Jones who is present with me very unwell unable to write you at present, the proportion though small is well worth receiving. the Gentlemen all desires to be remember to you, you will write by the first opportunity—
Yours &c

To Henry Knox

Dear General   Chester [N.Y.] Octor 1st 1779
    have only by this to inform you that the Eleven 12 Pound pieces of Ordnance which I mentioned in my last to be on the road here have arrived—and that the bearer Mr Stephenson is forwarded to procure a

sutiable Vessell to carry them to West point—if there is any Occasion for additional Orders you will please to give them—the powder I expect every moment—

Yours

To William Stephenson

Sir   Chester [N.Y.] Octo 1st 1779

Your will immediately upon the receipt of this repair to New Windsor and wait on the Dy Q M Genl or whoever is in charge of the Vessells, and procure such as are sutiable to carry Eleven twelve pound Cannon to West point—these you will have brought to the Wharf that they may be ready to take the Cannon of board the Moment they arrive, to prevent loss of time and insure the use of the Gin untill the Cannon are safe on board—you will call on General Knox and leave the Letter you have for him—and call on him also upon your return to know if he has any commands—

Yours

To James Pearson

Dear Sir   Chester [N.Y.] Octo 5th 1779

I have the pleasure by the return of Mr Baker to Acknowledge the receipt of your kind favour by him and one other by Mr Lucas, also of forwarding the General Return; in the last I am inform'd that the honble Board have order'd the Clarinets to be made this I am glad to hear on many accounts, as the inspector of Musick has been so disgusted at the delay that he has been almost ready to resign any further charge of the band—indeed the Man has Merited attention by indefatigable endeavours to promote the science of Musick in the Army—As to the shells sorry I am to say they were badly perform'd in every perticular—it really hurts me to find fault with our own Manufactories, I am sensible it is discouraging in their infant state—but duty and faithfullness oblige me to Notice every imperfection that may occasion disapointment and its consequences—

After this you will inform'd that the Vents of the eight inch shells were not big enough to receive the five an half inch fuses, all of which have been cut bigger. Numbers of sand holes which you migh[t] peirce to the centre, but the greatest fault of all was the irregular thickness of the shells, which was and can be discover'd no other way but by the proof, which was by the introduction of the Nose of a pair of double blasted bellowses secured so as to be wind tight in the vent of the shell then put the shell into a tub of water and fill the shell with a sudden blast which if free from any vacuum will occasion no irruption if not make the water blubber if they stand this proof we take them out and strike them all round gently with a Mawl or hammer about six pounds weight. by doing which if there is any thin place in the shell or any cavitty fill'd with dirt that enabled them to stand the first proof it may be easily discovered. so thin were some of those sent that they broke—however a Number of them it is judg'd will answer very well—I have been the more perticular, at your perticular request—

The Cannon by Mr Baker came safe to hand for which he has my receipt—with respect to the Sappers Fusees I have received no late Orders respecting them, for which reason I think it not best to forward them at present—As soon as convenient you will please to forward two hundred thousand Musket Cartridges Nineteen to the pound for as you justly observe by far the greatest part made use of by our Army are of that size. also the fifty drum[s] but especially the drumheads as the demand for them is become very pressing—

I am exceeding sorry to hear the Colonel Flower has return'd without being able to regain the inestimable treasure health hope however soon to hear that is the case or at least a mitigation of the extreems of his illness permiting him with a good degree of comfort to perform the duties of his Office—you will please to present my regar[ds] to him—hope before this enjoy your usual state of health if not must be of you to relax in time in your attention to the business, had Colonel Flower done this perhaps his disorder might not have been so severe nor of so long continnuance I pray God yet to direct and bless the Means that may be used for his recovery—

No account as yet of the tools sent for the Armourers to Camp by Capt Austin what is become of them I am at a loss to determine unless as they came on with the Q Masters stores they may be deposited with them—could I find where they were left possibly I might find mine among them—the delay has perplext me much to keep the Men employed hope by some Means or other to receive them—

Inclos'd you have a duplicate receipt for One hundred and fifty dollars supply'd Mr Schutz which you will please to settle with him

and pay to my account of Credit—I shall close with requesting the favour of you to procure me sixteen cups jappan'd and the two first letters of my Name in cyphers Mark'd on them each holding a gill and two larger of the same kind holding half pint—if you have any person in the works that can do they as they are solely for the use of my Mess in Camp, I should suppose they would come chea[p.] if that is not the case without they ask a very extravagant price should be Oblidg'd by you getting of them done and forwarded the first Opportunity—
Yours

To the Board of War and Ordnance

Gentlemen Chester [N.Y.] October 6 1779

This day I received your favor of the 29th Septr. the first paragraph of which informs me that you have never received a List of the Officers in my Department, or warrants would have been forwarded in reply, shall only say, this is not my fault had the Honl Board requested it of me, I am certain their would have been no cause of complaint for delay. I must now inform the Board to prevent unnecessary trouble, that I have some time since given Genl Knox a list of the names of the Gentlemen at present in my Department with the Dates of the appointments of each and at the same time, informed him that it was the unanimous expectation of the Gentlemen to accept of nothing short of Commission explicitly determing their Rank, to this they are stimulated by the incessant reproaches of the Officers of the line, calling upon them to declare their Rank and dispising them, & treating them with ineffable contempt because they have none. to such a pitch has this been carried, that one of the Condrs. has been arrested by a Lieut: whom he lately commanded, for striking a Soldier who grossly insulted him. many other reasons might be urged but it gives me pain to recite them. the Board must, I am sure, be sensible that as the Department is equally exposed in the field, common justice demands they should have equal rewards. behold them excluded by every act of their own Assemblies from all present and every future reversionary grant, at the very time they are hazarding their Limbs & Lives and abandoning their connections, for their peace & security, and this without the Shadow of any future reward and say if it be not discouraging.—In the next paragraph you say. "We are conscious of the difficulties you & your Department labour under and would gladly give us relief but at present it is out of your power." for Gods sak[e] Gentlemen can't you do as much for us or are we not so deserving as those of the CGM Stores Departmt: one of which namely Mr: Collins, I am informed you have lately given an order on the Clothr Genl. at Boston , to draw a handsome suit of Cloaths for himself, and the other Gentlemen in the Springfeild Department. because we are at a distance from you, is that reason good, that we should be neglected. I would rather think, the Honl Board perfectly knowing our circumstances, would communicate unsolicited every advantage you will excuse my freedom as the whole of my department are clamourous at the above information coming directly from one of my Department just arrived from Boston, who was present at the purchase. untill this time, I have kept them tollerably easy, with telling them my expectations in which indeed upon the footing of equal justice, I have been very sanguine, but shall now wait, indeed as they must, untill some more favoura[ble] period arrives. several of the Department have waited on General Knox, to know whether the late resolve raising the rations to 100 Dolls: each extends to us. he refers them to his Excellency who declares he cannot tell, they now call on me I fly to my dernier resort, and request to be inform'd by you. should this pass in the Negative I know the consequence, but this I think not possible; the wing of time must determine this—

I am very much oblidged by the information respecting the mode of settling the Conductors expences, think it will fully answer my purpose which the first opportunity I shall make certain if not, shall wait on you for further assistance

Yesterday I forwarded the General Return which you will perceive contains the Stores at Fish Kill. Mr: Greene by Letter informs me that his Returns for the future shall come regularly from Rhode Island shall endeavor to have them inserted for the future that at one veiw you may see the whole of the Stores with the main & eastern Armies—

I think it proper to inform you that I have lately had a draught or rather liberty to purchase about £8 Pena. Curry. worth of articles from the Continental Store, to be delivered after the Line were served, and at four time the advance, by which I obtain'd a serjeants Shirt for myself & the others of my Department together with some other small articles. this is the only time we have even been allowed to purchase to the value of six pence, and this not withstanding my having a full

Captn of Artilleries Commission from the first moment of my entering the Service—

But I forbear to enumerate Grievances on the known Candor & Integrity of the Board I rely for ample Justice, in confidence of which I subscribe myself—

Your Honors most obedt Huml Servt.

To Henry Knox

Dear General   Chester [N.Y.] Octo 11th 1779

Your favour of this day is just come to hand its contents perplex me much—having on the appearance of a sudden remove been very busy in overhawling, and yesterday loading all the waggons I had—with which I shall just make out to move the whole provided I can get horses, a sutiable number to put to the waggons—for which I have this day sent to Mr Thompson WMG—I have forty six waggons loaded, but at present have only thirty seven setts of horses and the same Number of drivers but am encouraged to expect the full number in a day or two—the intended journey to Kingwood for the shot, will again oblige me to unload twelve of the waggons, and render the horses unfit for any other service for some time—und[er] these circumstances I shall try to get them on in some of the quarter Master's teems very shortly, if that cannot be done will send my own without loss of time—Yesterday I forwarded Nine hundred 18 pound shot to West Point by the person in charge of them I was inform'd that a Conductor of M stores by the Name of Clumberg was on the road with several thousand more—perhaps I may get some of his teems to return and fetch those from Kingwood, at any rate as it is your orders they shall be on speedily—

With respect I am Yours

NB should have sent of the powder sent for yesterday but have no horns here if you chuse will send it in paper—

To Henry Weisner

Sir   Octr. 19th 1779

You will please to send me word by the Bearer what quantity of Salt Petre and Sulphur you have in your possession belonging to the

Publick. As the General has ordered me to make enquiry and draw upon you for what you have in favor of Colo. Stevens, you will accordingly without further advice, send such a part or the whole, if wanted to his or my order which I shall find most convenient to send

We have a quantity more of Damaged Powder here and at Fish Kill which I shall order to your Mill to have the Nitre extracted

I am Yours

To John Ruddock

Sir

General Knox again calls on me to furnish four Conductors to join Genl Sullivans division. I have inform'd him, two only can be supplied at present, one of these must come from you, the other I shall send. you will immediately send me one to be instructed and furnished for that purpose—I am much surprised that the person directed has not to this hour joined the Brigade of Light Infantry, and now request you to forward him without a Moments loss of time—if you have any Waggons under your care sutiable for them you will inform me—

Yours

NB—if you know any person's sutiable for Conductors desirous of joining us by a line informing me their Names I will appoint them—

To Robert Erskine

Sir   Chester [N.Y.] Novr: 10 1779

Your Favor of 8th Novr. came safe to Hand, am much obliged By its Contents—but am much surpris'd that Mr Kiman permitted The Waggoners to unload, without having fallen upon some mode to get them On to this place. he must be sensible that I Have no waggons At my Command, to send and pick up the stores left on the Road, a mere Accident enables me to send for these, but the shot at Present with you and What Other stores may arrive in future I shall Expect he will forward on

With esteem I am Yours

Erskine was the distinguished map maker and engineer, who had been geographer and surveyor general to Washington's Army since July 1777. He also operated Ringwood Ironworks in New Jersey.

To James Pearson

Sir   Chester [N.Y.] Novr. 11 1779

This day I received yours pr Mr: Baker have only time to say, that I am with you (under our present circumstances) perfectly clear, that it is best to keep the old hands employe[d] making musket Cartridges. under this conviction, I did all in my power to get the waggon master to go to Fish Kill with his Brigade where I undertook to load them with Lead but entreaties were useless and finding the Teems were private property, and not knowing the internal police of the state by which they were engag'd, after stating the great want of the article, I left it to the determination of the W. M. who thought it not best to go

However I shall use every possible means in my power to get it on it might have come on, had they been instructed to take up lead at Fish Kill. I perceive this will furnish you with a hint, against the next opportunity—

The pitch I have already prepar'd and am much oblidged by the seasonable supply of the other articles—

By the next opportunity will send the exact dimensions of the Calibre and chamber of the 10 & 8 Inch mortars and Howitzers as I intend to measure them myself to prevent mistake—

I have been waiting a number of Days for a conveyance for Returns. Mr. Baker has them in charge inclos'd to Colo. Flower

My compliments to all enquiring Friends In hase [sic] —I am Sir Yours &c.

To James Pearson

Sir

Mr Warner brings with him a receipt for all the stores forwarded except the Arms. A Mistake in the Invoice, and seven of the Chests, being left at Ringwood puts it out of my power to receipt for them at present—In the Invoice No 21 is said to Contain 55 Muskets, this I know to be a Mistake for reason that it would be impossible to handle or transport a Chest of such dimensions—In the Casting up the invoice there is Another Mistake—five hundred and sixty should have been five hundred and Ninety then the total instead of 1005 would have been 1035. to correct these errors I shall immediately send for the other seven Chests at Ringwood and Carefully count the whole and send you a receipt for the Number found the first Opportunity— The horses under the charge of Mr. Finley that came with Mr Warners stores being much immaciated, I though it a fit Opportunit[y] to get on the damag'd stores, which would give them light loads to return with—if they are able some of them may still call and take in some portion of the Iron Ordered from the furnace—Inclos'd you have an Account of the stores sent—

My box with its Contents came safe to hand for which accept my thanks—

My compliments to Col Flower   Yours

NB I forgot to Mention the Invoice contains thirty Eight Chest of Arms, Only thirty seven can be Accounted for by Mr Warner and I am ready to conclude no more were forwarded, I shall examine what Number is wanting upon examining the Invoice and Chest this will appear—

To Robert Erskine

Sir   Chester [N.Y.] Novr 14th 1779

The bearer drives one of the two waggons which I have sent to take on the remaining Chests of Arms which you kindly took in Charge—You will please to deliver them and if you have any forage on hand supply them with what is Necessary to return with—None at this post at present—As to the shot you will be kind enough to inform Mr. Kinnan (if present) they must remain until he has some convenient Opportunity of sending them on—if any should Offer from hence I shall send my self

I am with esteem Yours

To John Jacob Faesh

Sir Chester [N.Y.] Novr. 16 1779

Your very polite Letter by Mr: Ford I have received, and although my visit shortly intented, [*sic*] is prevented, I expect the pleasure of calling on you some time the beginning of next Month, to make a settlement for the Shott & Shells, making under the last order, should the furnace, as I suppose it will, be out of blast about that time—

Agreeable to Genl: Knox's order I have sent you by Mr. Ford, 35000 Dollars for which, have taken his receipt and pass'd to your account until final settlement—

I am Sir Your huml Servt:

To Ebenezer Branham

Sir Hannover Decr: 10th 1779

It being inconvenient for the late Condr. M Stores to General Muhlenburgs
Brigade to march with them at present, and as it is proper some person should immediately be appointed, to take the Charge of the Stores, and do the Duty of Conductor in the Brigade, I have appointed you in consequence of your application through Mr. Taylor, and by his recommendation to that trust. your Pay which it to commence from this Date, and which is at present 80 Dollars pr Months and 10 Dollars Subsistence is to be drawn as usual in Detachments, by a special warrant from the officer commanding the Brigade. as likewise what necessary expences you incur travelling on the service of the Brigade this must be made out seperately and sworn to after which you will receive the amount in the mode directed above—Mr. Taylor will deliver the Stores forwarded for the Brigade, and you will receive & receipt him for them—

I shall depend upon your utmost exertions to prevent loss and damage to the Stores, and that in every instance of Duty you will prove your self worthy the trust reposed in you—

Branham was appointed a Conductor of Military Stores on December 10, 1779, and a Deputy Commissary of Military Stores on August 1, 1781.

To Whom It May Concern

Hanover Decr. 10th. 1779

This may Certify that Mr. Taylor Condr. M Stores has Receiv'd the Whole Pay & Subsistence & Expences Due him in my Departme[nt] to ye 1st. of the Present Month from which time his Pay Subsistence & Expences is By General Knox's Direction to Be Drawn By a special Warrant on the Pay Master that Pays the Division or Brigade to which he is annexed. His Pay Eighty Dollars Pr. Month subsistence ten till further Orders and His expences incurred travelling on the Business of the Brigade as Pr Account sworn to, before the Commanding officer of the Brigade as usual—

To John Jacob Faesh

Dear Sir   Suckisunny Plains [Succasunna N.J.] Jany. 1st. 1780

The extremity of the weather alone has prevented me the pleasure of your Company this day. to morrow I shall wait on you, & happy should I be, could I fully comply with your request, but fate has for the present determined otherwise, of which I expect to hear particularly when I see you. I shall bring 30,000 Dollars with me that must suffice for a few Days

As to the Shells the Board of War concludes to have no more made for the present, you will govern yourself accordingly. I shall take dinner with you tomorrow, and drink a happy new Year to the freeborn Souls of America—

my respectfull compliments to Mrs. Faesh

Yours sincerely

To William Brower

Sir   Suckesunny Plains [N.J.] Jany 9th 1780

You will immediately repair to the second Pennsylvania Brigade and apply to Coll. Johnson the commander for an order on the person who at present has the military Stores belonging to the Brigade in charge to deliver them to you, informing him at the same time that you are to do the Duty of Conductor to the Brigade. You will also make enquiry into the State of the Armourers of the Brigade who

acted under Mr. Robinson the late Conductor, and inform me what sums, if any are due them. the commencement of pay, and the time they were employed, must be certified by the commander of the Brige., unless you can find the person that paid them last, in which case a certificate from him will answer—
    Yours &c

NB a Copy of this Mr. Eben Branham CMS to Jersey Brigade

To Henry Knox

Dear General   Suckesunny [Succasunna N.J.] Jany 9th 1780
    Yours of this day I have received accompanied with one other, that was left with you yesterday; for the speedy conveyance of which be pleased to accept my thanks
    Early this morning I sent off Mr Wm. Brower to take charge of the Stores with ye. 2 Pena Brigade, and act as Condr. to the sam[e.]
    The yellow Ochre the bearer takes with him the Spanish white and pasteboard, or press paper I have none at present, have sent you some of the stiffest paper I have supposing it possible in might make a substitu[te.]
    I expect to be down in a few Days which I shall do myself the pleasure to wait on you and attend to any further orders—
    Yours &c

To John Lillie

Dear John   Suckesunny Plains [Succasunna, N.J.] Jany 9 1780
    Yours of to day came safe to hand am oblidged by your kindness in sendg. me notice of your going, and kind offer of taking on any thing else, besides the peice Linnen and Letter which Captn. Nichols has, and shall accordingly trouble you with another small Bundle and a Letter, as on your care and kindness I know I may safely rely. you will please to put them in your portmanteau to prevent their being stole out of the slay by being loose
    Captn. Nichols will deliver them he has as I sent him word you would call for them both Linnen & Letters—

The money requested you have inclos'd and my best wishes that you may have an agreeable journey accompanies this from Your Friend

Lillie was a Captain in the Third Continental Artillery Regiment.

To Mr. Cooper

Sir Suckesunny Plains [Succasunna, N.J.] Jany 10th 1780
Last evening I had seven horses belonging to the public, lately annexed to the Brigade of Light Infantry, under charge of one of my Condrs returned in to me—as these are much wanted, I should have kept the whole, but recollecting the difficulty of getting forage I have selected four only and sent the rest to Mr Church at Morriss town: our forage is all exhausted, must beg the favour of you to call upon me and let me know whether in addition to our riding horses you can supplied the above Mentioned. if you can General Green would rather have them kept and employ'd than depend upon the teems of private persons—you will let me know immediately—Yours

This is addressed to Cooper as an Assistant Quartermaster.

To Henry Knox

Dear General Jany. 10 1780
Yours pr Fisher I have received and shall use my best endeavours to comply with its Contents in every particular
The note subjoin'd mentioning your having no return since Novr. oblidges me again to inform you that notwithstanding the most pointed orders repeatedly given to have the returns sent to me from Litchei[ld] Fish Kill & West Point the last day of every month at farthest those for Novr have jus[t] arrived. those for Decr. not yet come to hand but I have sent for them, and expect them every hour. after I receive them you shall have the return for both months as quic[k] as they can possible be made out, or mine alone if they should not soon come—
Yours &c.

To Henry Knox

Sir   Suckesunna [Succasunna, N.J.] Jany 11th 1780

This Morning I received your's Pr Serjt Scott directing me to send on all the shells and their apparatus, an answer must inform you that every species of these kind of stores, we have on hand, which is very triffling, Vizt 6 empty shells 2 fix'd and 468 fuses are at Pluckemin, the rest, having been delivered to Capt Craign of Col Proctors Regt. and should have been inserted in the Return for that Month but could not, as the deliveries, did not come to hand, till after the return was given in. this will be set right in the return for Decemr which togather with the Jany you may shortly expect to receive—The other stores sent for I expect to be able to get down this day
Yours

To Unidentified

Sir   Suckesunna plains [Succasunna, N.J.] Jany 12 1780

Noting further particular then only to desire you to send on with the next return, a particular return of what Stores you have delivered to every Division Brigade Regiment or Corps except the Artillery, since the first of march 79 to the first of January 1780 tis wanted for special service

I have procured two very good Shirts for each Gentleman in the Department at the moderate price of four Dollars each I shall embrace the first opportunity to send on those that belong your way—

You may inform the Gentlemen with you that I have procured a Resolve of Congress by which they are intitled to receive 100 Dollars pr Ration as Subsistence from the 18 Augt: 1779. also a genteel suit of Cloaths for the past and every future Year they remain in the Service. these advantages I hope will continue them in their present employments and enable them to appea[r] in Character, and live equal to their reasonable expectations.

I mentioned to the Board of War and Colo. Flower, the want of money to finish your former affairs. they say you never wrot[e] a line upon the subject, and they expect before they send any on, to have a well authenticated account of the Debts &c. to whom due. this you may remember I told you was necessary and to prevent loss to those to whom the money is due, must aga[in] advise you to apply in this way immediately

Your returns must if possible come more regular or it is impossible for my Genera[l] Return to go in any thing near the time due you may indeed you must send one of the Gentlemen on purpose to bring on yours together with that from Litchfeild and West Point which I have ordered to be forwarded to you for that purpose. as we are at a distance the person who comes may possibly serve those with you and those in the vicinity of you your attention to this particular Business I shall depend on

Yours &c.

My compliments to the Gentlemen with you

To Henry Knox

Dear Genl   Suckesunna [Succasunna, N.J.] Jany 14th 1780

A few days since I wrote you that I had sent Mr Even Branham CMS to Genl Maxwell's Brigade this Morning he returned, with the enclosed Letter I have once more instructed him and sent him to attempt General Stark's's [*sic*] Brigade. perhaps the Genl order alluded too in the Letter may again return him, should that be the case I shall wait for perticular application before I send him again—

I have also enclosed a Copy of the instructions for receiving the stores with which he was furnish'd—and shall conclude I have obey'd your orders and in this instance done my duty—

Your Most Humble Servant

NB Must request the favour of you to direct Major Shaw to send back the return from Pluckimin and the inclosed Letter after you have perused it—

To Henry Knox

                     Suckesunna [Succasunna, N.J.] Jany 15th 1780

Dear General   half past 3 °Clock PM

Have this Moment received your's but how to comply with its request, I am at a loss every sley belonging to this place is with you have sent the guard to press the Number, wherever found expect to be able to get them down in the course of the Night, rest assured

Nothing on my part shall be wanting, doubt not shall succeed to your wish, as I just hear of tow sleys, [sic] about two Miles off, have sent in quest of them—

With esteem I am

To John Stark

Sir   Suckesunna [Succasunna, N.J.] Jany. 16 1780

Your favor of this day pr Mr. Whittlesey I have received and should be happy to comply with your wish therein exprest in confirming the appointment of Mr. Whittlesey, beleiving him from the trust reposed in him by you, and by other testimonies to be a suitable person, but duty to the publick, the spring and moving cause of all my actions forbids, having already a sufficien[t] number of Conductors, to answer every purpose it would certainly be out of character, to create any more.—

Mr. Whittlesey mentioned his being continued to the end of the present month to this I have not objection of which having settled the Business as far as he has been concern'd in it, I will pay him the same sums, as is usual to any other Conductor or if he rather chuses upon reflection to quit at once I will settle with him immediately—

With esteem I am Sir yours

Stark was a Brigadier General from New Hampshire.

To John Ruddock

Sir   Suckesunna [Succasunna, N.J.] Feby. 20 1780

Since my return from philadelphia I received your Favor by Mr. Gordon CMS & Mr. Boyer now waits on you to answer its requests he comes prepared to make a full Settlement up to the 1st. instant from which time I quit the Department and immediately after having settled the Department which I expect will be by the last of the month I shall return to Philadelphia to take charge of Colo. Flower's Department at which place shall be happy to have it in my power to render you or any in the Feild any service—

Mr. Boyer has Mr: Gortons appointment except the date of his commencement, which when you furnish he will insert it, likewise the shirts to deliver to those for whom they were drawn—

A doubt having arisen whether the double pay will be continued as the Subsistence was dated back to the same time that it was granted to the Line, and I being desira[ ] considering it under the present circumstances an act of justice have given my judgemt. in favor of the Department, and have ordered it paid accordingly. however! as the matter is in doubt, I have sent an agreement for the whole to sign, to refund the double pay should it not be allowed upon settlement of my accots. and as this is an exertion to serve the department in future, as well as the present time I have no reason to think but that the whole will readily sign it—

I have nothing further to add only an affectionate farewell to you and the Gentn. present with you and an assurance that my services are at their command—

Mr: Frothingham take charge of the department here, for the present you will continue to make your returns and conduct the Business as usual at the post where you act—

With Esteem I am Sir Yours &c.

It being impossible to determine what sums are due on expence accounts I have directed Mr Boyer to settle the accounts as usual and give notes for the amounts after which the Money shall be left with Mr: Frothingham for their redemption—

To William Richards

Dear Sir   Suckesunna, [Succasunna N.J.] Feby 20th 1780

The multiplicity of business that has crowded on me since I had the pleasure of seeing you has also deprived me of time to answer the many favours I have received from you but now that I am called to quit the Department I could not think of taking my Departure, without an affectionate farewell

Your pay & Subsistence up to the 1st. instant I have settled with Mr. Jones, which suppose he will inform you by this opportunity. I expect to get my matters settled & set out for philadelphia by the last of this mon[th] there to take the sole charge of Coll Flower's Department. Mr: Frothingham takes the charge of the stores in the Feild for the present. you will continue to forward Monthly Returns, as usual, and make such applications in future as you may find

necessary. I have nothing further to add but a free tender of my services when at Philadelphia, an assurance that it wil[l] afford me sensible pleasure to contribut[e] to the happiness of any of the Gentlemen I have had the honor to command in the Field. you will present my most respectfull compliments to Mr. Buell, his Brother & family and inform, should Business again call him to philadelphia I shall be happy to wait on him at my Quarters
 farewell—

To Thomas Frothingham

Dear Sir   Suckesunna [Succasunna, N.J.] Feby 20th 1780
 The Board of War, have thought fit to appoint me to the charge of the Stores at Philadelphia, which appointment I have accepted, I have sent Mr. Boyer to make a full settlement with all belonging to my Departmt in the region of the north—in which direction you and my old friend Mr: Banks fall accordingly with my respects he waits on you. the settlement comes up to the 1st Instant and as it was impossible to determine with any precision what expences might be due I have directed him to settle the accounts as usual, and give notes for the Balle. after which the money for the redemption shall be left with Mr. Frothingham, with whom they may be left for payment— Mr: Frothingham takes charge of the Stores in the Feild at present. you will continue your Returns as usual—
 Nothing further remains but an offer of my services, an assurance that it will give me pleasure to be any way usefull to those who compos'd my last command[.]
 My particular respects to Mr. Banks I hear the Brat is come to town. possibly she may answer as a washing woman at the point in which case as it is good Business and ready pay you may find a way out of your difficulty, keep up a good heart my Boy and beleive me in all tim[es] of Distress—
 Your Friend

In May 1778 Frothingham signed his Oath of Allegiance as "Conductor of Military Stores." Hodgdon addresses him as Deputy Field Commissary of Military Stores.

To Henry Knox

Dear General   Suckesunna [Succasunna, N.J.] March 3d 1780
   When I had the pleasure to see you last you mentioned my Brigade Return was not so full as you could wish to make your's accurate on acct. the deliveries at Fish Kills not being included this I have obtain'd and together with another Copy of my own inclose for your use—
   Some small deliveries have doubtless been made at W. Point these time would not permit me to procure should they be found necessary they may be had in a few Days—
   With esteem I am Yours &c.

To William Thorne

Sir   Philadelphia March 22 1780
   It appears by your account, which I was fav[ou]red with yesterday, that one hundred & five thousand, one hundred & eighty five pounds, fourteen shillings & nine pence, have been drawn from Mr Rittenhouse in consequence of the last warrant for three hundred & seventy five thousand pounds consequently there remains a Balance in his hands of two hundred & sixty nine thousand eight hundred & fourteen pounds, five shillings & three pence, two hundred thousand of which must be reserved for its appropriate use.—and the other seventy thousand eight hundred & eighty five pounds, fourteen shillings & nine pence applied to the most material incidental charges of the Department, the only difficulty that arises is from the nature of the present payments to know which to pay first, and the only answer that can be given is, when you receive large Sum[s] make an equal divided among the Iron masters in proportion to the several sums due them. at the same time carefully keeping a proportion for the incidental charges of the Department, without this as credit seems not to be expected, we shall run aground a circumstance carefully to be guarded against—I shall be particularly carefull of drawg. untill I know you are properly supplied with money, which I hope will be soon, as measures are taking for that purpose—Yours sincerely

Thorne was Paymaster for the Military Stores Department.

Benjamin Flower to the Board of War and Ordnance

Gentlemen   Philadelphia March 28, 1780.
 The frequent applications of the Iron Masters lately employed casting shot & shells, and the distress[ed] situation they represent themselves to be in, by being kept out of their Money has determin'd me to make out all ,their accounts and lay the state of them before your Honble Board, and after representing my own inability and occasion of it, to give them any assistance, request your powerful assistance on their behalf
 On the 3d. of Jany. 1780 you may remember an Order pass'd in Congress on the Treasurer of this State for supplying me with one Million of dollars, for the express purpose of paying off the Contracts which in their behalf I had officially made. this was received & presented for payment, but so great & pressing have been the demands on the Treasury that notwithstanding three Months are near expired since the draught not one third part of the order is yet received. and even of this a considerable sum has been used for inevitable incidental charges under these circumstances I have inclosed the several sums due the Iron Masters, humbly hoping that the Honble. Board will join with me in endeavors to fall upon some mode for the payment thereof could this be done, I am of opinion that the other supplies for the Army expected from my department may be procured & the Officers & Men kept in countenance by the sums that may be receiv'd from the Treasurer from time to time by virtue of the with[in] mentioned Warrant.—
 The Honble. Board will excuse me for appealing to them again on the Subject, as nothing cou[ld] induce me to trespass upon their time for a moment but the distress that seems likely to pervade the department, and prevent the necessary supplies, should no methods be fallen upon to supply the requisite sums for its support
  With due respect I am Gentlemen Yours &c.

To the Board of War and Ordnance

Gentlemen   Philadelphia April 1st. 1780
 By looking over the papers in the Office I found an order of your Honble. Board for sending several species of Ordnance to Pittsburg, among other[s] one 8 Inch howitzer. upon enquiry I find we canno[t]

comply with this part of the order, untill an application is made, and one of those lent to this State obtained, would request to be informed whether the Board will make the requisition themselves, or direct in what I shall apply to procure one for the above purpose.—

Mr. Evans has by Billet inform'd me that if the publick occupy his Stores any longer they must pay double Rent Vizt: No: 1 will be £60 No: 7 £50 and the loft £50 Pr month would wish to have the direction of the Board upon the subject.—

Must again beg the Favor of the board to determine how much shall be allowed Pr Gill, for the liquor retain'd of the mens rations, and who shall pay for it. would propose for the consideration of the Board, whether after the price is ascertained it would not be as well for our own pay master to discharge these accounts, if not to keep the men (as they are at present) chearfully employed in confidence that they shall finally receive compensation shall be happy, the board would point some more eligible m[.]

With due respect I am Gentlemen Yours &c:

To Robert McFee

Sir— Philadelphia April 1st 1780

You will immediately set out for Princton in the state of Jersey, and when arrived there deliver the Letter & Papers you have as directed to Jno. Denton Esqr. the purport of which is to obtain a settlement of the acct: Current inclos'd between the U. States and the State of Jersey the Ballance of which in favor of the U. States you will see is drawn and amounts to 8700 Pensa: Currency this you are empower'd to settle & give a full discharge for the whole or such part of the Balance as you may receive and for so doing this shall be your warrant—Having finish'd the Bussiness you will return to this City with all convenient speed, paying a proper attention to the charge you may have with you You will be frugal in your expences I wish you a prosperous Journey.—

Yours &c.

McFee was a Conductor of Military Stores.

To John Denton

Sir   Philadelphia April 1st 1780
By order of the Honble. Board of War and in compliance with your request, often repeated I now incl[ose] you the acct: Current of the U. States, for Stores deliver'd Your State, which you will please to settle & transmit the Balance by the Bearer whose receipt shall be a [sure] discharge from—Your very huml Servt In behalf of the U. States.

Denton was a merchant in Princeton, New Jersey. A merchant of the same name also lived in Philadelphia, probably the same person.

Benjamin Flower to John Denton

These may Certify that the above sign'd Samuel Hodgdon is appointed by the Honble. Congress Depy. Comy. Genl. of M Stores and as such he has full powers to settle all accts: in my Department, and give discharges for the same[.] As the Department is in great want of money occasion'd by a general Stagnation, you will very much serve the publick as well as oblidge us by sendg. the Ballance by the bearer Mr: McFee as above requir'd
Yours &c.

While this is not dated, it accompanies the document immediately above.

Benjamin Flower to the Continental Congress

May it please your Excellency   Philadelphia April 3d. 1780
The distress of my department occasion'd by the want of money, and the consequent loss which will innevitably ensue to the States join'd to a fear that a relaxation in procuring the necessary supplies ordered and expected from my department, may involve me in the fatal effects of a disappointment, has induced me from a sense of duty to the publick as well as an earnest desire (as an act of justice) to alleviate the distresses of a number of poor people, to whom considerable sums are due for Labour, and others for materials supplied, to lay the following before the Honble. Congress, as the reason of our present embarrassments, humbly requesting that they

would take such order thereon, as to remove them or kindly direct to some other way of removing the difficulties, the Department at present labours under—

On the 3d. of Jany last a warrant issued by order of Congress on David Rittenhouse Esqr: Treasurer of this State for one million of Dollars for the use of my Department, of which sum (notwithstanding the pres[ent] demands at that time) only two hundred & eighty thousand, four hundred & ninety five Dollars & 37/90 parts has yet been received, and by an application this day it appears very uncertain when any further Sums may be expected. under these circumstances Congress will I humbly trust, perceive the propriety of the present application for direction, the season of the Year now permits, and invites to great exertions. advantageous purchases may be made of the necessary materials, use[d] in the several Manufactories, the workmen properly employed, and every article expected from my department be obtained, provided we are properly supplied with Money—but it gives me pain to declare the reverse is at present, the prospect having not a single Dollar on hand, and being unable to purchase a single requisite without the Cash, we are thrown into a state of anxious inactivity—I shall take up no more of your time than just to request Congress to take the foregoing into consideration, and grant us such relief as they in their wisdom shall judge best, to give Spirit & Energy to the business. I have recommend to their Notice—

With the most profound sentiments of esteem—I am Gentlemen Yours &c.

To William Egerton Godfrey

Sir   Philadelphia April 4th 1780

After having waited a week for your return which was ordered to be made without a moments loss of time I have now to inform you that your charge in the Laboratory is to be this day delivered up, with every thing under your care therein to Captn. Coren and with him you will acct: for the tools & stores delivered you when put in Charge, and all others which you have since receiv'd

---

Godfrey was a Captain Lieutenant in the Artillery Artificer Regiment, then in Philadelphia.

To Isaac Coren

Sir   Philadelphia April 4th 1780
    I have ordered Captn. Lieut: Godfrey in a Letter I have sent him to deliver up his charge in the Laboratory, together with every thing he has in trust belonging to the publick to you this day. in order to facilitate this Bussin[ess] you will please to repair to him at the Laboratory—Inform him of your orders & compleat them as quick a[s] possible. You will be carefull to see that you have every article that you receipt for, and make return to me thereof soon as convenient after you receive them
    I am Yours &c.
    Yours—

Coren was a Captain in Flower's Regiment of Artillery Artificers. He had been working in the "laboratory" since early 1777 and was cashiered on June 30, 1780.

To the Several Officers Commanding Companies in Colonel Flower's Regiment in Philadelphia

Sir   Philadelphia April 5th. 1780
    The unwarrantable combinations and unsoldier like behaviour of your Men under various pretences, has awakened a spirit of Discipline, which now calls aloud for attention. but willing to give warning before its effects takes place must request you will inform them that I am authoriz'd and empowered to pay the value of the Liquor at present retain'd agreeable to their due Bills, as soon as Cash can be obtain'd for that purpose after this declaration you may inform your Men, that is in an unalterable resolution to admit of no more applications, even for real grievances, should any exist by the whole Body[.] thro' their Officers and no other way, will they be heard in future—as it would give me pain to be oblidged to deal with them according to the severity of Martial law I am in hopes they will return and continue peaceably to their work, and observe the within mention'd orders, which will prevent disagreeable consequences to themselves for what is past, and ensure kind treatment and ample justice from the publick and the Officers under whom they act.—
    Yours &c

To Isaac Cox

Sir   Philadelphia April 17th 1780
    Agreeable to my promise I have advised with the Gentn. who rent estates in this City, consequently proper Judges what in specie is a valuable consideration for those rented at the present Day. upon their reports, and my own Calculations I am led to think you have set yours improv'd by us for the publick too high. this I have reported and am authoriz'd & directed to offer you the sum you demand for rent, and agree to pay one-half the Taxes that may arise during the time we improve them. if you accede to these proposals, by signifying your consent in a line to me I will wait on you and settle the matter for the present Year immediately—
    I am Sir Yours &c.

Cox, a Philadelphia merchant, had served as a Paymaster for Pennsylvania troops and owned, or shared the ownership of, several privateers.

To Gustavus Risberg

Sir   Philadelphia April 17th 1780
    I am informed by Mr. Pearson Comy. M Stores that you have an account open in your Books against Mr: Ebenr. Cowell for rations supplied a number of men under him, employed as armourers some time ago. if that is the case, as I am about settling with Mr. Cowell for work done at that time for the U. States, must requested to be favor'd with your acct:, that proper stoppages may be made.—
    With Esteem I am Sir Your huml Servt.

Risberg was in the Commissary General of Issues Department, then in charge of the department in the State of Pennsylvania.

To John Mitchell

Sir   Philadelphia April 18th 1780
    There is at Elizabeth Furnace Lancaster County about Forty Tons of Shells which are wanting in this City. if you can make it convenient to procure Teams for this Service, you will greatly serve the publick as well as oblidge Your hum Servt:

Mitchell was a Deputy Quartermaster General at Philadelphia.

To Samuel Sarjant

Sir,   Philadelphia April 19th 1780

Inclosed you have the Copy of an Invoice of Ordnance and Stores ordered by the Board of War to Pittsburgh, also a duplicate receipt of the part sent from here consign'd to you.—Captn. Craig of Colo. Procter['s] Regiment will be with you to compleat the Invoice and receipt for the whole I have referred him to you for such part as by your return I find you can furnish which with what I have sent will amoun[t] to the whole of the order. as it is of the greatest importance that the Captains command arrive at their destination without loss of time, you will please to afford him all possible assistance to get him on his way from Carlisle.—

The 2 six pounders with implements compleat one 3 pdr. with do. two 5 ½ Inch Howitzers with do. & the 8 Inch Howitzer which will rive with its apparatus with this, with the stores hereafter mentioned together with these forwarded as Pr Invoice you will perceive, nearly complies with the Return 100 8 Inch She[lls] 200 5 ½ Inch Shells, 100 lbs Slow match, 1 Rheam Cannon Cartridge paper 1200 lb powder and some other articles I have referr'd to you to be supplied. one waggon sets off to morrow with 3 pound ammunition and some Case shot for howitzers. the remainder will be sent as soon as waggons are furnished. I must beg you would send down one Barrell Sweet oil the whole of the Copper Ladles on hand and the 6 pd. round shot, the 3 pd. Rd. Shot & the strap'd heads 3 pds. likewise the strap'd heads 6 pds. in order to have fix'd with Flannells as there is a considerable demand for those Sizes. also the empty Flanl. Carts. two Bbls Tin, & all the Ladle heads. these are wanted & must shortly be procured if money can be obtain'd. unless forwarded Soon. you will please to bear this on mind [sic] & forward the Oil in particular as quick as possible

I am—Your most obedt. Servant

In March 1778, Sarjant signed his Oath of Allegiance as "Superintendent and Keeper of Stores in Cumberland County, Pennsylvania. In 1780 he was still in charge of the works at Carlisle. In the *Journals of the Continental Congress* the last name appears as Sergeant. In the manuscript of this letterbook it appears as Sargeant/Sarjent/Sargent/Sarjant. As the man himself signed his name as "Sarjant" this is the spelling used here.

Deserter Notice

Philadelphia April 22d 1780
DESERTED the 14th & 16th from Lieut: Alexr. Dow's Compy in Colo. Benja. Flowers Regt: of Arty & Artificers the followg. Soldiers. Vizt: Wm. Latimore about twenty four years of age by trade a shoemaker, 5 feet 5 Inches high well set wears his hair tied which is black, answering to a Brown complexion.—James Trusdall an Irish Man about twenty six Years of Age, 5 feet 6 Inches high, a slender fellow, black Curled Hair, has a remarkable lump on the back of his hand and a smaller one over his right Eye.—Jona. Arnold a native of new York twenty nine Years of age 5 feet 8 Inches high swarthy complexion black hair tied up, a well set fellow, speaks coarse.—Jno. Guilliam twenty four years of age born in London 5 feet 5 Inches high a thin fellow, fair complexion curled Hair—it is supposed they are gone to Sea, or are on board some of the Vessels in the river in either case the concealer, or carrier off in case of detection may expect to experience the utmost rigour of the Law whoever apprehends and confines any of the above deserters shall receive 100 Dollars Reward for each by applying to the Comy. Genl. M Stores Office in this City.—

Discharge Certificate for George Marshal

These Certify that George Marshal a soldier in the late Captn. Jesse Rae's Company in Colo. Benja. Flower's Regt. of Arty & Artificer has served faithfully the term for which he was enlisted which was three Years from the twenty third Day of April one thousand seven hundred & seventy seven. in consequence of which he is at full liberty to employ or engage himself in any Service, he thinks fit, being hereby honorably acquitted and discharged from the abov[e] mentioned Company & Regiment.—

Given under my hand at Philadelphia this 25th day of April 1780 Whom it may concern

Thomas Procter, Rental Agreement With Hodgdon

Philadelphia April 25th 1780
This day I have agreed with Major Saml: Hodgdon A C Genl. M Stores for the rent of a dwelling House at present occupied by Majr. Jona. Gostelowe Comy. M Stores as a Store & Drum Factory, situated east of Walnut Street a small distance as the rate of Fifty pounds in Gold or Silver, or the exchange when paid, which is agreed to be quarterly. the Taxes arising on the premises to be paid, as usual by myself or Attorney, the whole being vested in the United States for their use one Year, for the above mention'd Sum of Fifty pounds, by virtue of this agreement, which I acknowledge to be my act by signing—

Procter was Colonel of the Fourth Continental Artillery Regiment.

To Gabriel Ogden

Dear Sir   Philadelphia April 28th 1780
I have waited impatiently for a line from you for some time, and no favourable opportunity has presented, for my writing to you. consequently I have been at a loss to know how to conduct in your affair, respecting the payment of your acct:. have now to inform you that on account of the distrest situation of our Finances, the whole of the Iron Masters have accepted payment in Loan office certificates, your's is the only one that remains unpaid. Mr. Faesh's I have received this day in part & shall have the remainder next week. must request for your good, that you will either come yourself, send some person to negotiate your Business, or direct me explicitly how you wish to have it done, in this case if you chuse I should do it. you must enclose me an order, full to the purpose, and I will undertake to settle it, but if as convenient for you, as I am exceedingly engaged, should be glad you would depute some other person or come yourself. your account is accepted, certified, and passed and only waits for payment. should my advice be asked, I should recommend it to you by all means, to accept the Certificates, as from present appearances you will not get one farthing of money for a long time, and Certificates are almost as much used as money and make part of the present commercial Medium. the interest makes them very acceptable,

however! you will direct as you think best, and for old Friendship's sake I shall give you every possible assistance.—
  With esteem I am Your very Huml Servt:

Ogden owned Pompton Furnace in New Jersey.

To Daniel Burrell

Sir,   Philadelphia April 28th 1780
  Your favor of this day I have received must request you to inform me before I engage to have the Coals burnt, what Terms the Man will agree upon, that I may know how much they will turn out a hundred on the Bank. if you will please to let me know this I will send you an answer immediately. perhaps it might be best for you to employ the man. in this case you will be able to inform me, what you can afford to deliver them Pr hundred Bushell. I am so engaged that it is not possible for me to come out—
  I am respectfully Yours &c.

Hodgdon is referring to making charcoal, which was used for metalworking as well as the manufacture of gunpowder.

To Isaac Coren

Sir   Philadelphia April 28th 1780
  By particular Order Serjeant Jones is attached to Captn. Jordans Company and sent to work with Mr. Perkins in the Armoury. you will consequently consider him as seperated from your company and govern yourself accordingly—
  Yours &c.

To George Perkins

Sir,   Philada. April 28 1780
  The bearer Serjt: Jones being recommended as a Gunstocker, the Colo. thinks it best he should be employed with you. you will please

to set him to work and return him as a draught from Captn. Jordans Company untill further directions may be found necessary.—
Yours &c.

George Perkins was Superintendent of the Armoury in Philadelphia.

To the Board of War and Ordnance

Gentlemen, Philadelphia April 29 1780

I should be glad to be inform'd whether any quantity of Lead may be expected soon, as our Men employed at the Lead Furnace, will shortly be idle, and our Cartridge makers consequently stop'd as we have no returns from, Boston cannot say what quantity of Lead may be there but perceive a mere Trifle at springfield from whence I expected to have been supplied. as the number of Musket Cartridges on hand is by no means sufficient, must request the Board will please to direct where we may apply to obtain a supply of Lead to keep the Business going on.—
With Esteem I am Gentlemen Yours &c.

To William Egerton Godfrey

Sir Philadelphia April 29th 1780

I have received yours, informing of your arrest in answer must inform you, that as it appears from your own account, that you are arrested agreeable to the articles of War, the character of a Soldier requires you to stan[d] the arrest and confront your accuser. if you are found innocent of the charges exhibited against you, you will be honourably acquitted. if not as justice requires, you will be punished, in such way and degree, as the nature of the Crime makes necessary. permit me just to hint, that the reluctance you discover, to coming to trial, is no inconsiderable evidence of your guilt. having stood trial yourself the way is open for calling Captn Coren to the same Tribunal in either case, as my Duty does not make it necessary, I shall not interfere in the matter—
Yours—

Despite his arrest, Godfrey continued to serve in the Department until August 1780.

To John Jacob Faesh

Dear Sir   Philada. April 30th 1780

With this I send you a Letter I wrote some time ago, expecting Mr. Peirce would, as he then expected have been to Camp soon after its date—Since writing that I have got your stove mould finished, and Colo Procte[r] is oblidging enough to endeavor if possible, to take it on with the hats, which are in a Box directed to the General, from whom you will receive yours. the mou[ld] is neatly made by comes high, as you will perceive by the inclos'd Bill which I have paid & carried to you[r] account the fate of your Ticketts you shall hear by Mr. Peirce who expects to leave this for Camp next Wednesday I want to see Doctr. Leddell, as I have already received half your debt in Certificates, and shall have the other half next week, and I am anxious to know whether you approve of my plan, to let me use the Certificates, and pay you in Cash when it comes to hand. although as it seems to be your wish to have the other half in Money and no readier way can be devised to get it I think you will not object—in confidence of which should any considerable contract present for providing materials for the Department, I shall run the risque of doing for you in this case, as I would for myself—put them away, and repay you when the Treasurer pays me. should be happy however, to have your sentiments on the matter as quick as possible, upon the receipt of which, I shall govern myself accordingly

Inclosed is a Letter for Mr: Odgen which I would thank you to forward by the next opportunity shall send the Gun and any other necessaries requested—

Nothing new only an account is just arrived that five privateers belonging to this port, are taken & carried into Nyork. a Ship is also arrived here from ,Boston with 220 Hhds Sugar, 10 of Rum, and some wine belonging to the Continent—have nothing further at this time but my most respectfull compliments to Mrs. Faesh & the Ladies which with my determin'd Friendship closes this from—

Your most Obedt Hum Servt

To Joseph Eayres

Sir   Philada. May 2d. 1780

In behalf of Coll. Flower I have to acknowledge the receipt of your Favor of the 25th Ulto. with its enclosures which notwithstanding the neglect of inclosing the form, answered the purpose. have only to request in addition to know, what two Companies those are that refuse to make regular Returns, and what reasons are offered in Support of their refusal. if they belong to the Regt: of Arty & Artificers, they are under your immediate command. if that is not the case, should be glad to be inform'd, how they originated & how they are supported, and under whose command they consider themselves. this is of the utmost importance to them to have explain'd, as a special Committee are now employed arranging every Department, before whom I have been already, to endeavor to give them a general Idea of the Regt: the necessity of its being enlarged, and encouraged, by stating its importance. but these Companies upon their present footing however necessary must be neglected, as I have no official knowledge of their Situation, the reflection of which gives me pain, as I am determined to exert myself in support of every usefull Man or body of Men, however remotely situated belonging to the Department I have the honour to Superinten[d.]

As to the supplies of Money requested I am fully Sensible they are indispensable to procure Materials and pay Wages, at so large & important a post as Springfeild, and from this conviction, have made it the subject of representation to the Honble. Board of War. they too are convinced of the impropriety of keeping up a post, unless it can be supplied. but at present I must confess that appearances are against us in this respect, so general is the Malady that not a Dollar is to be found in any Department, consequently we ourselves involved in perplexity. hope however that light will spring forth speedily, the rays of which will be seen in Hemisphere where you dwell & desireable as the light of the Morning—

As to News can with pleasure inform you, that an express has arrived this Day from Charlestown which he left the 9th Ulto. at which time all was well & our Army in high Spirits. hope the event will be glorious.—

Coll. Flower tho' much better is yet very unwell and only waits for the weather to set out on his intended Journey, to try what a change of Air, and gentle exercise will do towards the recovery of his health, his compliments attends this—

My respects to all who enquire after me, and best wishes for the prosperity of you & your amiable Family closes this long epistle from—

Your very huml Servt:—

Joseph Eayres signed the Oath of Allegiance at Springfield, Massachusetts, as "Major of Artificers." This was directed to Eayres at Springfield.

To Samuel Sarjant

Sir Philada. May 2d 1780

Yours inclosing Captn. Wylies return have come safely to hand, and in behalf of Coll. Flower must inform you that the necessity of the Mill being finish'd becomes every day more obvious. 100 Dollars is now demanded for a Bayonet, and the reason given for the extravagant advance is that they must pay 10 Dollars a peice for grindg. and 10 polishing. under these circumstances, join'd to those of the mill being thus far built, a single moment must not be Spent, to determine that the publick Interest calls for every possible exertion of its servants to complete this Business—

The price demanded by the Masons is great, but it will be but a few days (I should suppose) they will be wanted, and the works when bro't to perfection will amply make amends to the Continent. the greatest difficulty at present seems to be how they or any other persons employed in the publick Service are to paid the sale of the Bricks I am in hopes will afford you a temporary relief. I mean in the Business, for which the Monies arising on the Sale are appropriated. if Mr. Gibson finds it necessary to have some person skill'd in Mill works, to assist him the sooner such person is found and employ'd the better. doubtless you may find such about you and as the completion of the Mill is resolved on, the best terms, that the times will admit must be made, and carried into execution without a moments loss of Time

Captn. Gordon is still here and likely to continue some time to avail himself of the prospect of getting the Cloathg. for the Regt: by which time it is probable we may be in Cash, should that be the case, he will receive a proportionable part. he is employed superintending the works at the Ordnance Yard in the room of Captn. Joy who is to be absent on publick Business probably 3 weeks, as we judg'd it needless for him to come on without Money or Cloaths—

The Tin and the Oil sent for are much wanted. must request to have them—forwarded speedily—the other articles with all the Screw drivers as soon as possible afterwar[ds.] good paper for writing we have none at present shall forward a portion of the first that comes to hand—
With Esteem I am Sir Your very huml Servt.

To Daniel Burrell

Sir, Philada. May 3d 1780
By Mr. Brown I recd. yours but can by no means agree to the proposals made, must request agreeable to my former Letter to be inform'd what the Coals will turn out Pr 100 Bushells untill I know this I cannot contract as it is very possible they may turn out dearer than I can purchase them here. knowing what they will cost delivered at the Bank I can calculate the transportation and wastage and determine with certainty what is best to be done
With Esteem I am Yours &c.

To the Board of War and Ordnance

Gentlemen, Philada. May 3d. 1780
In compliance with a late order of your Honble. Board, I send enclosed an account of the number and Value of the Muskets & Bayonets received from on board the Ship Batchelor—that the value might be properly ascertain'd I directed Mr: Perkins to call two other smiths to his assistance and the enclosed is the price affixed by them taken from the report—
With due respect I am Yours &c.
Copy of report of the value & number of Muskets Fuzees Bayts. recd. on board the Ship Bachelor, as dld in to the Board of War—Vizt.

22 Chests qt. 689 Muskets		@ 45 each	£31005.0.0
	1743 Bayonets	@ 7.10	13072.10.0
2 do. qt. 59 Fuzees		@ 210	12390.0.0
	59 Bayonets	@ 7.10	442.10
		Pena Currency	£ 56910.0.0

To the Board of War and Ordnance

Gentlemen   Philada. May 4th 1780

After examining Mr. Barbers return and Mr. Perkins's am of opinion that is the 119 Chests said to contain Gun Barrells, Ramrods, Gun Mounting Pistols [sic] Cutlasses &c. or any part together with the Gun Locks part of Locks, and mounting, the Cask of Flints twenty Lanthorns (if Horn) and 2000 hand Grenades can be got on it will serve the Comy. Genl. M Stores Department much, as the consumption of the greatest part of those articles is great, and those not wanted may be disposed of for a valuable consideration at this time of general scarcity of money a circumstance that in our present embarrass'd Situation duty oblidged me to mention. I would just suggest as another reason for bringing them on that as the army is moving to the Southward it is probable the whole supplies will be expected from this post. if so the necessity of collecting materials already purchased appears obvious—Must remind the Board that our lead casters have finish'd the small potion [sic] of lead we had on hand, when I wrote them on the Subject and are now Idle. perhaps if any at , Boston, and an opportunity offers, the Board may think proper to order to on with such other Stores as may be coming on—

With due respect I am Gentlemen Yours &c.

To Mark Thompson

Sir   Philada. May 5th. 1780

I am informed by Mr. Humphreys that you have a considerable quantity of Bar Iron on hand the property of the United States made on their account by virtue of a contract, which he was empowered to make. the quantity agreed upon it Seems was five Tons to be return'd for seventeen & half Tons Pig Metal, but it appears by a Letter of yours to Mr. Humphreys, which I have just seen that on 13Tons..14h..3qrs..8lb has been deliver'd to you. how this happened cannot Say, but must request the favour to be inform'd how much Bar Iron you have on hand, should Suppose by the contract better than three Tons. as this is much wanted I shall immediately upon advice from you write to the nearest DQ MGenl. to have it forwarded. at the same time shall endeavour to furnish you with the remaining part of Pig Mettle [sic] to enable you to compleat the contract.—As to entering upon a new Contract, untill the old is finished, it is needless besid[es] did that objection not exist the terms would by no means answer, as experience has taught us we can do much better with pigs, for however bad they may be, we find all the Iron Masters fond of working them, and under our present circumstances it becomes necessary, that we should act in concert with people engag'd in private Business and make the most of every thing—

I am Sir Your most Obedt: Humble Servt.

Mark Thompson was a Colonel of the Militia from Sussex County, New Jersey. He operated Changewater Furnace at what is now Changewater, Warren County, New Jersey.

To George Ingells

Sir   Philada. 6th 1780

In consequence of Orders from the Honble. Board of War I am to inform you that the Military Stores at Lancaster under your charge are immediately to be disposed of in the following manner, and the post discontinued—the whole of the powder in Casks is to be sent to the Magazine at Carlisle and delivered to Saml: Sargent Esqr: Comy. M Stores at that place—the remainder of the Stores of every Species are to be brought to this City. to accomplish this Business with dispatch you will wait on Geo. Ross Esqr: D Q MGenl. deliver him the Letter you have for him, the purport of which is to furnish Teems for this Service which having obtain'd either in part, or sufficient for the whole removal, you will begin as directed and finish with all convenient Speed—

I am Sir Your huml Servant

Ingells was Commissary of Military Stores at Lancaster, Pennsylvania.

To George Ross Jr.

Sir   Philada. May 6 1780

The Honble. Board of War having ordered the Military Stores at Lancaster to be removed, and the post discontinued, I have directed Mr. Ingells agreeable to my Instructions from the Board to wait on you for teems to enable him to comply with his orders. one part are to be sent to Carlisle the other to this City. I am informed about 30 waggons will answer the purpose. if it is convenient to furnish the whole at once, they may be removed by two or three draughts, but I would wish to have the Business compleated as soon as circumstances will admit—

I am Sir Your very huml Servt:

Ross was Deputy Quartermaster General for part of Lancaster County, Pennsylvania.

To Samuel Sarjant

Sir, Philada. May 6th 1780

By this you will be informed that the waggons have returned & delivered the Stores agreeable to Invoice have now to request of you half a dozen Chest Locks made of the kind, the best, such as was made by one of the Men for Captn. Jordan. they are wanted for Book Chests, for our own use & the Board of War, should be oblidged by having them speedily—In your last Letter but one to Colo Flower you informed the Hessians prisoners with you had deserted. as there is a call for their return, from whence they were taken, must beg of you to inform me whether any of them have been apprehended. if not you will enclose an account of their Names, and the time they deserted certified by Captn. Gibson whose immediate charge it appears they were under Colo. Flowers compliments attends this, he remains much the same—

Yours

To James Pearson

Sir Philada. May 8th 1780

The Honble. Board of War have informed me that you have been with them on the subject of settling your accounts and requesting the means to accomplish this necessary Business, you having inform'd them that it is not convenient to do it at your own house as suggested in a Letter from Colo. Flower—in complyance with their request, I have agreed to appropriate the File Room to your use, and any other

part of the Hall occasionally except the Room I do my own Business in, and for Clerks Mr. Jones and Dayley are at your service, till this Business is compleated, or the Honble. Board shall order otherways—
  I am Sir Yours &c.

To Samuel Sarjant

Sir Philada. May 8 1780
  The bearer Mr: Robt: Cluggage has been for some time past in charge of a number of Cannonand Stores at Fort Roberdeau, for which service he has this day received his Pay. the Honble. Board of War now direct that the whole of the Cannon & Stores at that place and Huntington, be immediately removed to Carlisle. you will upon receipt of this procure & send off an Officer, and suitable command to compleat this Business. a report having prevailed here that Some sculking parties of the Enemy were lurking between your post & the Fort, you will see that the Men who go on this Service are properly supplied and notified to prevent any Surprize. Mr. Cluggage has kindly offered to accompany the party, you will need to furnish him with Provision in common with the rest—

NB. Inclosed you have an Invoice of the Stores as delivered us by Majr: Cluggage. you will please to look at the Entry of the Stores forwarded to Fort Roberdeau, and let me know upon Receipt of these now sent for what is the Deficiency—

To the Board of War and Ordnance

Gentn. Philada. May 10th 1780
  Inclos'd I send a Copy of two Indents of Stores wanted in Camp, for the order & direction of the honbl. Board. they were received by last post—
  With respect I am Yours

To Seth Harding

Sir   Philada. May 10th 1780

In consequence of an Order from the Honble. Navy Board, the bearer waits on you to receive & deposit the Powder safely, which you have on board the Confederacy untill called for—

I am Sir Your very huml. Servt.

Harding was Captain of the Continental frigate *Confederacy*, which had arrived from Martinico, now Martinique, a short time before.

To Seth Harding

Sir,   Philadelphia May 11th. 1780

As we have only two Carts to employ this day in removing the ammunition, from your Ship to the Magazine, which will make but slow work, I have thought best to propose, if you can make it convenient, to load the whole in your long boat, and let her run up to the Continental Wharf as that is contiguous to the Magazine. great time may be saved, and the Ammunition be moved with much more safety than transporting it such a distance in Carts, through the Streets. if you approve this method by signifying I will order the Carts to attend at the place mention'd

I am Sir Your very huml Servt

To Jonathan Gostelowe

Sir   Philada. May 12 1780

You will immediately have the following articles got ready for transportation Vizt:—

    1500 Muskets, Bayts: & Scabbards
    1500 Carte Boxes new Construction
    1500 Bayonet Belts
      50 New Drums & Carriages
    1000 Brushes & Wires
    1000 Gun worms
    3000 Flints

To John Mitchell

Sir   Philadelphia May 12th 1780
   Since I saw you last I have been with the Board of War, on the Subject of transporting the stores to Camp. they are clearly of opinion that they should go by water to Trenton. by a calculation I find it will take twenty waggons to take them from thence to Camp. you will please to order the Vessell that carries them to Trenton to the Armoury wharf to load—and give the necessary directions for the transportation from thence to Camp[.] I shall send some person to see them safely deliver'd as directed—
   I am Sir Your very huml. Servt:

To Jonathan Gostelowe

Sir   Philada. May 13 1780
   You will please to exchange thirty Sides of sole Leather with Mr. Martil G[eu]il for thin Leather at the usual rate of pound for pound, as it will procure a supply to keep the Men employed, which can be obtain'd no other way at present
   Yours &.

To Jonathan Gostelowe

Sir   Philada. May 13 1780
   The Schooner which is to receive the Musketts & other Stores will be at the wharf immediately. I shall send Mr. Warner (who is to go on with the Stores) down to see them put on board. when that is done you will send me an Invoice, for which I will give you a receipt and credit in my Books, this being the most regular as well as eligable mode of doing Business of the Department—
   Yours &c.

To Philip Van Rensselaer

Sir   Philada. May 13th 1780
   I have received your Favor of the 7th Ulto. inclosing an indent

for several Species of tools and Stores, and as far as was in my power have complied with its contents as you will see by the inclosed invoice which was forwarded to Mr. Richd. Frothingham DFCM Stores yesterday with direction to send them on to you with all possible dispatch. the other articles to compleat the Invoice shall be forwarded with all the dispatch that circumstances will admit, and notice given you when they are sent on—

Colo: Flowers compliments in return for yours he remains much the same, next monday week he setts off to try the effects of a change of air. shall be happy to hear from you every convenient opportunity, and shall endeavor to supply you will every needed article, as early as possible after being made acquainted with your wants—

My particular compliments to Mr. Lansing & Wife and all enquiring Friends—

With Esteem I am Sir Your very hum Servt.

To Isaac Warner

Sir   Philada. May 13th 1780

You are early on monday morning to proceed to Trenton, and there take into your charge the Arms & Military Stores mention'd in the Invoice that will be given you, and after procuring the Number of Teems necessary, which must be done by applying to Peter Gordon Esqr. DQM Genl. or in his absence the person acting as such, you will see them carefully loaded and proceed with all possible speed to Head Quarters of the Army, and deliver them to Richd. Frothingham Esqr. DFCMS, and take his receipt for the whole you have in charge. you will keep with the waggons and dispose matters to the best of your Judgement so as to prevent loss by embezzlement or any other way—You will be as frugal in your expences as possible and make all convenient speed in the discharge of this Business. I wish you a pleasant & prosperous Journey—
cond ms

Warner was a Conductor of Military Stores.

To Richard Frothingham

Sir, Philada. May 13th 1780

Inclosed you have an inventory of Arms & Military Stores, forwarded in consequence of a requisition from his Excellency, and the Indent forwarded by you. circumstances has prevented my sending every species mention'd in the Indent but shall send on the remainder as quick as possible—I am desired by the Board to inform you that all orders for Stores must be countersigned by Genl. Knox or Officer commanding the Artillery previous to their being sent here, without this they cannot be attended to in future. if any further supplies are wanting, in addition to those already notified you will enclose them by Mr. Warner—the Medicines cannot be procured at present. perhaps the Teems which brings the Stores may be able to load with the damaged Arms you have on hand, and take them on to Trenton. should this be the case Mr. Warner will take them in charge—the Stores sent to your care a few days ago for Mr. Ranselaer, you will endeavor to forwarded immediately, as they are exceedingly wanted—

We have nothing new, Mr. Eayrs and Copeland went on without being able to obtain a single article of Cloathing. I have heard from Mr. Jones, he expects to be on the last of this month, but I fancy he will not come to the Field, as the Board inform me they intend to send him to the Southward—can with pleasure inform you that by a late resolve of the Assembly of Massachusetts Bay the Staff are included in the act for making up the depreciation, a Copy of the resolve you have enclosed. you will present my regards to Mr. Randolph & Wife, to uncle Bishop Colo. Drake & all enquiring Friends. tell Uncle Bishop I have not forgot the Spectacles, but I have not as yet been able to get a pair that I thought would answer his purpose. should the Idol at whose shrine so many worship & adore be present you will make my compliments if possible acceptable. my Love to Colo: Stevens and his wife. you will as soon as possible deliver the enclos'd Letter to Colo. Lamb—

Yours &c.

To John Lamb

Dear Sir   Philada. May 13th 1780

Being about settling my publick accounts I am under the necessity of requesting the favour of you to inform me in what way it will be most convenient to account the 1000 Dollars supplied you on my account by Colo. Stevens before your late tour to Springfeild. if you should settle your acct: with Mr. Frothingham the present Feild Comy and leave it in his hands it will answer me very well, as he can remit it any time. or if the acot is settled in any other way, and the money credited the publick a Certificate will enable me to acct: but the most eligible way I should suppose, would be to enclose your account with that sum credited, to the Honble. Board of War, who will doubtless order their Secretary & Pay Mater to adjust the account, and forward the Ballance as the service was performed under their immediate direction. I have suggested this Mode as the most regular, but I presume not to dictate. I should be happy to hear from you on the subject, as soon as conveniency will admit, as I cannot close my publick accounts untill I know whether it is to be inserted, or not, a circumstance that is in Some degree mortifying under the present apprehension of people at large, who suppose, that scarce a publick Officer can be found (I mean of the Staff) who wishes to come to a Settlement, for fear of loosing his ears, or what is worse his importance—

We have nothing new but are anxiously waiting the fate of Carolina, a week perhaps may put us out of suspence—

With esteem I am Sir Your very huml Servt:

To Peter Gordon

Sir   Philada. May 13th 1780

There is a considerable quantity of Bar Iron belonging to the publick, made under Contract of the Comy. Genl. Mily Stores at Colo. Thompsons works at change water. as it is much wanted and lies contiguous to your post, you will exceedingly oblige me and Serve the publick by falling upon some measure to forward it speedily to this City. the quantity on hand supposed to be from 3 to 4 Tons it being of a kind peculiar for makg Steel is the reason of its being so

much wanted—
   I am Sir Your most Obedt. Servt.

This was addressed to Gordon as Deputy Quartermaster General at Trenton, or the person acting at that post. Mark Thompson owned Changewater Ironworks in New Jersey.

To Thomas Potts

Sir,   Philada. May 16th 1780
   I have forwarded the remaining part of the pig Metal to compleat six Tons, as you will perceive by the Invoice inclosed, and should be glad to receive some of the Steel in return as soon as you can possibly make it convenient. at present we have none on hand and the demand begins to be pressing—
   I am Sir Your very huml Servt.

Thomas Potts was an Ironmaster who was part owner and operator of Warwick Furnace and Coventry Forge in Pennsylvania.

To Isaac Coren

Sir   Philada. May 17th 1780
   You were perfectly right in not quitting the Laboratory, in consequence of your arrest, as store[s] must in that case have been exposed to embezzlement, and you would have been accountable. you will continue to carry on the Business of the Laboratory as usual untill you receive further directions—
   Yours—

Discharge Certificate For Christopher Lane

These Certify that Christopher Lane having procured an able bodied Man by the name of Richard Obrian, by trade a Carpenter to serve during the War in his room & stead, free of charge: of inlisting on Bounty Money to the United States, is discharg'd from his enlistment in the Regt: of Artificers, commanded by Colo. Benja. Flower, and is at full liberty to dispose of himself as he thinks proper—
   Given under my hand in behalf of Colo. Flower this 17th day of May 1780   All whom it may Concern

Benjamin Flower to the Board of War and Ordnance

Gentn.

Captn: Jordan says the Gap where the Mill is now erecting is about six miles from the works, to the Boiling Springs four & half, and three to Mrs. Callender's propos'd Mill seat—Quere "upon what terms can either of these places be obtain'd—the old Mill at Mrs. Callenders as situated at present, can't work more than 8 months in the year. he thinks that there is no better situation at Mrs. Callenders than where the old Mill now stands—the Idea he says of raising a shed to answer the purposes of a Mill is too ridiculous to deserve a serious refutation—the road to Mrs. Callenders mill seat from the works is tolerably good. the others to the Gap & Boiling Springs equally bad, being both pretty rough or rocky.—Mr. Perkins says he gave a draught of a Building suitable for a Boring & Grinding mill when the building was first contemplating, and having a thorough knowledge of the Business at the time he gave it, it must be impossible for him to suppose any other will answer now. the Mill erecting nearly resembles the one he proposed & described as he is informed. this is the only construction for a durable & usefull work of the kind—an open Shed will by no means answer even in the most favorable weather—his draught was calculated for a stone Building which on all accounts, he supposes best & cheapest in the end."— From the above, these questions, for the information of those concerned will naturally arise Vizt: can the Seat at the Boiling Springs, be obtain'd and upon what terms. if obtain'd upon equal terms, all circumstances considered will it answer better. would a temporary Shed, suppose it would answer, be equal to the works, or preferable to that now proposed in the end—upon what terms can Mrs. Callenders place be had, should the terms be agreable, and a wooden Building answer Quere "whether such a temporary affair, from circumstances in the present case, would not come to near the cost, of that now in hand, to make it eligible to prosecute it—the Stone of that new Building is on the spot, the sand within one Mile, and the lime already for rise; on the other hand Timber scarce and dear the Sawing more than the cost of the Logs and the transportation equal to either—The rise of my Mill and the Timber on my land proper to compleat the Mill now building, you have without any Cost of transportation, and the Seat for the Mill you have upon your own terms. the reverse of this is the case with either of the other places contended for but I would be understood only to sugges[t] the above, upon the plan urged of oeconomy by no means to influence, as envy would suggest—as I feel myself perfectly indifferent, what may be the final result. I have stated facts upon my own knowledge, and best information, and as a publick Officer shall just subjoin my opinion which is briefly this, that it will be for the Interest of the United States, to perfect the Mill already begun if upon enquiry that shall be the judgement of the Board, they will give order accordingly

This and the following two letters refer to the ordnance works Carlisle, Pennsylvania. It was planned to move much of the Artificer operations from Philadelphia to that place.

Benjamin Flower to the Board of War and Ordnance

Gentn.   Philada. May 17th 1780

In consequence of the objections raised by Genl. Armstrong to finishing the Borring & Grinding Mill began at Carlisle upon the present Spot agreeable to the order of your Honble. Board forwarded to Mr. Sargent in your Letter of the 19th of October last, I have again recurred to the principles that gave rise to the application, supposing that the disgust that shews itself in the garb of oeconomy springs from the supposed selfish disposition in me, of recommending to the Board the Mill seat in question—I am sensible I need say but little to convince you, that no selfish or sordid views at that time, in that case, was harboured in my Breast, "but as a Gentleman in publick Character, demands a reason for this ill judged measure, attended with expence without a prospect of the ends being answered." as he is pleased to suggest. I have with great attention and calmness, look'd once more into the matter determining if I found we have been deceived, and acted wrong to join Issue with him, and as a publick Officer divested of all prejudice, in favor of myself sollicit the Board to endeavor to find Some more convenient place for the purpose— you are sensible of the Offer that attended the first mention of the mill being built on my land, being then fully aware of what I now experience in this Gentlemens objections, was the reason I then made them & now review them with pleasure—but if my intentions are insufficient to keep envy asleep, actions shall be called in aid. after declaring, that the publick good was my sole motive in the part I have taken in this matter I must request the Honble. Board, to give order for stopping the men employed at the Mill, untill they shall be convinced, and be able to convince Congress that under circumstances which I trust will appear upon investigation, it is their Interest to order it completed—should I be mistaken, and a more Suitable place can be found I shall chearfully prosecute your order in procuring the place and building the Mill, and as I am determin'd to Suffer no more imputations of having acted from my own partial authority, must inform you to prevent any undue influence in your decision, that I stand ready to take the Building in question to myself after it is covered, and refund the publick the Monies advanc'd in carrying it on thus far. if this is not accepted I shall conclude that my place is best calculated for the buildg & terms most advantageous to the publick, and shall consequently expect your Honble. Board will give such explicit orders for the completion of the mill as will remove any further objections the opinions. I have taken on the Subject I have subjoin'd for your consideration—

With due respect I am Gentlemen Yours &c.

Benjamin Flower to the Board of War and Ordnance

Thoughts respecting the removal of some part of the Regt: of Artillery & Artificers—in answer to a question from the Honble. Board of War on arrangements, submitted to their consideration with the substance of enquiry annexed.—

Mr: Perkins says that so many objects present themselves, from which difficulties arise, that inlisted men cannot be managed with that ease, as they might were they employed by themselves, especially under their present circumstances. hired Men in a City may be employed, or discharged as circumstances may make it necessary, and about six or eight would answer for small repairs, and inspection of Muskets and Bayonets or might be augmented or reduced at pleasure.—

With respect to the Brass Foundery Mr. Beyers proposes to undertake the whole casting himself and let the whole of the finishers be sent to Carlisle[,]three of them being inlisted men the other two hired men, which may if thought best be discharged. Mr. Byers will undertake to furnish the whole mounting for the Department—should this be adopted the present Foundery may be occupied for that purpose: and armour[er] and File Cutters being quite sufficient for these Branches—

In answer to the question is it best to remove the wheelwrights and carpenters from Carlisle to this City. upon examining Captn Jordan and referring to other circumstances we find, that the wheelwrights may be much better employed here, and the major part of the Carpenters for the following reasons. Vizt: timber difficult to be had at Carlisle, and such as can be obtain'd not good of the kind, and as the mounting of the Cannon appears to be necessary, it can be done much better here than there, having the Cannon on the Spot, they may be more compleatly fitted to their Carriages. the Stuff quite as high at Carlisle tho' not as good, as that procur'd here and the cost of transporting Carriages, (from Carlisle to this City after they are finished) considerable not one wheelwright at present in the Ordnance Yard here, and daily repairs in that branch wanted. should the wheelwrights be removed from Carlisle to this City it is tho't that six smiths might be spared from there to accompany them. these are much wanted, and indispensably necessary as the heavy work will be principally done here—

The reasoning of Mr. Perkins seems to be just for notwithstanding experience has taught us we must not depend on hired Men for supplies yet, when we have to combat with hunger, they may be discharged. not so the Soldier his food is all the compensation he expects for his Services, when that falls short, business stops. besides, great Saving will be made in Rents as the works at Carlisle are sufficient for their reception.—

Mr: Byers may be agreed with the case every article by the pound. these in the rough may be sent to the finishers cheaper than the materials and a Sufficiency of Brass furniture, upon an easy lay, thereby be secured. or if though best the two hired Men may be continued with or without Rations, as we agree and employed as usual by the day. the saving of Rent here again occurs. the present armoury and Leather Factory will receive the Stores deposited in other places, which may then be given up, and an annual Rent of £100 hard money be saved to the States—

Reason suggests that where an Ordnance Yard is established, there in all possible cases Cannon should be mounted, and their apparatus completed in it. in the present Instance circumstances makes it more convenient to compleat the Cannon there, than elsewhere, and if the necessity of the wheelwrights being bro't, here should occasion an order for their removal, it can be done no where else in our works, consequently determines the matter[.]

The Leather Factory on all accounts may be carried on better at Carlisle then in this City Leather the principal material, may be procured upon equal terms there, and we have reason to beleive better than here. the Men not having so many objects to call off their attention will perform their daily task, more steadily and perhaps contentedly, then here[.] consequently there will be more work done, desertions will be less frequent and as there is room for them to live in the Barracks at Carlisle, a considerable saving will be made in Rents, which is now paid for the houses they occupy. six of them under the care of a Serjeant. will be necessary here for the purposes of daily repairs;—as to the objection that may probably arise on the expence of transporting their work to this City (when finish'[d)] must inform the Board, that there is now on hand here as many Carte Boxes, Bayt. Bel[ts] &c. as is likely to be wanted this Campaign and when it may be necessary to transport them from Carlisle, 300 of each may be bro't in one waggon, consequently the expence but trifling[.] I will just add that the oil is already there and the thread used mostly spun there, and poplar wood most suitable for Carte Boxes may be had there in great plenty—

Having offered a few of the most weighty Reasons in support of the removal shall submit the decision to your Honble. Board—

With respect I am Yours &c.

Benjamin Flower to Robert Patton

Sir   Philadelphia May 22d 1780

I have just Received yours of the 17th. by Colo. Hughes Requesting to be Supplied as Qr. Master to the 2nd. Battalion of Militia with Arms and Accoutrements for Eight Light Horsemen—it is not in my power to Comply with the request, as we never Supply the Militia with any thing unless they are called out into Actual Service and then only on Application of the Governor to the State (to the Honble. Board of War) who is made Accountable either to return what Military Stores he may have Received or to pay for them at their Value if lost in Service.

I am with great regard Your Hum. Servt.

Patton was Deputy Quartermaster General for part of Lancaster County, Pennsylvania.

Six pages are missing from the letterbook at this point.

the whole department at Springfeild wants to be new Modelled and arranged, and a proper person appointed as DCGMS capable of commanding the whole—

To the Board of War and Ordnance

Gentn.   Philada. May 24th 1780
     Must beg to be inform'd whether Mr Godfrey can with propriety take the charge of Cap[tn] Corens company, and employ them as usual in the Laboratory—the men are stroling about and the publick I fear will suffer for want of some species of Stores which we cannot obtain elsewhere—The Commissary of Provision having dealt out a single ration of Bread only for the men, they have again quit work for the publick and are seeking employ in priva[te] Shops to prevent themselves & families from starving. must request to be inform'd how to proceed to do them justice and get them to work—A Serjeant Trested formerly oversee[r] of the armoury and furnish'd with house room which he was oblidg'd to give up, having a family requests the Board to order a part of the rent, he has now to pay, paid by the publick as the request, from the Circumstances, of the publick been oblidg'd to find him Barrack room, and his inability to pay the whole himself which is £400 Pr year out of his present Pay appears reasonable should be glad the Board would direct what part (if any) I must pay—
     With respect I am Gentlemen Yours &c

Benjamin Flower to the Board of War and Ordnance

Gentlemen   Philadelphia May 1780
     Having Obtained leave of absence for the Summer season from the Honble. Board of War and Ordnance—in consequence of my ill state of health was preparing for my Journey when I received directions from your Board to have all my Accounts with the public

adjusted for a final Settlement—since which time I have as far as was in my power so Arranged matters—that all my Accounts of Expenditures will be made up and closed to the first of June—but from unavoidable circumstances it will be Impossible to come to a final Settlement by that time—my own Accounts and those of my Paymaster Mr. Wm. Thorne will be ready and shall be delivered agreeable to Order—but as I Inform'd your Honours there are several Accountables at distant Posts who have not brought in their Accounts as directed—I have now ordered them to immediate Settlement on failure by the time appointed am determined to Arrest and prosecute each delenquent in the whole sum advanced them—and as soon as a Settlement can be Obtained will deliver them with the Vouchers &c. for a final Settlement. thus having done all at present in my power—and being Advised by my Phisician to leave the City as soon as possible, request permission of the Honble. Board to refer them to my Deputy Major Hodgdon—who will attend to the Settlement as directed produce my Books and give any further information relative to the Expenditures of the Department that may be required—under these Circumstances hope the Board will dispence with my personal attendance for the present—

With due respt. I am gentn. your most Obedt Humble Servt.

To William Egerton Godfrey

Sir   Philada. May 25 1780

You will upon receiving this immediately take charge of Captn. Corens Company and employ the men as usual in the Laboratory for the purpose of compleating the Stores already began and such others as you may receive orders for from the Comy Genl. m Stores Office—

You will apply to Mr. Thorne with the enclos'd order and receive from him one months pay for the Company, which you will pay them as usual taking every mans receipt, for your voucher on Settlement with the paymaster. other orders will be sent you as they are found necessary—

Yours

To Isaac Coren

Sir   May 25th 1780

You will please to deliver the Bearer, the whole of the Stores and materials belonging to the Laboratory, for which he will give you a receipt—

I am Sir Yours &c.

Benjamin Flower to Unidentified

Sir   Philada. 25th. May 1780

I have received yours of the 23d and in complyance thereto have directed that all provision Returns in future be Signed by my deputy Major Hodgdon—for all those Officers and Men in my Department—Capt. Coren as well as some other officers in the Department have heretofore been indulged with Signing their own returns but in future to prevent "impositions" they shall be Signed by Major Hodgdon—or in his absence by an Officer directed by him to do it of which you will be informed—the returns of the Officers & men drawing or making out [sic] will be delivered by the time required

I am your humble Servt.

To Joseph Watkins

Sir   Philadelphia May 25th 1780

The Honble. Board of Treasury upon preparing Mr. Sweers publick accounts for final adjustment find several sums of money charged advanced to persons therein names for the use of the Comy. Genl. of M Stores Department then under his Superintendence—

Among others you stand charg'd with the sum of £10217..10.0 said to be advanced to you for the above purpose—

To prevent any delay of proceeding to settlement, the Board have furnish'd me with a list of the names of the persons charg'd, and the sums said to be advanced them, and have directed me in behalf of Colo. Flower, to call on them to know whether they acknowledge the receipt if the Sums charg'd, if so, whether the whole was expended for the publick use, or any part return'd to Mr Sweers for which he has still to account, as no credit is given by Mr. Sweers for any part in any way returning into his hands—

In compliance with the above order, must request to favor to be inform'd, whether you acknowledge the charge and have already accounted for it, or stand ready when called upon to account that Sum—

I am Sir Your most Obedt. Servt.

This is marked as a Circular, meaning it was sent to others with details changed as appropriate. Watkins had been a Major and Commissary of Ordnance and Military Stores. In 1777 he had taken the lead downspouts in Philadelphia to be melted down for bullets for the Army.

Benjamin Flower to William Thorne

Dear Sir   Philadelphia May 29th. 1780

As I intend to leave the City to morrow, on a Journey into the Country and expect to be away all Summer Season—have to request that you will use your best Endeavours as Soon as your health will permit to have all your Accounts of expenditures made up and Settled to the first of June next Agreeable to the Orders of the Honble. Board of Treasury—& as soon as they are closed—let them be deposited in a Chest properly Arranged with such of the Accountables as may be in your possession for a final Settlement with the Auditor General agreeable to his directions—and as soon as you have matters thus prepared, inform Major Hodgdon who will attend to and direct the final Settlement thereof—if will be necessary for our Security to take a Receipt from the Auditor General for all Books, papers, Accounts or Vouchers delivered him or any other person

you will please to hasten the Completion of your Ledger Account and have an Account Current made out for each Individual that Stand on your Books Accountable for Monies advanced that they may be brought to Settlement as soon as possible and your Account Closed by their Vouchers &c—as soon as produced

I have Ordered them all to make Settlement immediately—if they neglect it am determined to punish them as defaulters.

I have sent a Chest to Deposite your papers in, also your General Account No. 5 with the Vouchers belonging to it—and Majr Lukens & Major French Account & Vouchers of Expenditures made by them—which you will Examine and give them Cr. for if allowed—I have also sent you the Books kept by Captn. Stiles whilst he Acted as Paymaster to the Department previous to your taking of it, to enable you to make final Settlement with the Accountables—you can also have reference to the Books kept by Mr. Sweers—should it be necessary in any of the Settlement[s] But Major Hodgdon on your Application will inform and Assist you in any thing that may appertain to this Business

I am with great regard your Obedt. Servt.

To George Perkins

Sir   May 30th 1780

There is some articles delivered into Major Gostelowe from on Board the Continental Ship Confederacy which are ordered to be appraised. you will please to see them and Certify in writing to me their value with all convenient speed—

Yours &c.

To George Parks

Sir,   May 30th 1780

You are to proceed to Camp at Morristown and deliver the Letters, and stores, you have in charge to Richard Frothingham Esqr. DFCMS either at that place or Suckesunna plains who will load your waggon with damaged Stores to be brought here on your return—

Parks was a wagoner.

To Thomas Wylie

Sir   Philada. May 30th 1778

I received your favor of the 3d instant was glad to hear the sword requested was in hand hope it will speedily be forwarded as Colo. Grayson is going to Virginia and presses hard to have it before he goes, as he expects from the character of the undertaker it will be elegant—

Have forwarded Mr. Sarjent some steel & four melting potts the steel is but poor but it was all we had on hand, and I supposed it possibly might answer the present purpose. shall forward some more soon and a quantity of spelter if it can be obtained in the City, this opportunity happening sudden prevents for the present am very happy to hear that the order for 3000 Gun worms and 10000 Screw Drivers is compleat. if your men are not otherwise particularly employed, should think they had better be continued at Gun worms till they have made 2000 more—

With esteem I am Sir Yours

Wylie, then at Carlisle, Pennsylvania, had been commissioned as a Captain Lieutenant in the Regiment of Artillery Artificers on February 17, 1777. He was promoted to Captain on February 1, 1778. He apparently spent the war years at Carlisle until his unit, then termed "The Pennsylvania Corps of Artillery Artificers" was orderd to New London, Virginia in November 1782. Spelter was what the metal zinc was often called.

To the Two Waggoners Going to Carlisle

May 30 1780

You will proceed with your teems as loaded to Carlisle, and deliver the whole to Samuel Sargent Esqr. Comy M Stores except the two Boxes and one small Cask, mark'd for Colo. Flower which you will deliver agreeable to their mark, at the plantation of Colo. Jno. Patton at Springfield ten miles above reading. you will take the greatest care of your waggons to prevent loss by embezzlement as you are accountable for what you receive—

To Samuel Sarjant

Sir   Philada. May 30th. 1780

By the two Waggons that comes with this you will receive a Small portion of Steel of different sorts agreeable to Invoice and a Box containing four Melting potts—this is all from us—the other Box[es] are Cloathing forwarded to your care by Captn. Jordan of which I conclude he has notified you—by the Return of these waggons you will please to send the Gun Worms & Screw drivers, and any other Articles you may have to forward—Colo: Flower set out on his Journey this day, since which I have received your Letter to him informing of the Mens Application for more Rations the Answer to which must employ the next opportunity

I am Sir yours

To Jonathan Gostelowe

Sir May 31st. 1780

You will please to inform me what number of Horsemans Swords, with Scabbards and belts, you can have ready for delivery in ten days from this date—also what number of pistols suitable for Horsemen you have on hand ready to deliver—

Yours

To George Perkins

Sir May 31st. 1780

You will please to inform me what number of pistols you have on hand which may be cut, repaired and made Suitable for delivery in twelve or fifteen days from this Date, provided all your people are set to work immediately

I shall be Obliged to you to give me an Answer to the above this day—

Yours

To William Thorne

Sir, Philada. May 31st, 1780

I am directed to inform the Honble. Board of War, immediately what sums of money are due the Department, on warrants already obtain'd, who they are drawn on, and what prospects there is, of getting the full amount shortly—you will by report enable me to answer those several questions to morrow morning—

I am Sir Yours

To Robert Lettis Hooper Jr.

Sir   Philada. May 31st. 1780

 There is seven Tons, and one hundred weight of pig metal belonging to the United States which lies at Mr Yamans Forge commonly called the lower Forge, at first intended to be drawn here, but circumstances prevented, and now to be drawn by Mr Geo. Ross at the Forge known by the name of Johnstons not far distant from Mr Yamans. if you can devise means to transport the above pigs from the place where they now are to Mr. Ross's works, you will greatly serve the publick and much oblidge—

 Your very huml Servt.

Hooper was Deputy Quartermaster General at Easton, Pennsylvania.

To Moses Yamans

Sir,   Philada. May 31st 1780

 You will please to deliver Mr George Ross Junr. or order the seven Tons, one hundred weight of Pig metal which by your acct: lately settled you acknowledge to have upon the bank near your Forge belonging to the United States for which delivery this shall be your sufficient voucher—

This forge was probably in the area of Bloomsbury, Hunterdon County, New Jersey, as a forge belonging to Robert Johnson, referred to in the preceding letter operated there.

To Alexander Dow

Sir   June 1st. 1780

 In answer to your letter respecting Mathias Ambrister must inform you that as he pleads sickness as an excuse to not performing his duty with you, and as you say he is a burden on your Company—I would recommend it to you to Deliver him up to Colo: Nichola where he may do duty as an Invalid and be thereby useful in some measure to the United States—

 Yours

Dow was a Lieutenant in the Artillery Artificer Regiment.

To the Board of War and Ordnance

Gentlemen   Philada. June 1st. 1780

In compliance with your Order I have enquired what time would be necessary to Compleat the five hundred pr. pistols, five hundred Swords and their Apparatus, intended for the use of Light horsemen—and find if the Men are furnished with provisions to keep them steadily employed, the whole of the pistols ordered, and about two thirds of the swords may be ready to be delivered in a short time after provided the workmen are furnished with Stock necessary to Compleat the[m.]

The Department has no Warrants for money except that granted by Congress the third part of Jany. last on David Rittenhouse Esqr. Treasurer of this State, which was for one Million of Dollars; Six hundred and Eighty four dollars & 63/90 parts of which remains to this hour unpaid—but by an Application made this day we are encouraged to expect one hundred thousand Dollars in all this week—part of which shall agreeable to your direction be paid Messrs. Caulaux & Co. the other part without the Special Interference of the Board I shall Appropriate to the payment of the men at Carlisle the payment of long standing debts and procuring materials to keep the men employed

I am Gentlemen Respectfully yours

To the Board of War and Ordnance, With Answer by Richard Peters.

Gentn.   Philada. June 1st. 1780

Having three tinmen at present belonging to the Department, and Mr. Murray's time being nearly expired, am of opinion his services as a tinman can be dispensed with and would recommend agreeable to his wish that he be immediately discharg'd. he wishes to be discharg'd by the Board, or I should not have troubled them further on the Subject

With due respect Gentleman I am Yours

War Office June 1st 1780
Mr. Hodgdon will give Murray his discharge
 By order—
  R. Peters

Peters, of Pennsylvania, was a member of the Board of War. See the following letter.

To Simon Murray

Sir, Philadelphia June 1st. 1780
 As the present Circumstances of the CGMS Department, can make it convenient, to dispense with your services, in complyance with your wishes the Honble. Board of War have directed me to discharge you from the Contract, by which you were engaged as Superintendent of Tinmen, annexed to the Laboratory in this City, for one year from its date, and you are discharged accorkdingly—
 Given under my hand at Philadelphia this first day of June 1780 whom it may Concern

To Robert Lettis Hooper Jr.

Sir Philadelphia June 1st. 1780
 To Compleat a Contract some time since made with Colonel Thompson by Mr. Whitehead Humphreys on behalf of the United States, Col: Thompson must be furnished with five Tuns five hundred one quarter and Twenty pounds of Andover pig Metal. as it appears there is several quantities on the Road between Andover & Easton, if you can by any means convey the above mentioned quantity to his Furnace immediately you will greatly serve the public, as the Iron he is to draw is exceedingly wanted for public use in the Comy. Genl of Military stores department—
 'tis probable we may want a considerable quantity more conveyed there shortly of which I will give you timely notice, but the above I must beg of you to send immediately as you have already sent a considerable quantity of Pig metal to Colonel Thompson on Account of the within mentioned Contract, should be much Obliged if you would favour me with an Account of the full amount, including

that now requested to be sent—as soon after if is forwarded as you can possibly make it convenient—

I am Sir Your very huml Servant

To Mark Thompson

Sir   Philadelphia June 2d 1780

I have been favor'd by Mr: Humphreys with a sight of your last letter; upon the subject of your Contract with the public by him am exceedingly surprized and sorry that you have not been furnish'd with the Pigs agreeable to your just expectation to enable you to furnish the Bar Iron, which we are much in want of whose faulty [*sic*] am not able to Say, but have reason to think Mr. Humprey[s] has done every thing is his power to have you supplyed—

In consequence of your Letter, I have look'd fully into the Contract with a determination to have it literally, fully, and immediately complyed with. I find by Mr. Humphreys report to the Honble. Board of War that you was to draw five Tons & half of Bar Iron of certain dimensions, for every Ton of which you was to receive three Tons & half of Pig metal. at this rate you should have had 19 ¼ Tons of Pig metal for 5 ½ Tons Bar Iron. by your account in a former Letter to Mr. Humphreys is [*sic*] seems you have received only 13 Ton 24 h 3 qr 8 lb so that if you have received none since that Letter was wrote there remains a Ballance of 5 Ton 5 h 1 qr 20 lb of Pig metal yet to be supplied you, which quantity you will perceive by the enclos'd open letter to Colo. Hooper or acting Quarter Master at Easton, I have requested may be sent you immediately which letter when you have read, you will please to Seal & deliver. should any delay in furnishing it be likely to happen, you will please to give me early notice, and I shall take such measures as will effectually ensure you the supply of the Ballance within mentioned you say you would haul it yourself, provided it could be paid in the metal therefor. this cannot be done, but to Serve the publick, and I would hope yourself in finishing the present Contract, I could wish you could make it convenient to haul it, and take your pay as usual—

Yesterday I agreed with Mr. Geo. Ross to draw a few Tons of Pigs, that lies contiguous to his works for which he is to receive four for one. as an act of Justice I mention this to you, to give you an opportunity if you are disposed to Contract for any quantity on the

Same lay. after the first contract is finished, you will please to inform me what time it will take you to compleat the 5 ½ Tons of Bar, provided you are supplied with the remainder of the pig metal immediately, and at the Same time what further quantity (if any) you would chuse to Contract for upon the new lay mention'd above—

I am Sir Your very huml Servt.

To William Egerton Godfrey

Sir Philada. June 5 1780

The bearer Serjeant Francis Stewart of Colo. Lambs Regt: of Arty being wounded and at present incapable of Feild Duty, is ordered to join your company and do duty in the Laboratory, until his wound will permit him to join his own Company. you will enter both him and his wife which he has with him in your return for provision and muster him in your next muster, and insert him in your Pay Roll and continue So to do untill further orders—

To Alexander Turner

Sir Philada. June 5 1780

Yours I have received and in answer inform you, that I would have you immediately load as many of the Shells at Colo Pattons furnace, as your Teems can haul, and proceed to this City taking special care to direct the waggon master that comes with them to See that none are left or lost on the road. I have wrote to Colo Patton to deliver as many Shells, as the waggons can bring taking a receipt of the waggon master for them. I am well pleas'd with your attention to the publick Interest which appears by you notifying, that the Teems could perform this service which will be a vast saving, the Shells being wanted here—

We have nothing new only a report that Charlestown is taken, but not believed. understanding by the man that came that, it would be more convenient to take them from Colo Pattons, is the reason of my directing you there, but if that should not be the Case, by shewing this Letter they may be loaded at Statels (or Colemans Furnace) the other place you mention'd—

Yours

This is directed to Turner as a Deputy Wagon Master General. Patton owned Berkshire Furnace in Pennsylvania.

To John Patton

Dear Colonel   Philada. June 5 1780

Being informed that there were a number of Continental Teems in your neighbourhood unemployed, I have wrote to the waggon master a Mr. Turner, and directed him to call on you for as many Shells as would load their Teems and proceed with them to this City. you will please to take duplicate receipts for the number and Size you deliver. by this means I shall know what you have left on hand

In haste I remain Dear Sir Your most Obedt Servt.

This was directed to Patton at Berkshire Furnace in Berks County, Pennsylvania.

To William Egerton Godfrey

Sir,   Philada. June 5th 1780

Mr. Hoffman informs me that the Smiths shop belonging to the publick which he superintends was broke open either the last night or the night before, and he supposes a considerable quantity of Iron stole—as their was a Centinel of your men there they must be the rascalls that has been guilty of the theft. you will immediately find out who was Centry there the two nights mentioned, and do your utmost to detect & bring to punishment the authors of this villainy. if we are not Safe with Centries we may as well discharge the whole at once

I am Yours

To Walter Stewart

Sir   Philadelphia June 9th. 1780

Colonel Flower being absent, your Letter respecting Drums, heads, Snears and Sticks fell into my hands I mentioned the Substance thereof to the Board of War They are averse to any Regimental deliveries from this post, for reasons that are obvious. however I have Supplied six new Drums and six pair of sticks. Drum heads, and snears [sic] we are not able to procure at present as soon as they can be Obtained shall forward them to the Field Comy. to whom you will please to Apply for a proportionable supply

    I am Sir Your very hble servt.

Stewart was Colonel of the Second Pennsylvania Regiment.

To Jonathan Gostelowe

Sir   Philadelphia June 9 1780

    You will please to pack up, and have ready for transportation at a moments warning as many of the undermention'd articles as you have on hand Vizt.—

    3000 Muskets, Bayonets & Scabbards
    3000 Bayonet Belts
    3000 Tin C Boxes & Belts
    3000 repair'd Leather C Boxes
    4800 Flints
    6000 Screw Drivers
    6000 Gun worms
    6000 Brushes & Wires

To Daniel Joy

Sir   Philadelphia June 9th. 1780

    You will please to call on Mr. Hoffman and request him to inform me what quantity of Tools will be Sufficient to set 10 Blacksmiths to work supposing them to be employed in the work common to an Ordnance Yard, with a particular Account what each Tool will cost you will Observe I mean only such Tools as are absolutely Necessary for them to begin to work with not those little Affairs that they can make themselves after they have once got to work—also I want to be informed what Tools will be necessary for 12 Carpenters to begin to work with and their Costs—also what Tools will be necessary for 12 Carpenters to begin with and their Costs—also what Tools will be wanting & their Costs to employ 4 Wheelwrights

    I am yours

Joy was Superintendent of the Ordnance Yard of the Military Stores Department in Philadelphia. In 1776 he had been employed by the Cannon Committee of the Continental Congress to "prove" the cannon being cast at various American iron furnaces.

To William Egerton Godfrey

Sir   Philadelphia June 9th. 1780
  I should be Oblidged to you to make me a Return this Afternoon of the particular Articles necessary for opening and carrying on a Laboratory Composed of about 30 Men I mean only the Tables and Tools that they must have to begin with; as we talk of founding a Laboratory in a distant quarter, I want to know what I must provide for the above number of Men to keep them employed. you will make the Calculation as small as will possibly answer the purpose—I want also to know what tools are Necessary for one Tinman and one Turner—
  yours

To Jonathan Gostelowe

Sir   Philada. June 10th. 1780
  Please to have the under mentioned Articles ready for Transportation at a Moments warning—Viz:
  250 Horse mens Swords
  250 pairs Pistols with Carte. Boxes
  250 Screw Drivers—
  250 Brushes and wires
  2500 Pistol Flints—
Inclosed you have an Order on Mr. Perkins for what Pistols he has finished and for perfecting as many more as is Necessary to complete the above Order—
  Yours

To the Board of War and Ordnance

Gentlemen   Philada. June 10th. 1780
  Inclosed you have a Return of the Number of Men & their

Different Branches of Business necessary for carrying on a Laboratory, Armoury & Ordnance Yard—Also the Number and names of the Tools, Absolutely necessary for them to begin their work—those with a Cross thus X at the end of the line are such as we can spare from our own works or have made Amongst our own people upon short notice. those with Figures signify the parts, that can be supplied of the Demands of the same line. Those not marked of which I have taken off and Inclosed a Copy are to be purchased, and the sums Annexed are the probable cost—The Tinmans Tools I had a fortunate Opportunity of purchasing all together at a Moderate rate, which I Availed myself off [sic] and they are now ready on hand—the whole of the Tools and the greatest number of the Men I have reason to think, may be Obtained in the Course of one Month, provided I am furnished with Money for the purchase of the first, and allowed to hire Men of the different Branches, as well as make draughts from Amongst our own Men—the whole of the heavy stock, such at Timber, plank, boards, Staves, hoops[,] Bar Iron, and Coals I presume may be purchased in the Vicinity of where the Men are Settled, the more portable Articles may be sent from here from time to time as their Circumstances and our Acquaintance therewith may render Necessary—

As to the Matter of the Boaring and grinding Mill I am clearly of Oppinion they are Unnecessary for these Reasons. it will be a Considerable time before they can Attempt any thing but repairs, and we shall be able to Send them as many Bayonets as will fully answer this purpose. Besides Bayonet makers & Millwrights or Grinders are not included in the above Calculation. should the Grinding after a while be found wanting, a stone fixed in a Grist or any other Mill which may be done for Little expence, and no Detriment, will answer every purpose—

If I am not sufficiently clear, or have Omitted any part of the Boards expectation from their order Communicated to me I shall be happy to wait upon them & explain myself or make any Additions—

With respect I am Gentlemen your very huml. servt.

Directions for establishing a standing Laboratory given in to the Board of War June 7

A suitable place being provided and a person capable of carrying on the Bussiness of a Laboratory being found, the following men are next to be sought for, as necessary for the purpose Vizt.—

  12 Carpenters 4 wheelwrights
  1 Turner   1 Painter
  1 Cooper   1 Tin plate worker
  10 Blacksmiths

and 30 Men for chymical preparation & finishing & packing Stores in the Laboratory the mechanicks to be under the Direction of two foremen, the one a Carpenter; the other a Smith, both of which are to be subject to the person who carries on the Laboratory that one spring may move the whole, and one person be made accountable to the publick for all monies materials, or Stores delivered for the use of the Laboratory. The duty of such person is considerable, the Men are to be paraded, at a certain hour for work, the supply of materials to keep them employed demands his attention next. all compositions must be compounded by his own hands and his Eye pervade them afterwards untill finished. the dimensions of Boxes and the manner of packing to prevent damage in transporting, should come from him, and his utmost caution must be exerted to prevent accident, as explosions in driving portfires without great care will frequently happen if only a temporary Laboratory of cannon Ammunition & making M Cartridges in the vicinity of an army is wanting, a Lieut. and twenty Draughts, providing materials may be had where they are, would be abundantly sufficient—

  These Gentn. are my Ideas of an establishment for a regular & usefull Laboratory, calculated upon a small scale but may be enlarg'd as circumstances may make necessary.

  With due respect I am Gentlemen Yours &c

To Moore Furman

Sir   Philadelphia June 13th 1780
  Mr. Aaron Day waits on you to request a Number of Waggons for the purpose of forwarding Military Stores to Camp—as it is of Importance that they should arrive will all convenient speed, must beg of you to furnish as many as will take on the stores he has in charge, perhaps Ten or Twelve may answer—
The Stores are on Board a Vessel, and Mr. Day is Forwarded by Land to give you the most timely Notice to Enable you to Comply

with our wish
    I am Sir your very huml. Servt.

Furman was Deputy Quartermaster General for the State of New Jersey.

To David Mason

Sir   Philadelphia June 15th 1780
    In Consequence of an Order of the Honble. Board of War—I have sent for Mr. Hoy to take Charge of and carry on the Laboratory in this City. I am at the same time directed to Acquaint you with this Order, and request you to give him every possible Assistance, to forward him immediately to his Charge—
    You will please to furnish him with Certificates, informing the time to which he is paid, and what pay and Advantages he has received at your post, and any other requisites which you may Judge Necessary—
    I am Sir Your very humble Servt.

In March 1778, Mason signed his Oath of Allegiance at Springfield, Massachusetts as "Director of Ordnance." Hodgdon addressed him as Colonel, but his rank was that of Lieutenant-Colonel.

To Benjamin Hoey

Sir   Philadelphia June 15th 1780
    The Laboratory at this place from whence most of the Stores for the Supply of the Army is expected—is in want of a Steady Capable Man to take its immediate direction in Order to Secure the Supplies expected—from my own knowledge of you, and the Character I have heard of you from others, on whose Veracity I could depend—I have recommended you to the Honble. Board of War, to have the above Charge—in Consequence of which they have directed me to send for you without loss of time—As to terms, can Only inform you that as the Business is important you shall have every reasonable allowance for your Service, more I think you would not desire—here is a fine Company of Artillery in the Laboratory, well used to the Business, tools, & Materials in abundance, so that your command will be equal

to your utmost wish—I could wish you would set off immediately for this City upon the receipt of this Letter—Your Charges on the Road coming shall be paid at your Arrival—I have wrote to Col. Mason to inform him of the Boards Order, and requested him to give you every Assistance to bring you on your way immediately—

My Assistance and Support you may depend on to enable you to Compass every reasonable wish—

I am sir Yours

Lieutenant Hoey did report to Philadelphia and took command of the "Laboratory Company."

To John Denton

Sir   Philadelphia June 15th 1780

Yours by Mr. Woodruff I have received and note the Contents Mr. Pearson Comy. Mily. Stores having Negociated this Business before my Arrival I enquired of him the Principles upon which the Account was made. he informs me that you Transported both the lead and the Iron, and brought in an Account amounting to £2080, with the Vouchers for the Charges, and that he Credited you for one half that Sum, which was Conformable to the Idea's of the Board for Settlement and appears to me to be just—

However if you Omitted any part of the Transportation or any other regular, and proper charge, we stand ready to rectify any mistakes upon proper vouchers appearing to Support the Charge—

I am Sir Yours

Discharge Certificate for George Smith

Philadelphia June 16 1780

These may Certify that George Smith late Soldier in Capt. Parkes Company, in consideration of his having procured an able Bodied Man, by the Name of John Lear who is now acting in his Stead, is Discharged from his Inlistment in said Company and is at liberty to employ himself as he thinks fit—
Whom It May Concern

Estimate of Necessaries Requisite for an Army of 40,000 Men

From 8 to 10,000 Tons of Shipping, and 4 or 500 tons of flat Boats or Batteaux, more or less May be required, with the Articles Necessary for those According to Circumstances of the Operations. The Article of Timber & Lumber Various and must be governed by the Demand.

Ironmongery

Scythes	2500 @ £37.10	93750
Scythe Rifles	600 @ 3/9	112.10
Scythe Stones	1250 @ £4.10	5625
Scythe Sneads	2500 @ £3	7500
Rings for do.	2500 @ £3	7500
Pounds of Spikes	12,000 @ £2.5	27000
Pounds of Nails Sorted	10,000 @ £3	30,000
Tons of Spike & Nail rods	4 @ £4500	18,000
Tons Bar Iron	30 @ £2500	75000
Tons best Steel	2 @ £5000	10,000
Tons Common do.	2 @ £4500	9,000
Setts Horse Shoes & Nails	4500 @ £15	675000
Cutting Boxes	250 @ £60	15000
Cutting Knives	250 @ £22.10	5625
Sickles	350 @ £11.5	3939.10
Beetles	150 @ £9	1350
Setts of Scales & weights	35 @ £52.10	1837.10
Pounds of Chalk	2500 @ £3	7500
Pounds of Glue	150 @ £7.10	1125
Pounds of Iron Wire	150 @ £15	2250
Pounds of Twine	1000 @ £11.5	11250
Frows	250 @ £15	3750
Crow Bars	300 @ £40	12000
Grindstones	100 @ £75	7500

Sadlers Tools

Knives	35 @ £3	105
Hammers	35 @ £7.1	262.10

Tacks Assorted	1500 @ £30 p m	45
Rubbers	35 @ £3	105
Pincers	35 @ £10	350
Needles	3000 @ £30 p m	90
Thimbles	35 @ £0.15	26.5
Creasing Irons	35 @ £3	105
Bridle Wheels	35 @ £11.5	393.15
Punches	35 @ £3.15	131.5
Pricking Irons	100 @ £7.10	750
Braces or Strainers	70 @ £90	6300
Brushes	20 @ £3	60
Mens Saddles Includg 900 Cavalry	1375 @ £150	206,250
Bridles	2075 @ £22.10	46687
Pack Saddles	250 @ £90	22500
Sides of Leather	250 @ £50	12500
Mail Pillions	250 @ £22.10	5625
Pairs Mail Straps	600 @ £11.5	6750

Smiths Tools

Pairs of Bellows	70 @ £375	26250
Vises	70 @ £180	12600
Hand Vises	70 @ £40	4800
Anvils	70 @ £600	42000
Beek Irons	70 @ £180	12600
Hammers	140 @ £15.5	2135
Sledges	70 @ £ 54	3780
Tongs	140 @ £ 11.5	1575
Pincers	250@ £18	4500
Cold Chissels	600 @ £4.10	2700
Pareing knives	250 @ £12	3000
Buttrasses	250 @ £9	2250
Rasps	250 @ £15	3750
Nail Stakes	35 @ £27	945
Screw Plates & Bitts	50 @ £24	1200
Travelling Forges	30 @ £4795	143850
Files Assorted	800 @ £15	12000
Bushels of Coal	30,000 @ £1.10	45000

Ships Carpenters Tools

Broad Axes	170 @ £56.5	9562.10
Pitt Saws	32 @ £157.10	5040
Augres	375 @ £30	11250
Sledges	100 @ £22.10	2250
Calking Irons	185 @ £6	1110
Mallets	100 @ £9	900
Scrapers	100 @ 18.15	1875
Gimblets assorted	600 @ £1.10	900
Sail Needles	10000 @ £1.2.6	11250

Intrenching Tools

Spades & Shovels	7000 @ £37.10	242500
Picks	3000 @ £30	90000
Wheel Barrows	250 @ £90	22500
Hand Barrows	600 @ £22.10	13500
Drilling Tools	2500 @ £12	30000
Hoes	500 @ £15	7500
Fachine Knives	2500 @ £15	37500
Mattocks	250 @ £22.10	5625

House Carpenters Tools

Falling Axes	1200 @ £30	360000
Broad Axes	400 @ £56.5	22500
Mortising Axes	150 @ £30	4500
Hatchets	350 @ £6	2100
Adzes	350 @ £45	15750
Whipsaws	100 @ £150	15000
Crosscut saws	100 @ £130	13000
Handsaws	600 @90	54000
Wood saws	100 @ £22.10	2250
Saw Setts	500 @ £3.15	1875
Files Sorted	300 @ £15	45000
Rasps	1200 @ £15	18000
Planes	600 @ £18.15	11250
Plane Irons	600 @ £4.10	2700
Drawing knives	400 @ £20	8000
Chissels	6000 @ £4	24000
Gouges	400 @ £4	1600

Augres	400 @ £11.5	4500
Gimblets	1400 @ £1.10	2100
Gimblet Bits	100 @ £1.2.6	112.10
Centre Bitts	100 @ £3	300
Bitt Stocks	50 @ £22.10	1125
Iron Squares	300 @ £11.5	3375
Rules	400 @ £9	3600
Compasses	400 @ £6	2400
Pincers	125 @ £9	1125
Hammers	1200 @ £4.10	5400
Chalk lines	1200 @ £2.5	2700
Gauges	200 @ £7.10	1500

Stationary

Rheams of writing paper	200 @ £112.10	22500
Rheams of wrapping paper	21 @ £60	1260
Papers of Ink powder	1500 @ £3	4500
Quills	25000 @ £15 p C.	3750
Pounds of wax	150 @ £37.10	5625
Pounds of wafers	100 @ £18.15	1875
Ink Stands	350 @ £3	1050
Penknives	500 @ £11.5	5625
Pencils	500 @ £2.5	1125
Ledgers	50 @ £150	7500
Journals	50 @ £120	6000
Waste Books	250 @ £50	12500
Blank Books	1500 @ £22.10	33750
Orderly Books	5000 @ £7.10	37500

Camp Equipage

Marquees compleat with poles	192 @ £3000	576000
Horseman's tents &c do.	1087 @ £1500	1630500
Wall tents do.	770 @ £600	462000
Common tents do.	8,000 @ £375	3000000
Camp Kettles	6,000 @ £37.10	600,000
Iron cups	1400 @ £3	4200
Iron Spoons	20,000 @ £3	60,000
Setts tin measures & Funnels	50 @ £56.5	2812.10
Wooden bowls	15,000 @ £1.17.6	28125

Buckets	3,000 @ £3.15	11250
Canteens	70,000 @ £2.5	157500
Knapsacks	58650 @ £15	879750
Bags	5,000 @ £15	75000
Leather portmanteaus	4,050 @ £112.10	45,625
Leather Valicees	1375 @ £90	123,750
Canvas Valices for Markees	192 @ £37.10	7200

To the Board of War and Ordnance

Gentlemen   Philadelphia June 17 1780

Upon examination I find we have two thousand eight Hundd. Repairable muskets in store, Eighteen Hundred of which may be properly repaired without stocking. One thousand of the best of which I can have ready in one week provided I am furnished with money to pay the workmen and they are Supplyed with their usual rations and one Gill of Rum each man p day—

A full supply of Cartouch Boxes for the above one thousand may be ready in the same time—

I am Gentlemen Your's

To George Perkins

Sir   June 17th 1780

You will please to employ as many men in addition to those you have at present under your charge, as are necessary to compleat 1000 Stand of Arms repair'd out of the best of those repairable on hand, in the course of the next week. your judgement with respect to the price of the repairs of such as are done out of the Shop will be relied on as just, and you will certify their accounts accordingly—

Yours

To Isaac Warner

Sir   Philadelphia June 17th 1780

Your will repair with the Muskets and stores, on Board the schooner which you have attended at loading, to Hallifax in the State of North Carolina by the following Route, and deliver them to Colonel Long D Q M G at that place and take his Receipt for the whole—You will proceed from this City to Christiana, when there Arrived apply to the D Q M G for the proper Carriages to take them on to the Head of Elk—The D Q M G there will furnish the Means to take by Water to Milleners near Suffolk from whence by another Application, you will Obtain teams to take them to their destination—having a Considerable quantity of Ammunition under your charge, you will be particularly careful on your Journey that no Accident happen. for this purpose you will suffer no fire to be made on Board any Vessell in which the stores are—And when transporting with Teams prevent their halting near any house—you will if possible procure a sufficient Guard to prevent injury & loss from ill disposed people—if they cannot be Obtained the Waggoners must watch themselves. On your prudence & exertion I rely to have them safely conveyed as directed—the Invoice of the whole you have with you.— I wish you a good Journey

All Quarter Masters, Commissaries, & Forage Masters are intreated to give every possible Assistant in the execution of this Business.

To William Thorne

Sir Philadelphia June 20th. 1780

Inclosed I send you an Order from the Honble Board of Treasury on the Subject of a General Settlement of the Accounts of the department the time to which it refers is short, you will please to exert yourself to have every thing ready for a final Settlement at the period they have set. if you want more help you shall have it, by acquainting me I should be glad you would Open Accounts in your Ledger for the Accountables immediately—and also favour me with a List of their Names, and the sums they are respectively Accountable for—that I may once more give them Notice of the determination of the Board to publish them as Delinquents, and treat them as such Unless they comply with the above Order.—should they Merit this by their Obstinate refusal, or neglectful disposition, the Accounts being regularly raised in the Ledger, and their receipts produced for the sums charged, they must and will be Accepted as Sufficient Vouchers from the Comy. Genl. and he will be discharged Accordingly—or should they appear to settle their Accounts it is proper that the final Adjustment should stand upon your Ledger—

You shall have the Chest containing Major Frenches & other papers any hour you call for them, and I will give you all possible Assistance to Accomplish this Necessary and desirable business

I am Yours

To the Board of War and Ordnance

Gentlemen   Philadelphia June 20th 1780

In Consequence of your Message in the Morning I have enquired and find the following Field pieces in this City—

2 Brass 12 pounders, belonging to the State
1 do   6 do   belonging to the Continent
2 do   3 do   do   do
3 do   5 ½ inch howitzer do   do
1 Iron   3 pounder   do
1 Brass 8 Inch howitzers [sic] at the Fort on the River belonging to the Continent—

With Respect I am Yours

NB all the Ordnance except the howitz, are in possession of the City Militia—

To Archibald Shaw

Sir   Philadelphia June 22d. 1780

You will repair on Board the schooner that has taken on the Musket Cartridges, which you have an Invoice of, & proceed without a Moments loss of time to Christiana. when there arrived you will enquire for Mr. Warner Condr. Mily. Stores—if he is there you will deliver them to him, to take on with his Other Stores to Hallifax in North Carolina—if he should be gone you will apply to the D. Q. M. G for Teams, and take them on to the head of Elk

If Mr. Warner should be gone from there before your Arrive you are to deliver them to Colonel Hollingsworth D. Q. M. G. take his Receipt for them, and request him to forward them to Colonel Long D. Q. M. G. at Hallifax in North Carolina immediately—

Having compleated this Business, Agreeable to these your Instructions, you are to Return to your duty at this place with all possible dispatch to prevent unnecessary expence—

Shaw was a Conductor of Military Stores.

To the Board of War and Ordnance

Gentlemen   Philada. June 22d 1780

Immediately upon receiving your verbal order to remove in a prudential matter, some of the powder, and other Stores from this City I applied to Colo. Mitchell to know if any Teems were returning the Lancaster road, he know of none. the Teems that were annexed to the Department having left it, I requested to be furnished with others. he informed me it was out of his power, nor could he at that time supply me with a Single team for that special purpose, but would as soon as possible. this morning I waited on him again, but no teems can yet be obtain'd. under these circumstances I find it impossible to comply with the order and am constrain'd to trouble the Board for further orders and directions upon the Subject

With due respect I am Gentlemen Yours &c

To George Ingells

Sir,   Philada. June 23d 1780

By this waggon I have forwarded a quantity of powder to be stored in your Magazine so much having arrived I have fill'd all the Magazines here and am not able to procure any other at present have avail'd myself of the return of this waggon to Send on one load, and shall Send more as opportunities present—

Must beg you would pay particular attention to See it properly aired and taken care of, as it is of the best kind, and now in excellent order—

As you must be detain'd to take care of it, you need not forward any more Stores at present, but take care of the whole on hand, and what may arrive untill further orders—

Yours

To Henry Knox

Dear General Philadelphia June 24th. 1780

I am desired by the honble. Board of War, to inform you, that the repeated draughts from the Main Army, and the great Supplies of Military Stores sent to the Southward, has so exhausted our Magazines, that you must turn your attention eastward for further Supplies, for a short Time, untill we recruit, especially for Musket Cartridges, a large quantity of which by the Returns, are at fish kills & Litchfield which 'tis probable may be Obtained with more expedition than they could from here.—Your Returns, for stores wanting, which we have already received, will be forwarded to their full Amount as fast as circumstances will Admit.—

For want of the necessary, I have not been able as yet to make the Settlement requested—the want of which has brought on a languor that portends a total Stagnation, but we have repeated promises, which keeps alive our dying hopes, tho' almost as repeatedly disappointed—the exertions now visible, bid fair to be permanent & to answer every reasonable expectations from one State. hope they will be followed by all that the Army the most virtuous of patriots now existing may experience the grateful returns of an Obliged people—

The sword still waits for a Suitable Blade I have one three Squares that would Answer, only I fear it is shorter than you would wish flat Blades of a proper length I have enough, but whether they would suit I am at a loss to determine. a line from you on the subject probably would remove my doubts—after which the sword shall for forwarded the first safe conveyance—

I have nothing further to add, but my respectfull compliments to Mrs. Knox, and a free tender of my Services whenever you may call, being never more happy, than when employed in grateful return to those from whom I have received repeated testimonies of esteem & friendship.—

I am Sir Your very humble Servt.

To Thomas Jones

Sir Philadelphia 26th 1780

I am directed by the honble. Board of War to inform you, that they have Appointed you to take charge of the Stores, with the

Southern Army, Subject to the command of General Gates. you will in Consequence of this information, Settle your Affairs in Camp & repair without a moments unnecessary loss of time to this City as it is of importance, that you make all possible dispatch to get on to your Command. when here Arrived, you will receive your Instructions, and any other Necessary Assistance, to enable you to proceed, & to act as directed—

I have nothing further to add but my best regards for all such as you know I have an Affection for—

Yours

To the Board of War and Ordnance

Gentlemen   Philadelphia June 26th. 1780

I enclose a Letter and a very Extraordinary Appointment just received from Fort-Pitt.—as the Gentlemen who is the Subject of them is very pressing to receive an Answer enclosing his pay—and Money to carry on I know not what—must beg to be favoured with your Opinion respecting him & his demands, before I write him on the Subject—as the same time submit it whether, if any Officer is allowed for the special care of the Military Stores at the Garrison of Fort Pitt a Conductor is not sufficient—if so whether Mr. Farrell if he chooses it may not be appointed

Yours Respectfully

To the Navy Board

Gentlemen   Philadelphia June 27th 1780

Yours of this day Address'd to Col. Flower, I have receiv'd. the demand for Powder being great, must inform you that the Honble. Board of War thinks it not Adviseable to spare more than Two Tons for the Use Mentioned. this quantity, and most of the Other Stores mentioned, are ready to be delivered when Applied for—Four pound double headed Shot, we have none, nor do I think they can be found in this City—the surest way to procure them, will be by sending to some Furnace, should Suppose you may have them made, at that, in this City—   I am Gentlemen Your Hble Servt.

The Continental Congress had established a Navy Board of "persons well skilled in maritime affairs...to execute the business of the Navy under the direction of the Marine Committee."

To Nathaniel Chapman

Dear Sir   Philadelphia June 30th 1780

Your two favours by the Post I have recd, Accompanied with several others from Gentlemen with you belonging to the departmt.—and do Assure, you their Contents gave me sensible pain; that Men who have faithfully served their Country, should be either Slighted or Neglected is too unnatural to bear Reflection—I have Communicated the situation of the Department to the Honble. Board of War, earnestly requesting their immediate determination, with respect to every Branch of the Department at Springfield, and have received for answer, that they have the Matter under Consideration, and will shortly determine upon such Arrangements as they shall find Necessary—

Hope by the next post to be able to inform you what is done and fall upon some Method to give you such Assistance as your Circumstances & Merit require—Inclosed I send the requested Return of Cloathing from Mr. Pearson, you own Cloathing he Cannot at present Ascertain the price of when, it can be Obtained shall be forwarded—have nothing further at present but my best respects to every Gentleman belonging to the Department, and my request that you would inform them, that as it is my duty, so it is my inclination to do every thing in my power to make them contented, & happy—their Letters I shall answer as Opportunity Presents—in the mean time believe me to be sincerely your friend & very Hble servant

Chapman was a Captain in the Military Stores Department at Springfield, Massachusetts.

To Ezekiel Cheever

Dear Sir   Philadelphia June 30th 1778

Some time since Colonel Flower informed you, of the Order of the Honble Board of Treasury, for Setling all Accounts under his direction by the 1st. June—since that I have received yours to him, assigning the Reasons that prevented your immediate Compliance— these have been Communicated to the Commissioners, and from them as usual to the Treasury—and the Inclosed is their deliberate determination—duty as well as Inclination, disposed me to give you the most early information to prevent the disagreeable consequence that might Possibly attend the failure of the Accounts being rendered by the time ordered—I have not as yet had the pleasure of a Line from you, perhaps reasons may Operate to prevent my expecting one— should this be the case, can only say that Conscious I have done nothing to merit your displeasure, I shall rest satisfied with discharging my duty to you as an Officer & friend, & leave it to you generosity (if I have given Offence) to inform me when & how, after which shall act as Reason Dictates—

With esteem I am Sir your very humble servant

To the Board of War and Ordnance

Gentlemen   Philada. June 30th 1780

In consequence of your request Yesterday that "I would in a frugal way prepare some Small Fireworks to be exhibited next Tuesday as a token of thankfulness and Joy for the return of the anniversary of that happy day on which the people of America determined to be free," I have provided one hundred & sixty nine Rocketts & 400 Serpents, and if time will permit shall prepare two Brilliant Fire wheels. the shortness of the time and the circumstances of our country (in my opinion) is a sufficient apology for no greater exhibition—

With respect I am Gentlemen Yours

To William Chambers

Sir   Philadelphia July 3d 1780

You will please to inform the men employed in the Laboratory under your direction, that their pay is Augmented to twelve dollars p day Commencing the 1st. Instant, and their Accots. in future are to be made out Accordingly—this generous allowance I hope will have a tendency to make the men exert themselves, at this time, as Cartridges

are much wanting, the Demand for them being very great—
   I am Sir Yours

NB such as have not received their pay for the Month of April by presenting their Accounts will receive an Order for it now—

Chambers was a Conductor of Military Stores.

To Lewis Nicola

Sir   Philadelphia July 4th 1780
   The honble. Board of War having directed me to prepare some small fire works to be exhibited on this transporting anniversary, and at the Same time, join the general Joy with the usual token of discharge of Cannon, I have taken this early opportunity to request you would be pleased to give Such orders to Captn. Lieut. Godfrey as may be necessary for the previous parade of the Company of Artillery at present under his Command, and regular performance of the discharge of three times thirteen Cannon of three pounders order'd for that Service—
   With Esteem I am Yours

Nicola was a Philadelphia businessman who was made Colonel of the Invalid Regiment in 1777, and a brevet Brigadier General in the Continental Army in 1783.

To John Mitchell

Sir   Philadelphia July 4th 1780
   In Commemoration of that day on which the Genius of America prompted her Sons to proclaim their freedom we are this day Ordered to Discharge our Cannon—
   You will please to furnish the Bearer with four horses for a few hours to take the pieces to and from the place directed for their Discharge—
   Yours

The horses must be harness'd two for the thrill[s] & two for leaders

To the Board of War and Ordnance

Gentlemen   Philada. July 6 1780

In the present circumstances of the Comy. Genl. M Stores Department with respect to money, I am at a loss to determine the propriety of the demands made on it from the post Office the Returns forwarded to this place, and the Letters that accompanies them at the present postage amounts to considerable Sum. one week I paid 165 Dollars and constantly from fifty to Sixty, if the Gentlemen who fills the Office of post master receives Commissions, I should Suppose it for the publick Interest, to order ours as well as other publick Letters frank'd I would wish the direction of the Board on the Subject—

Yours &c

To William Smith

Sir   Philada. July 6 1780

The situation of Mr. Chambers renders it very improper that he should go at large and especially, be about the Laboratory. must request that you would give immediate orders for receiving him into the hospital untill his health is restored, at which time as it appears he is unfit for his present employment, he will be discharged or employed elsewhere, as circumstances shall determine most adviseable—

With esteem I am Yours

Agreement With Simon Murray

These may certify that I Simon Murray Tinman have this day agreed with Samuel Hodgdon Esqr. ACMGS. for the Term of One Year to Act as Tinman in the works now establishing in the State of Virginia under the immediate direction of Captain Natl. Irish, upon the following Terms.—Vizt. for and in Consideration of my Services as Tinman faithfully performed, it is agreed that I shall receive Twenty Dollars p day and one Ration of Provisions, have my Wife with such small effects as may be Necessary to carry Transported at the publick expence to the place destined for the Works—

On these Considerations being faithfully fulfilled, I promise to Obey every Regulation, agreeable to the Articles of War, or Special Order of the Honble. Board of Signified by the Commander of the Department or abide the penalty annexed—Signed at Philada. July 6th 1780

By Virtue of the above the said Murray is to have the whole Charge of the Tinmans branch and under the Direction of Captain Nathaniel Irish (or the Commanding Officer for the time being) Superintend the men employed in it—

Signed in presence of us James Boyer
William Knox

Captain Nathaniel Irish had served in the Regiment of Artillery Artificers since February 7, 1777, mostly at Carlisle, Pennsylvania. In 1780 he was sent to the Southern Department to serve as Deputy Commissary of Military Stores in Virginia. In November 1780, he wrote to Hodgdon that he had found a barn at Westham, five and a half miles from Richmond. Virginia. The barn was used as a workshop and armory, and a laboratory was set up in a stable to produce fixed ammunition, portfires and tubes. He continued in the service until 1785.

To Charles Lukens

Sir   Philadelphia July 7th 1780

Yours of the 8th. June I have received with the Inclosed Account of Monies received of Mr. Sweers amounting as it said to £14,284.17.6—upon examining your Accounts left with the Treasury Board we find him Credited with upwards of £40,000—this Matter and the inclosed Order will point out to you, the Absolute Necessity of your Attending with your Accounts for a General Settlement immediately—I have it expressly in charge to inform you that your Personal Attendance will be expected that the Accounts Already exhibited, and all Others which you may have to exhibit—may be examined, and a final settlement Commence

With esteem I am Yours

Lukens was a Major in the Regiment of Artillery Artificers and Commissary of Military Stores at Carlisle.

To Samuel Sarjant

Dear Sir   Philada. July 7th 1780

By Captn. Wylie I have an opportunity to inclose you a late resolve of the honble. Board of Treasury, respecting the Settling the accts: of the Department, in compliance with which must request, you would have all yours ready, and as a very minute acct: of the propriety of every charge will be demanded, I think it best you should attend in person to facilitate this business. the time you will perceive is confin'd to the 1st. August and I am Sure you will join with us in this very desireable settlement, the completion of which will give a fresh confidence to the Department, and eventually have a tendency to procure that justice founded upon merit which the department has long had a right to expect—

As Soon as opportunity presents I must request you would forward in addition to the Stores formerly wrote for, the Carte Boxes mentioned in your return wanting repair one Barrell Linseed Oil, and 2 Bbls Tanners do. all the Screw Drivers & Gun worms and all military Stores proper for repair in the Laboratory. as to further supplies of money they shall be forwarded as fast as circumstances will admit hope they will be such as will enable you to continue to carry on with spirit have nothing further to add but to assure you

I am Your Friend & very huml Servt:

To John Jordan

Dear Sir   Philada. July 7th 1780

Your favor of ye: 22d. Ulto. came safe to hand was happy to hear you found things on your return better than you expected, such deserving men merits the kindest treatment and from me that shall have it. one source of my enjoyment shall be to administer to their happiness. the Shirts I am Sorry to Say are not yet to be had but would recommend it to you to come down immediately upon receipt of this for many reasons. in the first place it is proper that you should be furnished with money to pay the 100 Dollars to the men engag'd during the war likewise to try the experimt. with Such as are for three years of during the war as it is well worth while to make their Services during the war certain. thirdly as there is an expectation of a quantity of cloathing arriving every moment your being on the spot may be of service to procure a full supply and lastly your presence will be necessary here, to answer many little requisitions, that daily occur.—

As for the two gentlemen you mention faith and hope they are yet much caressed and with much reason, being the whole dependance of all publick Officers. but patience must be added to effect their kind Office & perseverance at the Same time demands attention, and respect to make the Composition Salutary. have nothing further to communicate but an assurance of Friendship while I have the happiness to Subscribe myself—

Yours

Jordan was commissioned a Captain-Lieutenant in the Regiment of Artillery Artificers on February 17, 1777. Most of his service appears to have been at Carlisle and he was promoted to Captain on May 7, 1780. He later served in Virginia and retired on January 1, 1783.

To the Board of War and Ordnance

Gentlemen   Philadelphia July 10th. 1780
having as Acting head of the Comy. Genl. of Military stores Department, Received Repeated Applications from that part of it stationed at Springfield in the state of Massachusets for Countenance and support in their present distressed situation and being also called upon to give your Honble. Board such information concerning it is in my power, it is my duty to lay before you the Complaints of the Officers there and the causes from whence they spring, together with such Observations of my own as will be necessary to give you that Knowledge of the post on which a new Arrangement of it so essential to the public Interest may be grounded.—

But before I proceed upon the Business so delicate in its Nature & consequences would just premise that Scituated as I am it cannot be Supposed I have any views in this Representation but such as are founded on a desire to promote the public Interest and the happiness of the department. yet as I am aware that my intention to serve the public, and do my duty may be by the persons affected construed into a specious pretence under which by insinuation or direct Accusation I endeavoured to Remove Officers long since know in the service to make room for Others more Acceptable to me, I beg leave to inform you that should you find cause to remove the persons employed at present in that division of the department I know of none whom I would choose to Recommend to supply their places.—

Inclosed you have a number of Letters from different Gentlemen in the department which will fully shew you their sentiments with respect to the present state of it. my own Observations on the spot previous to their complaints convince me that they were well founded. I shall accordingly proceed to relate what in my Opinion are the causes that has prevented the Beneficial effects expected from the post.—

Very early in its establishment the dispute about precedency arose between Col. Mason and Mr. Cheever, the Commissary of Military Stores. from this parties were formed and suspicions & Jealousies with their Mischevious Consequences Appeared and a Mutual hatred succeeded to that degree as to prevent the exercise of such Acts as were Absolutely necessary to carry on the public business. this Conduct gave a General disgust to the Inhabitants which finally broke into public Impeachments & put an end to every kind Office between them and the department and each pursued the Other with a most unwarrantable rancour from this moment the usefulness of the department began evidently to decline—by which means disappointment attended every Application for stores until they entirely ceased to be made—its importance being thus done away—its support was not so fully attend to—Nevertheless large sums of Money were still continued to be forward, but with very little advantage to the public, as the Stores provided there were indeed very trifling since 1777.—this and the growing clamour against the Principals at the post for their conduct in other respects, than those they had already been called to Answer too, not only from the inhabitants but some among themselves of both parties rendered it unsafe for the Comy. Genl. to forward any further supplies of Cash before those already received were Accounted for, and the department examined & Arranged anew indeed the public finances pointed out the propriety of Appropriating the partial supplies of Money that were to be expected to procure such articles as were found indispensibly necessary for the Army where they could be Obtained from these Reasons and others that might be Adduced the pay of the Officers & Men is greatly behind hand and called for immediate Attention to prevent a dissolution of the post—The situation of Springfield is favourable for carrying on the Business intended when the post was Established—good Timber may be had for Carriages of all sorts, lead for Musket Cartridges may be procured from Boston , at any time and most of the articles necessary for Carrying on an Ordnance Yard and Laboratory. the stores when made are perfectly safe there, the Air is healthful and nothing seems to be wanting to restore the department to its former Usefulness but the removal of some of its present Officers and the Appointment of a suitable person to superintend the whole. could such a one be found who would make it his study to cultivate a friendly Correspondance with the Inhabitants and Conciliate the Affections of the several Branches employed under him, I am certain every advantage ever expected from this post would be immediately experienced.—on the Contrary I have good reason to believe that should every possible encouragement be extended to the department and the present Principal Officers be Continued no Material Advantage would be derived from it to the Publick. as to those Officers who immediately Superintend the respective Branches of work, better men or between workmen can no where be found.— Major Eyres is an active officer and deserving Man, and should it be found necessary to have a person to do the duty of Major of the Regiment with that division, procure stuff &c. no man would answer better than he—The Captains Boulton, Faxon, Haws, & Boylston are excellent workmen at their branches, and their services can on no terms be dispenced with. the subordinate Officers I need not mention, I believe them in general to be good Men, but think there is more of them than are Necessary at the post—Perhaps I need say no more of the Principles, Colo. Mason & Mr. Comy. Cheever, than that the latter is far advanced in life—the frailties of which he every day exhibits and Colo. Mason is, and always has been detestible to the department. as both are evidently incapable of directing it neither of them I conceive ought to be Continued, but as they embarked early in the Cause of freedom, & have been useful I beg leave to suggest a suitable provision ought to be made for them to retire upon. Clear I am that the publick had better allow them pensions for life equal to their present Allowances & remove them, than Continue them in Office it they could & would serve with out pay—Thus Gentlemen without the least desire to injure any person unless a relation of the facts does it, I have endeavoured to discharge my duty and Comply with your request in giving you a true and faithful Account of the Division of the Comy. Genl of Military Stores Department at

Springfield. have nothing further to add but my hearty wishes that your honourable Board would immediately proceed to an Investigation and Arrangement of that Post, that Justice & happiness being extended to it the publick may reap those advantages from it, that under proper regulations it is capable of yielding—
    with due Respect I am Gentlemen yours

Discharge Certificate for John Spelerback

These Certify that John Spelerback having Procured an able Bodied Man, by the name of Jno. Christopher Paul, by Trade a Shoemaker, to serve during the War in his room and Stead free of all Charges to the united States of bounty Money, and the Man being this day accepted by the Officer Commanding the Company said John Spelerback is discharged from his Inlistment in Colonel Flowers Regiment of Artillery Artificers and is at full liberty to employ himself as he thinks proper in future
    Given under my hand on this 10th day of July 1780
Philadelphia   Whom it may Concern

To Philip Van Rensselaer

Dear Sir   Philadelphia July 14th. 1780
 This day I received your favor of the 1st: Instant inclosing the Return for the Month of June—and informing that the Armoury is in great want of the Articles mentioned in the indent sent here some time ago—the want of Money has Stagnated the business in every department and so severely has it affected the Q. Masters, that they have been unable to furnish Waggons upon the most pressing Occasions—however you may rest assured that as it is my duty do it is my inclination to give you every assistance in my Power—as the Army is removed towards north River it will have a tendency to facilitate the Transportation of such Supplies as you may have Occasion for—the indent on hand you may depend shall be forwarded as soon as the Articles can be procured & Transportation obtained— You will please to present my Compliments to Mrs. Renselaer, Mr. Lansing and family and Captn. Lamb if Present
 With esteem I am Sir Yours

To the Board of War and Ordnance

Gentlemen   Philadelphia July 15th. 1780

Last evening Captain Jordan returned from his Journey in quest of stores left on the Road belonging to the public. the following is founded on his report—4-12 Pound Cannon unfit for Service at Sweedes Ford—20-18 pound Shot at ditto—at Doctor Shannons formerly Bulls 40 Tons different Sizes mostly 18 & 12 pounders—at Colonel Berrys 230-18 pound Shot—at Valley Forge 1320-24 Pound Shot—2853-18 pound ditto—803-12 pound ditto—904-9 pound ditto—at John Jacob's 30 Tons different sizes mostly 18 pounds—at Colonel Gibbons 30 Tons of sizes mostly 18 & 12 pounders—at Christiana Bridge 99-18 pounders 113-12 pound ditto 100-9 pound ditto & 16-4 pound ditto—

By examining the Return brought by Captain Jordan & attending to his declaration respecting those mentioned as Tons—as their Situation prevented their being Counted—I conclude the following state will turn out pretty exact—Vizt.—

6 Tons damaged Cannon to run into Shott
1324 twenty four Pound Ball
8202 Eighteen do.   do.
7316 Twelve do.   do.
1200 Nine   do.   do.
100 Four   do.   do.

Should be glad to be informed whether the Board think is adviseable to send for them immediately—

With due Respect I am Gentleman Yours

To the Board of War and Ordnance

Gentlemen   Philadelphia July 18th 1780

In Answer to yours of this day must inform you, that Fifty four Thousand dollars is wanting to pay the workmen for the repairs of the fifteen hundred Muskets lately ordered to be repaired which are nearly completed.—We have now on hand three Thousand Stand of Repairable Muskets—which on enquiry I find will cost twenty Shillings each hard money to put them into proper repair—the whole may be Completed in three Months, the exchange will amount to four hundred and eighty thousand Dollars. five Thousand new Constructed

Cartouch Boxes will cost five hundred Thousand Dollars. five Thousand Bayonet Belts will Cost one hundred Thousand dollars. Total Amount for the above supplies agreeable to the stating is one Million and eighty Thousand dolls.

I would just suggest for your Consideration whether it is not proper that some more adequate provision be made for supplying the department with Money than that at present depended upon. the demands are already great & pressing & the supplies so partial & uncertain that I dare not anticipate the Consequences. one Million of Dollars as Ordered for the use of the Department by a Resolve of Congress so long ago as January the 3d. more than two thirds of which sum is not to This day Received. I need say no more as you are Acquainted with the expenditure of the Department, you will easily imagine the distress it is in

With due Respect I am Gentlemen—Yours

To Archibald Shaw

Sir July 20th. 1780

Your [sic] immediately to Set out for Trenton & there receive the Stores, agreeable to the Invoice you have with you, from on board the Schooner which you have attended to loading of—

The teems it is probable will be ready as the Quarter master is notified of the number wanted to take them in. which these when properly loaded you will proceed with all convenient speed to the head Quarters of Genl: Washingtons army and deliver them to Richard Frothingham Esqr DFCMS, and take his receipt for the whole agreeable to invoice this done you will return to this place—

Your are to be particularly carefull to prevent loss or damage to the Stores you have under charge and be very frugall in your expences on the road—

Yours

To Moore Furman

Sir Philada. July 20 1780

The Bearer Mr. Archibald Shaw CMS waits on you to be supplied with a number of waggons to transport the stores he has in charge to Camp. Colo. Mitchell informs me he has given you notice of the time when and the probable number, that may be wanted from this I conclude you will be prepared and no time lost.—

I am Sir You very huml Servt.

To Richard Frothingham

Dear Sir   Philada. July 20 1780

By the Invoice that accompanies the Stores, you will perceive a number to be forwarded to Mr. Phillip Van Ranselaer at Albany, which beg you would Send on, without a moments delay, as they are greatly wanted. presume you have forwarded those sent for him long before this time. I wrote Some time ago, by order of the honble. Board of War, for Mr. Jones to return to this place, and take his instructions agreeable to his appointment, and go on to the Southern army. whether this Letter miscarried, or he did not think best to accept the appointment, cant Say; but if present, should be glad you would desire him to inform me, that I may know what I have to depend upon. should be glad you would be very particular in forwarding the Returns as they become due, as I wish often to know the State of your Stores. the difficulty of obtaining Money, lays an almost unsurmountable Barrier in my way, of procuring such supplies as I know you stand in need of. untill this is removed I shall continue Such partial Supply as your circumstances shall make necessary—

I have nothing further to add, but my regards to all enquiring Friends—

With regard I am Sir Your Friend—

To Mr. Donaldson

Sir   Philada. July 20 1780

Missing some heavy peices of Ordnance belonging to the States I have made enquiry and find that of the number taken away, 1 18 pounder and 1 12 pounder, are on the Brig commanded by Captn. Barry, owned or fitted out by you. as there is special occasion for this Guns, and I am ordered to collect them, you will oblidge me very much by informing me whether any regular order was obtained for them and if so who from, as I am to report this Day—

I am Sir Your very huml Servt:—

To Blair McClenachan

Sir   July 20 1780

Upon the arrival of the Brig Fame Captn. Jno. Mc.Clanaghan, belonging or consigned to you I received a Bill of Lading for ninety Casks of powder shipt on board for the use of & belonging to the United States, which have not yet been delivered. upon enquiry I find it has been sent without any notice given to this States Magazine, by this means it does not appear on any publick Books, and therefore remains to be accounted for—

Mr. Stiles informs me he has another quantity belonging to the United States, imported in one of your Vessels, circumstanced as the above, which is in a ruinous Situation. if this is the case must beg the favor of you to attend to the matter & order a regular delivery, that I may be enabled to report the quantity and quality I receive, as there is probably [sic] a considerable demand for that article will be made Soon—

I am Sir Your very huml Servt.—

McClenachan rivaled Robert Morris as the one of the premier shippers, importers, and privateer owners in Philadelphia. In 1780 he and Robert Morris each subscribed £10,000 to found the Bank of Pennsylvania. He was later a United States Congressman.

To James Clark

Sir

Inconsequence of a certificate from Doctor William Smith certifying your inability to perform the business for which you Inlisted And your own desire repeatedly signified to me—You are discharged from your Inlistment in Colo. Flowers Regt. of Artillery Artificers, and are at full liberty to employ yourself, as your own circumstances & inclination direct—Given under my hand at Philadelphia the Twentieth Day of July 1780.—

He was a solder in John Jordan's Company in Flower's Regiment of Artillery and Artificers.

To the Board of War and Ordnance

Gentlemen   July 24 1780

In compliance with your orders I have made enquiry for Junk, and find I can procure the quantity wanted at a price not exceeding £1500 pr Ton. it must be purchased immediately, or it will be bought to employ the poor confined to the work house—

Shells may be had at the rate of £2500 p Ton shot for £1250 ditto—

As appendage to the estimate—
     5000 24 pound paper Cartridges
     20,000 18   do   do.
     15,000 12   do   do.
these will take 110 Rheams Paper which at 300 Dollars p Rheam amounts to 6000 [sic] dollars

     20 Galls. spirits of wine @ £40—£800—
these are all the appendages worth mentioning some others will be wanting, but there cost will be trifling—

With respect Gentlemen I am Yours—

The *Oxford English Dictionary* defines Junk as "Old cable or rope material, cut into short lengths and used for making fenders, reef points, gaskets, oakum, etc."

To the Board of War and Ordnance

Gentlemen   Philada. July 25 1780

Mr. Hoy the person I sent for to Springfield by direction of your Honble. Board to take charge of the Laboratory in this City is Arrived here and is ready to enter upon his charge—but the Intention of the Board (Signified to me some time ago) prevents my ordering him to his duty.—The Situation of the Laboratory here, and the present expectations from it, has induced me to believe his services here would be more beneficial, than they could possibly be should he proceed as designed to Virginia.—Captain Godfrey who at present superintends the Laboratory here, and on whom we must depend, should Mr. Hoy go on.—is by no means equal to the preparation of the Stores Mentioned in the Indent, w[e] have on hand, yet is quite equal to such preparations, as will be expected from the Laboratory in Virginia in its Infant State—the conclusion is easy, that, to insure a

Supply of such Chymical preparations with dispatch as are absolutely Necessary to facilitate the intended Operations—he should be employed here—shall only add, that as his services here will free me from a painful anxiety Respecting the immence quantity of stores demanded, and probably be attended with Real advantage to the publick, am disposed to hope the Board will see the propriety, and Accordingly Order him to take charge of the Laboratory in this City

With due Respect I am Gentlemen Yours

To the Board of War and Ordnance

Gentn.   Philada. July 28th 1780

To prevent loss of time in getting Mr. Hoy to work in the Laboratory 'tis necessary to inform you that agreeable to your verbal order, I have engaged him upon the following terms Vizt.—

To procure him a Lieuts. Commission in the Compy employed in the Laboratory under him, with all its pay and advantages, and additional allowance of 15 dollars p day, as director of the Laboratory. with this he is well Satisfied and if it meets with your approbation his future Services are Secured. his distressed Situation occasioned by the failure of former promises with regard to Cloaths, he desires may be mentioned to you, in hopes your knowledge of his circumstances may operate to his relief. he says he has never received but part of one Suit of Cloaths since he entered the Service, which together with his low pay, has reduced him to a Single shirt and as by resolve of Congress 2 Suits as described are due to him, requests that at least he may be enabled immediately to procure Such portions as are requisite, for his appearing decently in Character. under these circumstances I am Sure the Board will give him Such relief as his necessities call for and their Abililties admit—

The Situation of the enlisted men in the Regiment of Arty Artificers relating to Cloathing oblidges me to request the Board, that 2 Shirts, (such as were lately given them one each, as gratuity) may be ordered them at Such price as the Board shall direct th[em] tho' very ordinary as they are almost naked would be thankfully received, untill Such as they conceive, they have a right to expect can be obtained. inclosed you have a return of the number of Men, by which the number of Shirts necessary for the above purpose will be ascertained—

Captn. Irish has applied to me, to be informed in what way he is to be furnished with money to bear the expences of his charges to Virginia, and for the purchase of materials for the work when he arrives. this I could not determine but gave my opinion that the Board, would make Such additions to the Sum mentioned in the estimate to be necessary, for the purchase of Tools, as they should judge requisite for this present purpose. or perhaps, a special warrant on their paymaster, sufficient for his present demands and empower him on his arrival to draw on the Treasury, under the direction[n] of the Governor & Council (or if under a military command) the commander in Chief, for such further Sums as may be found necessary in the prosecution of the business he has in hand, and there or here as directed to account for the Same. should wish to be favored with the Sense of the Board upon the Subject, that I may inform him, how when & where to apply for his present & future supplies. have not as yet been favored with the promised order, for engaging the foremen of the Several Branches going to the Southward for want of which, and the Money to purchase to Tools, the Business is now at a stand—

With due respect I am Gentlemen Your most Obedt. huml. Servt.

To the Board of War and Ordnance

Gentlemen July 28th. 1780
One reason why the Company late Corens have not received their Cloathing, was owing to their never being annexed to any Regt., and on this ground I am informed the discharges given by Coren to several of his men have been confirmed by the Court of enquiry on those proceedings: as it appears to me to be for the Interest of the publick that such pretences should be done away and the men placed so as to know to whom they may apply for their dues shall take the Liberty to recommend the immediate annexing that Company to the Regt. of Artilly. Artificers knowing it in general the wish of the Men an believing in a publick Utility

To William Egerton Godfrey

Sir July 29th 1780
I am directed by the honble. Board of War to inform you they

have made choice of you to go with Captn. Irish to Virginia, there to direct the Men to be employed in the Laboratory to be carried on, at such place as he shall find convenient—

Having already mentioned the matter to you and given you to understand that an additional Sum to your present pay will be allowed you as director, it only remains to Say what that allowance shall be. this if you will call upon me we will endeavor to agree on, and any other requisites that shall be judg[ed] necessary, to get you on your way, as we expect the whole will go next wednesday—

I am Yours

Discharge Certificate for John Treacy

These Certify that John Treacy Drummer in Captain Lieut. Godfreys Company of Artillery & Artificers, having served the full Term of his Inlistment, is discharged from said Compy. and at liberty to employ himself as with the advice of his Friends he may think Best—

Given under my hand at Philadelphia this 31st Day of July 1780—

whom it may Concern

Agreement With Walter McFarland

Philada: Augt: 1st 1780

These Certify that I Walter Mc.Farland a soldier in Captn. Lieut: Godfreys company by trade a turner have this day agreed with Samuel Hodgdon Esqr. ACGMS to proceed to Virginia under command of Captn. Irish to undertake the Superintendency of that branch of Business in the publick works establishing there, under his direction.—

Upon the faithfull performance of which, it is agreed it is agreed that I am to receive, ten dollars p day in addition to my present pay, as Matross in said Company, together with one Ration p day, and my expences paid by the publick while on my Journey, to the place where I am to be employed.

'tis expected in addition to the Regimental engagements, that you will consider yourself subject to all orders, of the commanding Officer respecting the branch of Business immediately under your

direction. the above & foregoing terms, on the part of said Mc.Farland being fully complied with, I promise in behalf of the United States to make good their part of the Contract.—
    Sign'd in presence of us   James Boyer
                                 Peregrine Jones

Jones was a Clerk in the Military Stores Department.

Agreement With William Clark

                                                        Philada. Augt: 2d 1780
These Certify that I William Clark Armourer have this day agreed, with Saml: Hodgdon Esqr: ACGMS on behalf of the United States, to proceed to the State of Virginia under the immediate command of Nathl: Irish, to Superintend the Armoury to be carried on with other publick works at Such place as he shall direct, and in character of superintendent of the armoury, to act for one yea[r] from this date upon the under written conditions
Vizt: It is agreed upon the faithfulll discharge of my trust, that I shall receive thirty dollars p day one fatigue Ration, have my expences borne by the publick to the place destin'd to carry on the work and upon the expiration of the term, should I be disposed to Return to this City, by obtaining a Certificate from the Commanding Officer at the works, of my time of engagement being fully expired and having been faithfully performed, be entitled to my expences returning—
    These conditions being performed by the public I promise to Subject myself, to Such rules & regulations as are at first established, and all others that may be found necessary, during my term of Service.—
    Signed in presence of us John Jordan Capt, Arty. & Artificers
                                      James Boyer Clk

To William Egerton Godfrey

Sir   Augt: 4th 1780
    As you are appointed to the Directorship of the Laboratory intended to be carried on in Virginia, and are shortly to set out for your command you will please to deliver the Laboratory and

apparatus under your direction here to Mr. Hoey, (who is appointed to take that charge) this day. you will apply to me to receive such further instructions as you may need previous to your setting off to the Southward—

I am Sir Your huml. Servt:—

To Benjamin Hoey

Sir   Philada: Augt: 4 1780

You will this day call on Captn. Lieut: Godfrey to receive from him, the charge of the Laboratory and its apparatus in this City, to the directorship of which you were lately appointed—

Captn. Godfrey, being notifyed will deliver the charge as directed, when called upon—

I am Sir Yours

To the Board of War and Ordnance

Gentlemen   Augt: 5 1780

In compliance with your orders this morning (acompanied by Mr: Byers,) I visited the air Furnace, and find the following particulars relative to it, which I take the liberty to lay before your Honble. Board—

The Furnace is in perfect order, was in blast yesterday, and may be put in Blast any time at two hours notice. there is about 10 Cords of wood ready prepared, & fit for immediate use. the present workmen four in number say they understand the business of casting shot & shells, and are willing to engage, at reasonable wages provided they may be freed from Militia Duty to which they are now called. from this representation you will perceive I only wait your orders to Set Mr Byers at work. at the Same time you will See the propriety of giving Such orders to the Q Master as may be necessary to procure & transport to the Furnace Such further supplies of wood, as may be necessary to keep up the Blast after they begin to Blow. this may be done with dispatch, as I am inform'd great quantities are on the Banks of the River, belonging to the publick. the means for transporting of which are in the Q Masters hands, So that we easily obtain a full & timely Supply—

With due respect I am Gentlemen Yours &c

To the Board of War and Ordnance

Gentlemen   Augt: 7th. 1780

It gives me pain to be under the necessity of requesting your attention, while I renewedly recite the distress of the Department I have the honour to Superintend, labours under for want of money. sensible in Some measure of the embarrass'd state of the publick Finances, I have for a considerable time, contented myself, with making partial requisitions, but having never been able to obtain these, & being shut out of any prospect, fills me with apprehensions, for the consequences that I am certain will arise, without an immediate supply. it is needless I trust to enumerate the particular Sum[s] due, suffice it to Say, that the Regt: of Arty Artificers have received not pay Since March. the hired men a number of which are now ordered to Camp are in the Same Situation. having heavy Rents to pay large Sums due for Stocks and Materials the non payment of which has Sunk our Credit to that degrees, that a twenty shilling article cannot be procured without the money being paid down, the natural consequence of which must be, a total annihilation of the Business expected from the Department, and that at the only Season of the Year proper to carry it on to advantage. under these circumstances, a Sense of Duty oblidged me to make this representation, as a speedy supply of Money, (if to be obtained) may yet prevent a total dissolution of the department, and ensure the Supplies expected from it—should it be practicable, to procure 500,000 dollars, I am of opinion it might answer our present purposes less would afford but a very temporary relief—

With respect I am Gentlemen Your most Obedt. Servt.

To W. Nancarrow

Sir   Augt: 8th: 1780

Having received orders from the Honble. Board of War to get the air Furnaces in this City imediately to work, I waited on you as the owner or occupier to endeavor to agree on terms, to prevent any complaint of injustice at the conclusion of this Business, but after Several times calling without being able to See you, I am obliged to prevent further delay to inform you that I shall take possession of the works, with the necessary apparatus and wood to begin the Blas[t] to morrow morning 8 oClock, at which time if you will please to attend, an inventory of such articles as we want shall be taken which with the wood shall be replaced, in Such way, as is most agreeable to you, if not returned, when the works shall be given up—if you have any thing particular to communicate, must beg of you to call on me at Carpenters Hall Some time to day, as I am going on a Journey to morrow in hopes that every thing will be agreeable I subscribe myself—

Your Friend—

On July 26, 1780, the Board of War wrote to the President of Pennsylvania Joseph Reed informing him that General Washington planned a siege of New York City. The Board informed Reed that "We have in this city, materials for casting many tons, & there is an air furnace convenient for this purpose, now standing Idle; but the owner of it, a W Nancarrow, being a quaker, refuses to let us use it, if any instruments of war are to be cast at it." The Board asked that orders be given by the state government to "exercise of the authority of Government to obtain it" which was apparently done.

To Henry Valentine

Sir   Augt: 8th 1780

As I am going from this City for few days on publick Business, I supposed it necessary to inform you that I leave my Clerk Mr James Boyer in charge of my Business here, and you will please to accept his signature, on my behalf as I shall consider myself accountable for every publick act of his in my behalf during my absence—

With esteem I am Yours

Valentine was an Assistant Commissary of Issues.

To John Mitchell

Sir   Augt: 8th 1780

As I am going from this City, for a few days on publick Business, I have judged it proper to inform you that I leave my Clerk Mr James Boyer in charge of my affairs. you will please to accept his signature as mine in every application to you untill my return—

I should be oblidged to you to order twenty Cords of the dryest wood you have on hand to the air Furnaces in this City to be delivered Mr James Byers who is to Superintend the works. please to take his Certificate for what is delivered and I will receipt you for the whole on my retu[rn.]

With esteem I am Sir Yours &c.

To James Byers

Sir   Augt: 8th: 1780

In consequence of Orders from the Honble. Board of War, I have taken the air Furnaces in this City, on Rent for the United States for the purpose of reducing a number of damaged Cannon, and other useless metal we have on hand, into 10 Inch Shells and 9 pd. Bar Shot with direction to employ you to superintend the Business—you will accordingly immediately repair to the works, and in presence of Mr: Vancarro, if he chuses to attend, take an inventory of the apparatus, you will want belonging to the works, to carry on the casting of the Shells, and also a particular account of the wood at the Furnace, that we may make payment with exactness, when the accounts are exhibited—

There is four Men at the Furnace who wish still to be employed, you will agree with the whole of them, or such part as you may judge necessary, for compleating the Shells with dispatch. you may agree with them, with or without Rations, as you find most for the advantage of the publick

You will call on Mr: Boyer who will furnish you with Such orders as may be found necessary for transporting the Cannon & metal to the furnace for Patterns, and any other requisites—

You will compleat 200 rounds of Barr Shot 9 pds, the first work you do, as they are immediately wanted. your own pay shall be determined at a future Day, any matters not particularly mentioned, I leave to your prudence—

I am Sir Yours &c.

Byers, a brass founder formerly of New York City, had cast ordnance for the Continental Army early in the war. In 1778 he had made a contract with the Board of War to direct a brass cannon foundry, but on August 23, 1781, Congress authorized the Board to vacate the contract. Here he was ordered to cast scrap iron into shot and shells.

To Samuel Sarjant

Sir Philada. Augt: 8 1780

By Captn. Irish I have an opportunity to forward 10,000 Dollars which tho' a very trifling Sum is a quarter part, of what we have had on hand for a month past, and possibly may stand you in Some stead, untill further supplies can be obtain'd which I hope will shortly be the case. should it prove to be as I expect, by Captn. Jordan shall Send an ample supply. he has received & forwarded by this conveyance 10,000 dollars for a temporary relief to the men.—

By a special call from Camp, I have it in charge to direct all the Rifle Musketts at Carlisle to be repaired: in consequence of this must request that you would order them immediately repair'd and Sent here, to be forwarded to Camp. conveyance must be obtained for them, the moment they are finished, as the demand admits of no excuses or delay—

As Captn. Irish is going on command, you will furnish him with any articles he may request, that can be spared from the works, particularly 20 Steel plate Saws, 50 sheets Tin, and some stockers Tools. it is probable he will want a Smith & a Carpenter from the works to proceed with him. should that be the case, you will give him & them any needed assistance—

By a waggon going from this City to Carlisle, sent by Captn. Jordan (if not before) you will have an opportunity to forward the Oil and one Cask Tin, and any other article Sent for, to make up his load—

Some time ago I wrote you, requesting you would make inquiry for a certain Mr: Jno: Noble waggoner, and obtain repayment or stoppage of one hundred & sixty Dollars, furnished here to enable him to proceed with the Stores intended for Fort Pitt. pray write me word what is done, that I may know how to proceed to get my money—

Nothing further to communicate, only in answer to yours, to inform you that Colo. Flower by accounts from him this day, remains much as he was when he left the City. the Settlement of your accts: I have reason to think may be effected without your attendance. if not,

shall give your timely notice.—
I am With Esteem Sir Your very huml Servt.—

To William Thorne

Sir   Augt: 8 1780

In consequence of the information I receiv'd from you this morning, I have drawn on you for 10,000 Dollars in favor of Captn. Irish for Mr Sargent and 10,000 more in favour of 10,000 more in favour of Captn. Jordan to pay the inlisted men at Carlisle, and upon reflection I am led to think that we had better pay the inlisted men here one months pay with the remainder you have on hand. the application made yesterday to the treasury, will undoubtedly be answered with Some Cash immediately, from which the most pressing demands may be answered which as formerly I shall leave to your discretion to determine—

Should the warrant be drawn in my favor I have empowered Mr: Boyer who does my Business in my absence to receive it, and pay it to you entire. but should it be drawn in favor of Colo: Flower, the Board can and will empower you to receive it. should it be drawn in Flower'[s] name payable to me Mr. Boyer will receive and hand it to you as above—

Having not yet Seen Major Lukens, and it being impossible (under circumstances) for me to attend to the Settlement, would just inform you that you may receive his accounts, with any Ballanc[es] that may appear due thereon, after full satisfaction that all Sums paid him are accounted for, and give him a Certificate of the state of his acct: ballance received, and the number and amount of the Vouchers left to Support the charges in his acct: this is all that can be done at present as the Comy. Genls: accounts are to be taken up aggregately at which time should the Deputies be pass'd a full discharge will be given—

Relying on your exertions in every Branch of Business that comes before you, it is needless to be more particular—

I am Sir Yours

To John Jordan

Sir   Augt. 8: 1780

Captn. Joy being absent, and publick Business called me for a few days from Town, I am obligded to request you once more to take the Superintendency of the Ordnance Yard, and the men therein employed under your Direction; this day I have given orders for the pay due the inlisted men at this post for one month, this you will please to See regularly paid. you will call on Mr. Boyer (whom I leave to act for me during my absence) for any needed supplies to keep the men employed, and to him you will apply for assistance in any case you may deem necessary to keep the department employed. under our present embarassments you will assist Mr. Byers in collecting the damaged Cannon for the purpose of converting them into shot & shells, and deliver him those that are in the Ordnance Yard. as you are acquainted with the Bussiness you have on hand it is needless to be more particular, only let me intreat you to keep the men diligently employed this will ensure peace among themselves & make them usefull to the publick, the praise of which shall be fairly plac'd to the account of Captn. Jordan by his determined Friend—

Hodgdon gave Jordan the title of Superintendent of the Ordnance Yard.

To the Board of War and Ordnance

Gentlemen   Philadelphia Augst. 9th. 1780

Inclosed I send you a Letter and a Return for Cloathing which I received this Morning from Mr. Farrall, should be happy as soon as Convenient, to receive your Orders respecting both.—The Officer who brought them is to return in fifteen or twenty days—

With due Respect I am Gentlemen Yours

Extract From the Minutes of the Continental Congress

In Congress Augst 12th. 1780 The Board of War report, that pursuant to the Resolution of the 26th. of July, they have enquired into the state of the Department of Military stores and upon mature deliberation propose to retain in service untill the further order of Congress

One Commissary General of Military Stores—
One Deputy Commissary General of Military Stores
One Comissary at Springfield.
One Commissary at Carlisle.
One Commissary in Virginia, and two or three Commissaries or Deputy Commissaries at some subordinate posts and Stations.

That the pay of a Commissary of Military Stores be not less than 360 nor more than 1750 Dollars p Month.

That the pay of a Deputy Commissary & of the Conductors of Military stores be not less than 240 nor more than 1000 Dollars p Month.

That the pay of the Clerks be fixed by the Board of War and Ordnance in proportion to their respective merits and Services.

That the pay of a Captain of Artillery Artificers be 900 Dolls p Mon[th.]

A Captain Lieut 750 Dollars p Month—
A Lieut. 600 Dollars p Month—
A Serjeant from 150 to 200 Dollars p Month—
A Corporal Acting as foreman in any Branch of work the same pay as a Serjeant—
Other Corporals, Drummers & fifers & privates from 30 to 150 Dollars p Month.

That the pay of the Commissaries, Deputy Commissaries and Conductors to be Confined to the limits before mentioned be fixed According to respective Merit and Services by the board of War and Ordnance.

That the pay of the Non Commissioned Officer [sic] & privates be fixed According to their respective merit and Services within the limits before mentioned by the major part of their Commiss'd Officers who shall meet together Monthly for that purpose—

That a Daily Ration of Forage be Allowed only to such Commissaries & Conductors of Military Stores whose frequent Traveling shall in the Opinion of the Board of War require the same.

Resolved. That Congress agree to the said Report

Extract from the Minutes Charles Thompson, Secy.

To William Egerton Godfrey

Sir   Augt: 19th 1780

In consequence of an order from the Honble. Board of War, I have directed Lieut. Greer to call on you, as the commanding Officer of the Laboratory Company late Corens, for the following Men Vizt.

Rutledge	Baggs
Irvin	Hammond
Tinkfield	Hornkeith

to proceed with him to Virginia to be employed in the Laboratory establishing at that place. you will deliver them and give proper Certificates of the pay & cloathing due them up to the 1st. Instant

Yours

Certificate Regarding Services of John Rugan

These certify that John Rugan sergeant in Captn. Jno. Jordans Company Colo. Flowers Regt: Arty Artificers, being by trade a Carpenter have this day agreed with Saml. Hodgdon Esqr. ACGMS in behalf of the united States to proceed to Virginia under the command of Captn: Nathl. Irish to undertake the superintendency of that branch of Business in the publick works establishing there—upon the following conditions—

Vizt. Upon the faithfull performance of my duty it is agreed that I shall receive ten dollars p day in addition to my present pay as Serjeant in the above named Regiment to gether with one ration as usual daily and my expences paid, while on my journey to the place where I am to be employed—

These conditions on the part of the publick being complied with, I promise to pay all possible attention too, and comply as far as is in my power, with all orders of the commanding Officer respecting the Business I have undertaken at the post where I am employed—

In witness of which I have hereunto Set my hand this 20th day Augt: 1780   John Rugan
Signed in presence of us   Peregrine Jones
                            John Jordan Capt.

In addition to the above it is agreed that the wife of the said Jno. Rugan shall draw rations during his absence, he paying whatever shall be charged, by the united States for the Same—

Samuel Hodgdon

To the Board of War and Ordnance

Gent. Philada. Augt. 21st. 1780

In consequence of your orders, I sent a billet to Captn. Godfrey, notifying him with the requisition of the Board to me to furnish Captn: Irish with six men from the company under his command, to proceed to Virginia to be employed in the Laboratory, and at the same time inserted the names of the Men I thought Suitable for this purpose. his answer informed he that he cared nothing for me nor my orders, that he had received orders to go to Camp with his company, and that not a man should go from his company for any service without an order from Colo Nicola[.] this treatment, added to the numerous insults which I have before received from him (and attributed to his ignorance) has determined me to call upon the Board, either to dispense with my general Superintendance of the laboratory, or dismiss him from the command of the company, which is to prepare the Stores expected from it, being fully convinced while he has any command or influence over the men, nothing can be done. I have long laboured, to keep the bussiness going on, but this absolute refusal to obey my orders, dictated by your honble. Board and express'd so to him, I consider as a full absolution of any further expectations of or conduct of the Laboratory or Men employed in it untill I have your decision on the subject—

With due respect I am Gentlemen Yours &c.

To William Egerton Godfrey

Sir Philada. Augt: 21st 1780

Francis Mc.Glaughlin of your company lately attached to Captn. Dow's by his own desire having absconded, and hearing he was with you, I have directed Lieut: Dow to call upon you for him, and take him to his duty. you will deliver him accordingly—

To Thomas Wylie

Sir August 22d 1780

In consequence of Lieut: Greers being order'd (upon his own application) to superintend the Laboratory, in Virginia, the men formerly under his command annexed to your Company[.] as commanding Officer you will See that the Guards are properly kept up, and order preserved among the men—

They are in future to receive the same pay as the other men of the Regt:, and upon the Same principles. I suppose a trusty Serjeant under your immediate direction and inspection, will answer every purpose expected from the guard. pray desire Mr. Hall to let me know how the pistols come on—

To Richard Backhouse

Dear Sir	Philada. Augt: 22d 1780

A disappointment I met with after you left me, had well nigh prevented my sending the promised patterns. however! I have procured the most material, the 10 In Shell pattern the 8 In. do. & one 12 pd: Shot pattern you will receive by this conveyance. the centre Boards for the Shells, and the remaining shot patterns shall be forwarded in another team, which Colo. West expects in town to morrow or next Day. with this you will receive the profiles promised the inside Line of the two outside, [sic] is your direction as I am informed the shells rather swell, after they are cast, before they cool—

I am Yours

This was addressed to Mr. "Backhurst" at Durham Furnace in Pennsylvania. This was Richard Backhouse who owned the ironworks for a time.

To Nathaniel Irish

Sir	Philada. Augt: 23 1780

As you are about to Set off for Virginia to carry into execution the business for which you are appointed, and furnished perhaps a few Lines by way of instruction, respecting the most general parts of the service expected from you, may not be amiss. in confidence of this and as an act of duty I must request your attention to the following particulars

As it is your interest so also it is your duty to be very particular in making proper entries and demanding satisfactory vouchers for every article received, and delivered belonging to the publick, by which means you will be able to come to a settlement not only for the cash received, but also for the articles purchased—

Having already been furnished with the counter parts of the contracts of the Officers under your command, you can be at no loss to determine their pay, that being explicitly declared therein—Lieut: Greer being absent, puts it out of my power to effect a written agreement with him, however! I have informed him, that his additional pay shou'd be fifteen dollars p day, and have received his assent to receive as full compensation—you will govern yourself accordingly—

You will endeavor to make monthly returns to the Comy. Genl. of M Stores, of the state of the men and Stores under your charge. at the Same time noting any further regulations or assistance you may find necessary; your route will be by the way of Baltimore, from whence you will procure the most safe and easy carriage to Richmond. when there arrived, you will wait on Colo Carrington if present, who will kindly introduce you to the governor of the state. to him you will open the business you are designed to execute, who will give you such advice and assistance, as will enable you readily to begin the works, for which you were forwarded.—

A proper situation being found, suitable buildings for the works will engross your attention, perhaps temporary ones that will answer may be found. if so, you may soon be employed. this is of the greatest importance as the Stores, you are to provide are this moment wanted. should you have to erect any buildings, you will See the propriety of being most particular, to ascertain the advantages and dissadvantages that will attend their Situation in any proposed place—suitable buildings for quarters to the men must also be provided at the publick expence, agreeable to common usage, and in their case especial contract—

When the Stores are perfected, I conceive they are only subject to the order of the commander in cheif of the Southern army, or commanding Officer of Artillery in ordinary cases, and in extraordinary ones, to that of the Governor and Council. but this & all other matters not mentioned must depend on the nature of the demand, and your own judgement to render the Institution generally usefull—

I am Yours

Captain Nathaniel Irish had served in the Regiment of Artillery Artificers since February 7, 1777, mostly at Carlisle, Pennsylvania. In 1780 he was sent to the Southern Department to serve as Commissary of Military Stores in Virginia. In November 1780, he wrote to Hodgdon that he had found a barn at Westham, five and a half miles from Richmond. Virginia. The barn was used as a workshop and armory, and a laboratory was set up in a stable to produce fixed ammunition, portfires and tubes. He continued in the service until 1785.

To Ezekiel Cornell

Dear Sir   Augt: 24th 1780

Yours of the 18th instant inform that Congress had appointed a Committee, to make an estimate of the expences of the current year, & requesting me to furnish the committee with Such part, as will arise in the Comy. Genl. M Stores Department, I have received—have now to request, before I proceed in this Business that you would please to inform me, whether in the estimate you mean only to have included Such stores, as have been, or probably will be purchased in the present year, or whether you mean to include the whole expence of the department, Such as pay due the men in the Several Branches, and all Sums necessary, to procure materials to keep them employed. when the principles are ascertain'd on which you wish to have the estimate grounded, I shall with pleasure comply with the committees request—

with respect I am yours

Cornell was a Delegate to Congress from Rhode Island.

To Unidentified, Incomplete Letter

Sir   Augt. 24 1780

The honorable Board of War having dismiss'd Capt Lieut: Godfrey, as a useless Officer, and appointed you Lieut: of the company late his, with an order to take the command thereof for the present agreeable to the inclosed. you will immediately parade the men and call the roll, to know how many men are present. and inform yourself of the disposition of all the men, that were inserted in the last muster roll—(this I give as advice) previous to the mens being employed under you for chymical preparations in the Laboratory, to which as director you will be accountable for the improvement of their time, and all materials delivered you for preparations—

The publick having been deprived of the important Services of the company lately, owing to various reasons, particularly from their not knowing to what Regt: they were to be annexed by means of which the men have suffered many inconveniencies and are now in suffering circumstances with respect to cloaths in particular—This State have indeed included them with their Troops, and as Such they have a right to expect to be benefited by the stores, but as these Supplies are very uncertain and partial, and at present totally unnattainable you will inform the men, that the party of their Company formerly under the command of Lieut: Greer at Carlisle are annexed to Colo Flower's Regt: of Arty & Artificers, and are now entitled to receive [**top of next page cut out**].

To Samuel Miles, Incomplete Letter

also a flat load of sand at the same place, both for the use of the Air furnace, and immediately wanted. but after several Applications Vizt. at your Office, at Colo. Mitchells, and at the Waggon Masters I find myself utterly at a loss to procure waggons for the Transporting them—could wish to be informed where I am to apply for Services as dayly occur—in the present case six men remain idle untill Transportation can be Obtained, could wish have a team or two annexed to the department as usual to prevent frequent Applications.

Samuel Miles (1739-1805) had been Colonel of the Pennsylvania Rifle Regiment, suffered capture and imprisonment at the Battle of Long Island, and was exchanged in April 1778. In 1778 he was appointed Deputy Quartermaster General for Pennsylvania and served in this position until 1782. After the Revolution he became a state judge and was elected mayor of Philadelphia in 1790.

Top of next page cut out, at least one letter is missing.

To Timothy Pickering Jr.

Dear Sir　　　　　　　　　　　Philadelphia August 28th. 1780

Your's of this day I have received, in Answer shall inform you that the value of the Powder and refined Salt petre in every part of

America before 1775 were nearly equal and their Intrinsic value will forever remain so, with respect to each other, as Seventy five pounds of refined Salt petre will make one hundred pounds of powder.—by this you will readily perceive that 100 of Salt petre Afforded formerly a full Compensation to the powder Maker for his work and Supplies after returning 100 neat of powder, & in Similar Cases always will continue to do so.—perhaps the present high price of Labour and Sulphur may over balance the price of Salt petre—if so the exchange will rise Accordingly—but of this you will be able to judge after enquiring the price of each on the spot should the petre be in the rough a Sixth, Seventh or eighth part will be lost in refining, and should be estimated Accordingly—

Perhaps the Contracting parties may be disposed to Agree for the pay in Cash. in this case I would inform you that the highest price I have paid yet for making is £60 Pennsylva. p hundred, but do not expect to have any more made under Seventy five pounds, perhaps ninety.—but even then it would Answer to have our Materials made up—should this last mentioned mode of payment be agreed on, the following will inform you what quantity of Sulphur will be necessary for 100 pounds of powder, by which you will Compute any greater or less quantity—Vizt. 75 pounds Salt petre, 13 ½ Sulphur, & 11 ½ of pulverized Charcoal, is the proportion of every 100 neat of powder.—

With esteem I am sir your very humble servant

To the Board of War and Ordnance

Gentlemen   Philadelphia September 1st. 1780

The following Stores on hand ready for Transportation wait the Orders of your honble. Board—Vizt.

      347 Pistols for Horsemen—
      533 Musquets, bayonets & scabbards—
      290 Horsemans Swords

With due respect I am Gentn. Yours

To Archibald Shaw

Sir   Philadelphia Sept. 1st. 1780

You will immediately proceed with the Teams loaded with Military

Stores, by the nearest and Safest route to new Windsor on North River. when there Arrived apply to the person in charge of the Water craft and procure a suitable Vessel to take the whole to West point, and deliver them to Mr. Thos. Frothingham DFCMS. or the person Acting as such at that post—as the same time take his receipt for the Amount of the Invoice and inform him they are for the use of the Main Army, and must be forwarded intire to Richard Frothingham Esqr DFCMS. as quick as possible—

You will be very particular in frequently examining the Stores to prevent damage or loss by embezlement. when the Teams have Occasion to halt you will direct it to be done at a Considerable distance from any house or building where fire is kept, and take special care that the drovers don't attempt to light their pipes which driving as a Single Spark may announce your fate and be attended with loss & disappointment to the Continent

You will be very frugal in your expences as none will be admitted but such as were evidently unavoidable—I wish you a prosperous Journey—

Yours

To Richard Frothingham

Dear Sir   Philada. Sept. 1st 1780

By a Brigade of Teams that leaves this City to day under charge of Mr. Archibald Shaw, I have forwarded a Number of Military Stores as per Invoice that Accompanies them—the powder being ordered to West point I was Obliged to send the whole of the Stores there—as we could not separate the Teams and supposing you to be in that Vicinity I judged it might be as well, as transportation (should you be below) will be very safe and easy by water—the other Articles for which Indents are lodged will be forwarded as fast as Circumstances admit—the destruction of our Southern Army you will hear long before this comes to hand, therefore shall not enlarge—my Compliments to all the Gentlemen present

To David Mason

Sir   Septr. 6th 1780

The Honorable Board considering it my duty has imposed on me the dissagreeable task of inclosing the within resolve of Congress, excusing you from any further service at the post of springfield. their reasons for this I shall not attempt to assign, only in general terms I understand that the Services performed bear no proportion to the expence of the post upon the present footing, and that our distresses for money makes every possible retrenchmt. necessary, and that for the future, the bussiness at your post shall be carried on upon a Smaller and better adjusted plan than formerly, producing more Services from less expence—

As a final settlement of all accounts in immediately intended you will please to transmit a list of such as you stand obligated for, without you chuse to exhibit them to Colo Cheever, who in that case can forward the whole together as usual, when after inspection and finding them right, a Sum sufficient for payment will be forwarded for their discharge—

The tools & stores in the Laboratory, wrought & unwrought you will please to deliver to Captn. Bryant who I understand is to carry on the Bussiness—

Requesting you to consider the foregoing as a part of duty, and not a desire to communicate intelligence that I have reason to think will give you pain I conclude & subscribe myself—

Your very huml Servt:

Lieutenant Colonel Mason superintended the laboratory at Springfield, Massachusetts, and had been dismissed by a resolve of Congress of July 26, 1780.
On October 18, Henry Knox wrote to General Washington and stated that Mason, had been "making fuzes, a species of laboratory preparation that requires peculiar skill and nicety. In case of a siege the whole success of a bombardment must depend on the accuracy with which they are executed. His practice and perfection in this branch have produced fuzes whose exact operation cannot be surpassed by any made in Europe." Despite Knox's plea, Mason was not retained.

To Joseph Eayres

Dear Sir   Septr. 6 1780

The inclosed will inform you that the post at Springfield has been under the consideration of Congress, and Sorry I am that my situation makes it my Duty, to forward such dissagreeable intelligence to my Friend. reason dictates to me that you will want to know the reason that operated to give birth to the dissmmission couch'd under the term "excused." can only say in general, that the post is said to be too expensive, and not to answer the expectation that there are too many Officers, and too many heads, and in your particular case that such an Officer is needless, as the Captn. of each branch is Sufficient for the care and conduct of the men and the commanding Officer at the post is in future, to procure all supplies for the work. the accounts brought by Mr: Cheever for settlemt. in which yours were included, I have inspected and finding some of them so deficient as renders them inadmissable, I have returned the whole with Such remarks as I thought necessary to put all concerned right, and secure an easy liquidation. most of yours are destitute of any vouchers, except the persons names, in the face of accounts, which on no terms can be admitted as an authentick voucher for the payment of its contents. indeed the popular cry of missapplications of Cash advanced the Staff departments, has called up a spirit of examination, which will tend in the sequel to the honor of honest men, but probably prove a scourge to those that are otherwise. no person concerned can entertain the least doubt, but that you have paid the sums which you have charg'd, yet method must be attended to. you will therefore please to call on Mr. Cheever for sight of the minutes he is furnished with and in the shortest time possible comply with those respecting your account rendered and add what others yet remain open, that a general settlement may take place—

I have nothing further to add, but only that you would consider me in the foregoing as acting in my Official Character, which harrows up the friendly feelings of my heart gladly would I have been excused from this Service, but a mandate from the honble. Board of War reducing it to duty, makes it unavoidable. I shall be happy to render you any service in my power, which in case of any commands shall be manifested by your determin'd Friend & very huml Servt.—

On August 30, Congress resolved that Eayres and Captain Nathaniel Chapman "who have been employed at Springfield in the department of the Commissary General of military stores...be excused from farther service.

To Nathaniel Chapman

Dear Sir   Sept. 6 1780

At length the arrangement of the division of the Comy. Genl. M.

Stores department at Springfield is completed, and in consequence I have the dissagreeable service arising from duty to enclose the resolve of Congress respecting you the perusal of which I doubt not will much surprize and perplex you. as an alleviation to your embarrassment while casting around for the reasons, let me inform you that it is not founded on any complaint, but merely upon the score that numbers have been dismiss'd from the Line Vizt: as a supernumerary, and as such Congress have it under consideration to make up both yours and Major Eayrs depreciation to the time of dissmission, or allow both one years present pay

The department is to be carried on in future upon an entire new plan, and I am informed nothing but Captn & Foremen to the respective Companies will be admitted, and that each shall superintend forty men. Cols. Cheever & Mason being excused from further service by a subsequent resolve—A new head vested with necessary & well digested powers, and accountable immediately to the Comy Genl M Stores for his conduct is to be appointed to Superintend the whole—

The inlistments & other papers relative to the company, you will either forward here or deliver them to the person when arrived who is next to superintend the department as described above, who will probably come supplied with money to answer every demand of the present department—

I have nothing further to add but a tender of my services, whenever you may find them necessary and be disposed to command them

With esteem I am Yours &c

To William Hawes

Dear Sir   Philadelphia Sept. 6th. 1780

Your favour of the 17th Ultimo I received in answer must inform you that your fears of being Affronted arising from my silence are entirely Groundless—Business my dear sir must be my Apology—should that cease you would soon be sensible by my frequent Scriblings that my Attatchment to you remain as strong as ever—thus in Answer to yours—Shall now proceed to give you an Account of the new arrangement of the Department at Springfield as you are immediately interested in it, and must remain in doubtful (perhaps painful) suspence untill it is properly Announced, and Clearly ascertained, what part you are to Act, and on what ground your services are to be Accepted of in future

To prevent prolixity in a Letter I have enclosed a Copy of the Resolve of Congress respecting the principals of the department—and the pay to be Allowed for those retained—the Board of war are Anxious to make the Service agreeable to the Capts. Haws, Faxon, Boylston & Bolter—who it is intended shall preside at their different Branches, at thirty dollars p day, as you will see by the resolve—no Lieuts. will be admitted but a foreman is Substituted, which upon encouragement given they conclude will answer every purpose—one person acting immediately under to Com: Gen: Mily. Stores is to Superintend the whole, and will shortly be Appointed and forwarded with explicit orders and a Sufficient Sum of money to direct and enable every one to do the duty Assigned him, with that Spirit so necessary to render the public the Services which they have a right expect from every well Supported body of men acting for them

I have nothing further to add but to Assure you that I shall always feel myself happy when I have it in my power to render you Service—you will therefore I trust command my Assistance when your exertions for the public good shall render them necessary—my best regards to Capts. Bolter Faxon, Boylston and all Friends—

With regard I am sir your very hum. servant

This was addressed to "Captain Haws." In March 1778, William Hawes signed the Oath of Allegiance at Springfield, Massachusetts, as "Captain of a Company of Harness Makers."

To Ezekiel Cheever

Sir   Septr. 6 1780

I am ordered by the Honble. Board of War to furnish you with the resolves of Congress of 26th July last, in which you will perceive that honorable Body have dispenced with any further Services of yours and Colo Masons' at the post at Springfield. their motive for this you are sensible it is not my bussiness to investigate, but as far as it lies in my power it is my duty to direct and assist you, in the duty expected from you while you continue to act, which must necessarily be, untill your accounts are Settled and the Stores delivered to your

Successor—

The accounts bro't with you of the expenditure in the department, being not admissable in their present State, for reasons given you at large in the minutes annexed to them, in their return to you, will naturally command your first attention and I would recommend it to you, which they are putting right to call, for all other demands on the department during your administration or superintendence that a general Settlement may immediately commence, as the future usefulness of the department greatly depends on the present debts being discharged. this being done you will take an accurate account of the Stores on hand, which will enable you probably to account for those purchased, and facilitate the bussiness when delivery is requested. Colo. Mason if he thinks proper may exhibit any accounts for which he is obligated on behalf of the publick, to have paid to you, and deliver the Stores he has receipted for, and has on hand to Captn Bryant who is still to Superintend the Laboratory. Maj Eayrs having acted under your direction will naturally apply to you for settlement, and should Captn Chapman stand charged with any publick stores, he will settle where he receipted for them—

Thus having attended to the letter of my orders and given you Such direction as time and ability would permit, have only to request that you would consider me as acting officially and not take offence at any thing suggested in the foregoing Letter, as I declare every line was dictated by a sincere desire to render you Service, by directing your attention to the essentials necessary to convince the world that you have acted well and discharged your trust with fidelity a consolation in my opinion my valuable than the mines of Peru, and which I hope and trust you will obtain—

With respect I am Sir Your very huml Servt:

Extract From the Minutes of Congress, July 26, 1780.
In Congress July 26th 1780
Resolved that Ezekiel Cheever Esqr. & Lieut. Colo. David Mason who have been employed at Springfield in the State of Massachusetts Bay in the department of the Comy Genl M Stores be excused from further service at that post—That the Board of War & Ordnance be authorized & directed to remove any unnecessary Officer at that & any other post in the Department of the Comy. Genl. M Stores and to arrange the affairs of the whole department in such manner as they

shall deem most conducive to the publick Service, reporting their proceedings to Congress

 Extract from the minutes Geo. Bond D Secy

Extract from the Minutes of Congress, August 30, 1780.

In Congress Augt: 30th 1780
Resolved, that Major Joseph Eayrs and Captn: Nathl: Chapman, who have been employed at Springfield in the department of the Comy. Genl. M. Stores be excused from further service—
 Extract from the minutes Thomas Edison for Charles Thomson Secy

Hodgdon had the date wrong in the first extract. The resolve took place on August 30, 1780. Edison was a clerk in the office of Charles Thomson, Secretary of Congress. He resigned the post in 1781 and was captured at sea and taken to New York City. There he learned of and may have participated in a plot devised by Benedict Arnold whereby two British soldiers were to steal secret documents from the Secretary of Congress. The plot was discovered and the three were arrested in November 1781. The two soldiers were executed as spies but Edison managed to convince Congress he had joined in the plot in order to expose it. On December 5, 1781, Congress commended him for his fidelity and granted him $266.00.

To Henry Knox

Septr. 6 1780

 By Colo. Pickering I have an opportunity to inclose the account transmitted me for settlement, with Genl. Mifflin with other papers annexed, having made best Settlement in my power or indeed in his, hope it will under circumstances be satisfactory I have every reason from appearances to judge it will be final the amount you will see of the Ballance was 2890 dollars 2500 of which I received by Mr. Cheever. the Ballance you will please to forward when you can make it convenient by some safe hand. the receipt inclosed for £105 plainly appears to have been intended for that credited of £150 and by your direction, I have settled it accordingly. however you have it that if you should think otherwise, you may use as occasion may offer—
 The sword I hope to have elegantly finished in a few days. any other commands will be punctually attended, to and executed with as much accuracy and dispatch, as ability will admit—
 With due respect I am Sir Yours &c:

Timothy Pickering Jr. to Joseph Hiller

Dear Sir, Philadelphia Septr. 7th. 1780

I know not what business you are at present engaged in, whether lucrative or otherwise; on which however may depend your determination on the proposal I am now to make; because should your business be profitable, I can hardly expect that you will abandon the Advantage for a publick employment from which more than a decent maintenance is not at present to be expected—

You have known that there was a Laboratory established at Springfield under the direction of Colo. David Mason, and Mr. Ezekiel Cheever (usually I believe called Colo Cheever) was Commissary of Military Stores. besides fixing Ammunition divers branches of work were carried on, as mounting of Cannon, making of Harness, and Accoutrements for Infantry, and Repairing of Arms, there required Carpenters, Smiths, Armourers and Harness makers. The works were pretty well conducted till the close of the Year 1777, Since which the public have not reaped from the Establishment benefits proportioned to the expence of it, and for more than a Year past it has been in great disorder from its having too many heads whilst neither of them appeared adequate to the direction of the whole business. The Board of War therefore on the most Satisfactory evidence reported to Congress that Messrs. Mason and Cheever should be dismissed (or excused) from further Service. Some other dismissions have since followed and the department at present stands thus Arranged—Captain Haws director of the Harness & Accoutrement makers—Captain Bolter of the Carpenters—Captain Boylston of the Wheelwrights & Captain Barton of the Armourers— and it is expected Captain Faxon director of the Smiths may be induced to return to the post on this new Arrangement. Captain Bryant of the Artillery directs the Laboratory & a Mr. Collins is Deputy Commissary of Military Stores. From this Arrangement much good is expected, provided a Gentleman suitable qualified can be found who will take upon him the Superintendence of the whole and amongst all my Eastern Acquaintances I can think only of you. I think the nature of the Business will hit your taste. it will give scope to your Ingenuity—Employment to your Industry and abundant Occasion (which the times so distressingly demand) to evince the Integrity of your heart[.] All these excellent qualities I know you possess, and I therefore most sincerely wish the publick may benefits from them. I confess that an honest man in the public service cannot expect to make a fortune, unless he does extensive business on a handsome Commission; and few men therefore who are engaged in private business to Advantage will relinquish it for a publick employment; but from the proffs you always gave me of your virtue & patriotism no body would more willingly sacrifice their private gain to the publick good.—The depreciation of the currency has heretofore been highly injurious to publick Officers; but all pay will ere long be fixed in specie and paid in that or an equivalent in other Current money. This is already done on the department of the quarter master General. The pay of the Commissaries of military Stores is not fixed, but depends on the extent and importance of the business under their direction. The post at Springfield would demand a handsome allowance, a Commissary of Military Stores lately appointed to Superintend a Laboratory in virginia was allowed 1750 Continental dollars a Month, one ration a day, and Forage for a horse. This is moderate pay: but the Gentleman had been in the Service on much lower pay, & was Satisfied with the Addition that increased it to the sum above mentioned. Without limiting the pay beforehand, I should be happy to know whether the Appointment to be head of the department at Springfield would be Agreeable to you, and on what terms you can consent to serve the public in that station. I need not urge all the motives which should induce you to Accept the Office: Your discernment and zeal for the public welfare will suggest to your every Argument I could mention.—Should it be impossible for you to Undertake this important office, (an event I should exceedingly regret) I shall be Oblidged to you for information of a suitable Character for the place. a Letter from you will find me at the head quarters of the main Army.

 I am, dear sir with great regard & esteem your Affectionate friend & humble Servant

P.S. I forgot to mention that Mr. Saml. Hodgdon formerly your intimate Acquaintance has long been in this department, is now at the head of the business as deputy Commissary General of Military Stores, and will be made happy by your taking the direction of the post at Springfield. His experiance in the business of the whole department will enable him to give you every information you can wish for & which he will take pleasure in Communicating.—

A Joseph Hiller had a shop in Salem, Massachusetts. Hiller was apparently interested in the job, but it appears that he never took the office. In 1781 Luke Bliss was put in charge of the operation at Springfield.

Discharge Certificate for Philip Clumburg

These Certify that Mr. Philip Clumburg has Acted as Conductor of Military Stores in the Comy Genl. of Military Stores Department from the 27th day of October 1778 to this day, during which time as far as has came to my knowledge he has Supported the Character of an Active Officer and honest Man, and is now discharged at his own Request—
 Given under my hand at philada. this 7th. day of September 1780—
Whom it may Concern—

To John Bryant

Sir							Philada. Septr: 7th 1780
 I am directed by the Honble. Board of War to inform you, that in consequence of a resolve of Congress of 26 July, Colo: Mason is excused from further Service at springfield, and that they wish to retain you as director of the Laboratory at that place for which Service they mean to make your pay equal to the Capts. of the other Branches employed at that post. if the offer should meet with your acceptance, you will please to communicate it to me by the most early conveyance, and I will announce it to the Board. I must add to prevent misunderstanding, that the Laboratory and its principal is to be under the immediate direction of the principal at the post, in the Same manner as the other Branches, it being intended that like a well regulated Machine one spring shall move the whole. all applications for every species of materials must be made to him, and all Stores perfected return'd to him as he is immediately under the direction of the Comy Genl. M Stores. such orders & assistance will be forwarded from here to him from time to time, as the exigencies of the States

shall render necessary, and his orders to the Several Branches it is expected will always carry them into effect—

Should any thing operate to induce you to decline this Service, you will please to give immediate notice, that measures may be taken to further the future expectations from the post—

With esteem I am Yours &c.

Bryant had been a Lieutenant in Knox's Artillery Regiment, and had an arm accidentally shot off on July 12, 1776. He continued to serve as a Captain in the Laboratory at Springfield, Massachusetts. The name often appears as Briant.

To the Board of War and Ordnance

Gentlemen Philadelphia Septr. 8th. 1780

In consequence of yours of this day, I have examined the Contracts lately made and find 402 T. 13 H 0 qrs. 20 lb weight of Shells and 345 T 14 h 3 qrs 4 lb weight of Shott, have been Contracted for, at the several Furnaces in this State and Jersey, the amount or which in Specie or its Equivalent is £ 28250.—a third part of which being immediately paid, and an Assurance that the remainder shall be paid when the contracts are fulfilled will Satisfy the Iron Masters and ensure the Supplies.—

The Muskets on hand wants considerable repair having been often cull'd—but with a Supply of Money equal to the expence I have reason to think 5000 Stand may be compleated in three months[.] to Ascertain the cost exactly is impossible, but I immagine upon an Average it will not exceed 17/6 hard Money, for each Musket Bayonet & Scabbard; by once more taking out the best 3000 may be got ready for service in Six Weeks, in either case the necessary Sum may be computed from the above Estimate

With due Respect I am Gentlemen Yours

To John Stith

Sir Septr. 8 1780

Inclosed you have an Invoice of Stores intended for the Cavalry of the southern army which the honble. Board of War have directed me to forward to your care

I am Sir your very huml Servt.

Stith was a Captain in the Fourth Virginia Regiment.

To The Acting Quartermaster at Head of Elk

Sir   Septr 8th 1780

 By order of the Honble. Board of War I have forwarded by the bearer Mr: Nathanl. Triplet Condr. M Stores sundry boxes qt. as p Invoice, to your care to have forwarded with the Letter he has in charge to Captn Stith at Baltimore for the use of the southern Cavalry. as it is of the utmost importance to have them got on immediately, I must beg the favor of you to direct them to the care of Colo Long DQMr: at Halifax, should Captn Stith be gone from Baltimore before they arrive—

 I am yours

To the Commercial Committee of Congress

Gentn.   Septr: 9th 1780

 I have several times called at your Office to inform you, that the two quanties of powder imported in the Fame, Captn. Mc.Clenaghan, belonging to the United States have never been deliver'd at the Office of the Comy Genl. M Stores, nor put into the continental Magazine, consequently the continent have no account of them. the last quantity imported in the Governor De Graaff Capn. Lyle is Said to amount by Invoice to 5000 neet pounds, of this only 2950 have been received. I have waited on Mr. Blair McClenaghan the owner of the Vessells mentioned above. to be informed what became of the remainder. he Say's the Bill of Lading was wrong, the quantity mention'd in it having never been put on Board. that he stop'd one third part of what was ship'd, and that it is all the satisfaction I can obtain on the subject. as the whole appears to me a very extraordinary transaction, I must refer myself to your Honble. Board for light & direction. In the last instance the Captn sign'd the Bill of Lading for the quantity mark'd in the margin, and 10 p Ct: was agreed on for freight. the contents of the Bill is now called in question and one third part confessedly stopt for freight if this is to be admitted, and Settlement made accordingly, I wish to have notice, and I shall give myself no further concern—

 With due respect I am Gentn Yours &c

One of the concerns of the Commercial Committee of the Continental Congress was promoting the imports of needed goods and materials.

To Philip Van Rensselaer

Dear Sir Philadelphia Septr. 12th. 1780

This Moment I received yours of the 1st. Instant, enclosing the Return, am much obliged by your punctuality in this respect. The Brass requested or the Mounting finished shall be forwarded the first Opportunity and the remainder of your Indents shall Accompany them.—A Bill of yours for 39,000 Dollars was lately presented the Honorable Board of War, by a Mr. Judah, but sorry I am to inform you that neither the Secretary nor our Paymaster could give any Account when it would be possible to answer it, and it was Accordingly Returned, I am Afraid to the Detriment of the holder.— At present we have not a Dollar in the Office.—please to deliver the Inclosed to Captain Lamb.—

Yours—

To Charles Lukens

Sir Philadelphia Sepr. 13th 1780

In compliance with my Orders which you have inclosed, I send you a resolve of Congress excusing your from any further service at the post of Carlisle

you will please to consider me as acting officially which will free me from any imputation—as I am pained at the recollection of the disagreable sensations that may Naturally be suppos'd to arise from the perusal—

When you can make it convenient I should be glad you would attend the final adjustment of the accounts lately given in—I mean so far as the Comy General of Military stores is impowered to make it—

I am dear Sir Your Most Obdt

In Congress August 20th. 1780

Resolved
That Major Charles Lukens employed in the department of Military stores at Carlisle be excused from further service—
Extract from the Minutes
Thomas Edison for Charles Thompson [sic] Secrey

To Samuel Sarjant

Dear Sir   Philada. Septr: 13th 1780

I wrote you the other day, upon the subject of the return but thro' haste, as the person was waiting. I conclude the directions given were imperfect, however! I trust they were sufficiently clear to set you to work, as the very being or continuation of the post now depends on a conviction of its usefullness. I must beg the favor of you to make out an accurate return upon the following principles, and forward it to me immediately—

You will first insert the inlisted men, commencing the return from the 1st: Jany. 1780, and ending it the last of August following, agreeable to the inclosed. after which you will insert the hired men, determining the pay they have received within the periods mentioned, and carry out the Sum total of each drawn in a line for that purpose. you will next insert all the purchases of materials used in the above time, and in the work which the department is to be credited for. you will then insert the Number & value of the rations drawn by the whole in the time alluded to. this being done & the expence of the department fully ascertained, you will make an accurate return of every species of work performed by the men, and its present value from this you will raise and state an account current, on the last leaf of the Book you make the return in, the Balance of which will determine the propriety of keeping up the Post the importance of this Bussiness will engross your whole attention untill completed—

Captn. Jordan has had an opportunity of seeing my general return, and as I intend to forward him shortly, perhaps consulting him may set right any thing you may conceive in the foregoing not fully explained—

Pray inform me; whether the Rifles are not completed, as the application is repeated & I must Say, when they may be expected—

Colo. Flower is on his way to town, and I am informed he is on the whole better, expect him next Saturday—by a resolve of Congress of the 30th Augt: 1780, Major Lukens is excused from any further Service at Carlisle, notice of which (by inclosing the resolve) I have given him by this conveyance consequently his command is at an end this you will Signify to all concerned—

With esteem I am Yours &c

To Henry Knox

Dear General   Philada. Septr: 14th 1780

Some time since the Honble. Board of War, at the instance of the Council of this State, referred the expediency of annexing the Laboratory company late Corens to Colo. Procters Regt: to his Excellency Genl. Washington the Council promising if his approbation could be obtain'd, to consider them as part of this States quota and as Such furnish them with Such supplies as were furnished their other troops. the foundation of this application was the inadequate pay they received as soldiers, and a conviction that tho' consigned to a post, they were in Some way intitled to receive like advantages as those doing duty in the field. no annexment. in consequence of the above reference having taken place, the Men have hit upon another expedient, and have all but eight petitioned to be annexed to Colo. Flowers Regiment and enjoy like advantages as the Artificers, to be considered as Labortarians, and be subject to the Same rules & regulations as order'd for the Regt: the particular difficulties these Men have been subjected to from their not being annexed you will readily conceive. they are now almost naked and will be quite in a short time, if they continue in their unsettled State. from these considerations & the obvious ability of the measure, join'd to their own particular desire, the Board are desirous that they may be annexed to Colo Flower's Regt: and be provided for with them. but as the matter had been previously referred to his Excellency, and possibly might have been acted upon, they requested me to inform myself by writing to you, whether any thing had been done in their case. if not, the eight men will be sent to Camp, to be disposed of as you think best, and the remainder annex'd and retained agreeable to their request—

As this mode of proceeding seems well calculated to procure the Stores from this Post & do justice to the men, I hope his Excellency and yourself will recommend its being carried into execution, and that you will kindly give me the most early notice, that I may make immediate provision for the men who are actually at this moment in a Suffering condition, and know not where to apply for relief—Colo. Pickering can give you the past and present State of the company, to him therefore I beg leave to refer you, having already (I fear) trespassed on your patience—

With Sentiments of esteem I am Yours &c.

To John Jordan

Dear Sir   Septr. 15th 1780

Having procured an order on Mr. Stephen Dunkin, Treasurer at Carlisle, for the sum of twenty thousand Dollars for the use of the detachment of the Comy. Genl: M Stores Department at that post, you will please to prepare yourself to proceed with the order tomorrow morning the contents of which you will be authorized to receive and appropriate in the following manner Vizt: to pay the men belonging to the Regiment of Artillery & Artificers two months pay, and deliver the remainder to Saml: Sargent Esqr: Comy. M Stores for the purpose of discharging the most pressing demands of his Department. having compleated this Business, which must be done with all possible dispatch, you will apply to Mr Sargent for the return & estimate I wrote him for & return immediately with it. I have wrote him fully on the subject, but for fear he may not fully understand them, must subjoin that my interest is to ascertain the whole expence of the inlisted and hired men at Carlisle, the value of the materials used by them, and the number & value of the rations drawn by them from the 1st Jany 1780 to 1st Septr. following, and the total value of the work done by them in that time, that a Balle. may be drawn, from a clear stating, and the advantages or dissadvantages, arising to the publick from keeping up the post be ascertained—

With Esteem I am Sir Yours &c.

To Timothy Matlack

Sir   Septr. 16th 1780

Mr. George Hubener having delivered me a quantity of powder which he says is the remains of a large quantity contracted for by him with you for the united States, and being desirous to settle his account, I am obligded to request the favor of you to inclose me an account of the materials supplied him, and the terms on which he was to make the powder. if you have leisure for this in the course of next week, it will enable me to comply with his wishes, and be accepted as a favor conferred on—

Your very huml Servt:

Matlack was a Philadelphia merchant and state office holder. He was elected Secretary of the Supreme Executive Council of Pennsylvania in 1777 and served in that position until 1782.

To Benjamin McCowen

Sir   Septr 21st 1780

You will proceed with the teams (loaded as Pr Invoice inclosed) to Mr. Thomas Pott's forge at Coventry. their deliver the Contents, and take a receipt for delivery on the back of the invoice, which you will bring to the Comy Genl Mil stores Office, to cancel your's now lodged there—

You will go from Coventry to Warwick furnace and present the Order you have for shells which will procure them. with these you will proceed on your return to the City with all convenient speed—when arrived give Notice, and you shall have immediate direction where to unload the teams—

Yours

McCowen was titled a Wagon Conductor.

To Thomas Rutter and Thomas Potts

Sir   Philadelphia Septr 21st 1780

Please to load each of the twelve waggons under direction of the bearer Mr Benja McCowen Conductor of waggon's with Thirty ten inch shells, to be transported to this City—

This was addressed to them at Warwick Furnace, Chester County. The Rutter and Potts families were intermarried and owned numerous ironworks.

Thomas Potts, Agreement to Exchange Steel for Pig Iron

Philadelphia Sept 21st. 1780

These Certify that I have this day agreed with Saml. Hodgdon ACMS, in behalf of Benja Flower CGMS—upon the following terms to exchange any quantity of steel, made of Andover pigs—Vizt—For every seven tons of Andover pigs I engage to return one ton of good blistered steel the pigs to be delivered at the forge at Coventry, and the steel at the Cost of the said Potts at Philadelphia in witness and confirmation of the above I have sign'd
Thos: Potts

To John Jacob Faesh

Dear Sir   Philada. Septr 23d. 1780

By a brigade of Teams which leaves this for Camp this day I have an Opportunity to Forward the two Bolts of Oznabrigs promised in my last. each contains 72 Ells, or ninety English Yards, for which I gave thirty two Dollars & a half per ell, or 26 dollars per yard in Certificates.—which as things go at present, I think they will do very well—hope they will Answer your purpose and my Conduct meet with your Approbation.—

In haste have only to add that I have Ordered then to be left at Colonel Abeels, Morriss—hope they will come safe to hand—I expect a Considerable Sum of Money for the Iron Masters next week, of which shall write you fully.

To Nathaniel Triplett

Sir   Philadelphia September 24th. 1780

You will immediately repair to Camp with the Stores you have in Charge, and deliver the whole as pr Invoice to Richard Frothingham

Esqr. D.F.C.M.S. with the Army, and take his Receipt for them on the Back of the Invoice. the Box No. 2 which you have in charge Address'd to and directed for John Jacob Faish, you will leave with his Letter at Colonel Abeels D.Q. M G at Morriss—you will be very Attentive to the Stores to prevent embezzlement or Accident, to which purpose you will see the waggons properly Disposed of at Night, and if necessary the Waggoners must keep watch in Rotation—having compleated this business, you will return with dispatch to prevent unnecessary expence—

Triplett was a Conductor of Military Stores.

To the Board of Treasury

Gentm.   Septr 27th 1780

Inclosed I send you the requested attested Copy of the resolve of Congress of 29th June. Mr Thompson being unwell prevented my sending it before—

The allowances made by the Honble Board of War in consequence of the resolve, you will See by the vouchers, were conformable to the letter of the resolve, both in Sum and commencement of time—

With due respect I am Gentlemen yours

To Mr. Frothingham

Dear Sir   October 3d 1780

By Mr. Adam Willhelmn Waggon Conductor, I have sent on a Small portion of the Stores Remaining on Indent, as p Invoice which I hope will come timely to hand.—Others shall come as Opportunities present.—in the next Brigade I shall forward a large Quantity of Wadds made up fit for use from a 32 Pd. to a Swivell, the large for the Cannon in the Forts, the small for the Field, these I think must be wanting I have nothing further to add but Compliments to all Friends—

This was probably intended for Richard Frothingham.

To Mr. Hughes

Sir						Octr. 7th. 1780

In consequence of a requisition from Captn. Joy, I have forwarded 4 12 pd Shot patterns for the purpose of facilitating the completion of the Shot of that Calibre mentioned in the contract have only further to request that as the Season is fast approaching, which will render transportation difficult, you would make every possible exertion to finish, that may be forwarded to this City—

I am Sir Your Obedt:

Addressed to a Mr. Hughes in Baltimore, this was probably to either Daniel or Samuel Hughes, who had earlier held a contract with the Continental Congress for cannon manufacture, and operated Antietam Furnace and several forges.

To James Johnson and Company

Sir						Octr: 10 1780

A letter from you to Captn. Danl. Joy on the subject of contract for shot & shells has been communicated to the Honble Board of War, and they have directed me to report to its contents. In the first place am sorry to find any of the shells removed before they were proved, as this may subject you to an additional expence should they finally prove faulty. as to payment must inform you, that only one third part of the original contract can be paid at present this we have reason to expect will be ready in a few days. in the mean time it will be necessary for you to authorize some person here to receive the Sum design'd for you, as the advance Sums will only be paid in this City. the final Settlement it is probable may be ordered, when the contract is compleated, to be made by the person appointed to prove the work, and payment will commence agreeable to contract accordingly the deranged situation of out finances preven[ts] our venturing to encrease the number of shells by prolonging the time, as we are sensible payment could not be made so as to make it convenient to the Iron Masters, we would not wish to subject them to future dissappointments—

With esteem I am Sir Yours

James Johnson operated Catoctin Furnace in Maryland.

To the Board of War and Ordnance

Gentlemen   Philadelphia Octor. 19th. 1780

The Repeated interruptions the business of the Comy. Genl. of Mily. Stores Department labours under, & the Consequent loss the ensures from the partial supply of rations has determined me to propose the following plan, to less the Number in future to be drawn, which Method if you Approve the resolve of Congress of the 12th. August 1780, I concieve gives you full powers to carry into Effect.—

In the first place I would propose that no person in the Department, except those immediately belonging to the Regiment of Artillery Artificers be permitted to draw either Rations, or wood from the publick, and that the following Salaries be given in Lieu thereof.—

To a Comy. of Mily. Stores 1750 dollars pr. Month

To the Clerks employed, the Board to say the number 1500 Dollars p Month.—

To a Conductor 1000 p Month, the Board to Say the Number to be employed

I would further propose to employ none but hired men in the Armoury, that none but the best workmen be Admitted and that such when found be Allowed five shillings hard Money p diem or the Exchange, this to be Considered as full Compensation for their Services

The smiths necessary to Carry on the Business may be Obtained upon the same terms as the Armourers. the Superintendants of these Branches may be retained for Ten shillings per day or the Exchange and without an Assurance that this Sum will be paid in future for their Services, they are determined to quite immediately—

The Labourers, the Carters, the Men employed at the Lead Furnace; and the people employed making Musket Cartridges may be hire for little more than the Rations alone Cost the publick. As I have reason to think that those now at work might be engaged at thirty Dollars p day—

The File Cutters Rations may be done away, by Allowing so much more an Inch for cutting as shall be agreed on. Should you think the plan elligible after Considering, the only difficulty that I concieve stands opposite to it, Namely a fund to pay the Mens Wages as they become due, you will please to inform me that I may take Measures for carrying it into execution

Surely Gentlemen you will think with me that it is time to do something, when I inform you, that not a Man in the Department is this day at work for the Publick.—on Account of the Stoppage of the Rations, & Other grievances which they enumerate, and as I am Sensible that the Supplies for the Army which should now be prepared, will shortly be called for, I feel Distress'd for our situation, no Money, no Cloathing, nor Provisions for the Men.—what can be expected.—Yet large Quantities of Stores are daily called for, both for the Main, and southern Armies, and large Indents not Complied with Remain yet on hand.—In this situation I find myself Obliged to fly to you for Advice and Assistance.—Intreating you would take the premises into immediate Consideration that something may be done equal to the importance of the Case.

With Esteem I am Gentn. Respectfully Yours

To Ezekiell Cornell

Sir   Octr. 23d 1780

Inclosed I send an estimate of the expences of the Comy. Genl. M. Stores Department for one year; the pay is calculated at forty for one upon the Sum paid last year. the rents as they stand at present by contract, and the materials upon the prices now demanded in hard money, and the quantity estimated upon supposes a sufficiency to keep the present number of men employed the whole time. the whole I have endeavored to make as correct, as the means I had to act on wou'd permit, hope it will meet with your approbation—

With esteem I am Yours

Estimate of the Sum in Specie necessary to carry on the Bussiness of the Comy. Genl. M Stores Dept: for 12 months—

For Wages	£25867..7..6
For materials	15332..5..
For Rents	820.. ..
	£42019..12..6

To Joseph Hiller

Dear Sir   Octor. 24th. 1780

This Moment I received yours of the 11d. Instant, am happy to hear you have thought of Accepting the Appointment tendered you by Colo: Pickering.—having but an Hour for this & Several Other Disptches that goes by the same Conveyance, I am unable Accurately to point out the duties Attendant on the appointment in question.— Suffice it to say, that all the purchases necessary to keep the Men employed at the post, as well as their pay will pass through your hands; the perfecting every species of Warlike Stores and forwarding them as directed depends on you; tho' you are Apprized that there are heads to all the branches who will receive their Orders from you.— Yet like a well regulated Machine one spring must move the whole, this I am sure you are equal to, & therefore if the terms held out are no bar, must urge your Acceptance[.] the department at present is but small, yet well managed it is capable of yielding great support to the Army, while lying at or in the Vicinity of North River, as well as any detatchmts. that may be employed further East. the Laboratory is carried on by the same Men under the direction of Captain Bryant as formerly, and the Captains of every other Branch continued as Usual. Nothing is wanting but a suitable person to act as head, & pervade the whole, to make the post as useful as intended at its establishment, and nothing more than a General Knowledge of Business, founded on a good mechanical head is requisite in the person who superintends the whole. Mr. Boyer my Clerk who brings this is perfectly Acquainted with my mode of doing the Business, which to appearance has always given Satisfaction, to him I refer you for any further information—of this you may rest Assured that should you join the Department I have the honor to be in charge off, [sic] nothing shall be wanting in my part to render your services easy & Agreeable.—In the mean time with Sentiments of Affection and Esteem I subscribe myself your Frd. & very hble. Servt.

To Isaac Craig

Sir   Octr. 25th. 1780

You may remember in your distress for money in the month of April last, being then on your March to your present Station, I furnished you with one Thousand Dollars upon the express condition that you should immediately upon your Arrival forward me a Certificate of your having settled it, or your Attested Account of expences while in charge of the Stores—neither of these has as yet been done.—Consequently I stand Answerable for the Money. this I think unkind, as I told you at the time no Allowances for advance would be Admitted upon Settlement of my Accounts:—I have not enclosed a form of expence Accots. as they are pass'd here, and request you would Oblige me as far as you have yours made out in like form (if not already Settled in which case the Certificate will Answer) & transmit to me, and if any balance appears I will pay it to your Order.—

I am Yours

Craig was a Captain in the Fourth Artillery Regiment.

To James Boyer

Sir   Octr. 25th. 1780

You will immediately set out on the business you are appointed to transact in behalf of the United States; and Observe the following directions in their Accomplishment.—Vizt. You will call on Mr. John Jacob Faesh at Mount Hope,—and deliver him the Letter you have in charge, and Obtain from him an Accurate Return of Shot and Shells cast by him in Consequence of his last contract—you will them proceed and deliver the Letters you have for Genl Knox & Colol Pickering, they will probably be found at or near Totawa, the present head Quarters of the Army—There you will receive such Orders as are Necessary to put a Stop to the prosecution of the Contracts entered into with the Several Furnaces in the State of Massachusetts, with these you will without a Moments loss of time go on & execute— Should any of them be in blast in Consequence of the Contract you will by virtue of the documents with which you are furnished, put a Stop to their going on, and forward accurate Returns of the Number & weight of each sort cast which you concieve likely to stand proof:— that as far as they have proceeded, they may recieve compensation agreeable to the Contracts.—

Having finished this business you have leave of Absence for a Reasonable time to Visit your Friends in Boston, perhaps six Weeks may be found sufficient for every purpose mentioned in these Instructions.—On your return you will call on Colol. Cheever at Springfield, and bring on all his Accounts for expenditures while Acting at that post, and exact returns of the Stores on hand, the Materials at the Works, and the pay due, both in and out of the Department at that post up to the first of Novemr. for this purpose you will call on him upon your Journey down and give him Notice of the time of your expected Return, that he may be ready and prevent loss of time.—you will as Opportunity offers acquaint me with your proceedings, that if Necessary you may receive further Instructions.— all other matters not particularly mentioned; which may have a tendency to forward the general intention of this Journey, or be useful to the Department and thereby Subserve the publick Interest is Submitted to your own Judgement.—upon the best advice you can Obtain:—I Sincerely wish you a prosperous Journey and an Agreeable sight of your Friends, and a safe return at the period fixed:—

To the Board of War and Ordnance

Gentlemen   October 26th. 1780

Being taken at unawares yesterday, I did no recollect myself sufficiently to Obviate the Objection raised by Colo. Grayson on the Carlisle Estimate, which I find by looking over the papers, might easily have been done. I therefore in Addition to what I Offered yesterday, request the Board would attend to the following particulars. Vizt.—It was my first Idea when the returns were called for, of the expences of the Department,—to charge the publick with the work done in the Several Branches including the materials used, & Accordingly wrote to Mr Sargent to make it out from Carlisle in that way. in Consequence of which the whole Materials used a[re] Credited to the publick,—and the work performed including the Materials charged against it.—by some mistake the labour of the Carpenters without including the Stock made use of were inserted in the Return—Consequently to do them Justice, the Materials they made use of is added as appears in the Account current, and as all the Stock is valued at Sixty prices [*sic*] upon their former values in 1776 upon the spot, I conceive the Transportation is thereby included: and therefore not to be charged, which if Admitted destroys that Objection

and leaves nothing to be Accounted for, but the wood & Rent of the Publick Buildings, which you have inclosed, & if you will please to let me have the Estimate a few minute[s] shall be inserted, that an impartial state of that Division of the Department during the period in question may appear—
Yours with due Respect

To Samuel Sarjant

Sir   October 27th. 1780

By Captn. Jordan you will receive an Order on Mr. Stephen Duncan for Twenty Thousand Dollars state Money, and a further Sum of Twelve Thousand in the same Currency—by his own hand—This you will Appropriate to the payment of the longest standing Debts, and you will please to pay particular Attention to such Accounts (if any there be) that have Certificates on them—Altho' the delivery of the Articles has never been made, these Ought not to be paid as a Scene on Iniquity would be opened by Embezzlement and peculation, incompatible with the public Interest, nor will the Vouchers for such payment be admitted[.]

I expect to have an Opportunity shortly to forward some Crucibles, and a further supply of Steel, which I think is the Only Articles mentioned in your Letters to be wanting at your post,—You will please to forward on the repaired Muskets of every kind as fast as possible, as there is at present a pressing demand for them.—the Saws I wrote for have never come to hand, tho' there has been Waggons frequently Arrived since, please to inform me the reason.—& I should be greatly Obliged, if you would always reply to all parts of my Letters, as I am left in the dark often for want of knowing what I may expect, after I have made requisitions for stores and information—and Obliged to purchase articles of which the returns says we have plenty.—

Colonel Flower remains much as usual latterly—his & Lady's Compliments attend you, and Daughters.—Nothing particularly new.—

With Esteem I am Sir Your most Obedt.

The fate of your post is not yet finally determined but believe you have nothing to Apprehend from the late Enquiry—Should any thing Material respecting the post turn up I shall give you the most early information

To Benjamin Hoey

Sir   October 27th. 1780

Your conduct as Represented to me is very extraordinary—What do you mean by saying you have nothing to do with the Company immediately under your Command, to whom have you signified this; if you think to build your importance upon such conduct you are mistaken.—your refusing to do your duty by Attending to the supplies of the Turner shall be immediately enquired into, and you dealt with Accordingly—
Yours—

To the Board of War and Ordnance

Gentlemen   Novr. 1st. 1780

Agreeable to your direction I have made a Stating of the Account between the United states & Mr. Thos. Dickinson in which as the Board disavow any order for the making the Contract, I have proceeded by charging the Supplies, at the price paid for the same kind here, at the time they were delivered and have allowed the expences as charged in Mr. Dickinson's Account, and Added the Interest at 6 p Cent upon the whole Sum—the Credit is made upon the same principle.—by which it appears a Balance of £8066..12..9 is Due to Mr. Dickinson but as this stating is unsatisfactory to the Bearer Mr. Stevens Attorney for Mr. Dickinson, by reason of the depreciation not being Allowed, and I concieving it not just under the Circumstances of the Account, nor your expectation that it should be—have been Obliged to refer him with the accot. to your Honble. Board for your Sentiments upon the Subjt.
With due respect I am Gentn. Yours

Statement Concerning James Meck

Novr. 2nd. 1780

The Bearer James Meck having Represented that he has an Opportunity, and is desirous to go the Sea for the recovery of the use of his Limbs.—These are to Certify that he has full liberty to make Trial of the efficacy of a Voyage for the purposed mentioned.—and is recommended as an Object to the well disposed to favor, as his case requires, having behaved well as a Soldier.—

To the Board of Treasury

Gentleman Novr. 4th. 1780

In Behalf of Colo: Benjamin Flower, Comy. Genl. Stores I have to request your honble. Board to grant a Warrant on either of the States of Connecticut or Massachusetts—for the Sum of four Hundred and Eighty pounds, Six Shillings & three pence in Specie or the New Bills of Credit lately emitted—for the special purpose of paying a Balance equal to the above sum which upon liquidation of an Account between the United States & Thomas Dickinson, Appears to be due to the latter.

With due respect I am Gentn Yours

To Samuel Sarjant

Dear Sir November 6th. 1780

By the return of Mr. Hall I have an Opportunity to inform you that since recieving the Order from the Board for raising the pay of the Commissaries & Conductors as express'd in my last, I have waited on the Board and Obtained liberty for a Retrospect to the 12th. August last—instead of 27th: October—you will govern yourself in this respect Accordingly—and settle their Accounts upon the Old Establishment up to the 12 August, and commence the new pay from that time—

The Business Mr. Hall came upon was very irregular and would in my Opinion have proved very detrimental to your post, for which reason by my Advice the Letter on the Subject to the Board was not Delivered; the contents being told me by Mr. Hall, I found two parts out of three had been complied with before he Arrived—and the third was then under consideration having been previously preferred by the proper branch, these reasons on my part I hope will be satisfactory for my Advice.—Mr. Hall having come on this particular business, you will of course pay his reasonable expences.—

I am with esteem Your Frd.

Benjamin Flower to John Jordan

Sir   November 13th. 1780

I have recieved yours of the 6th. by Mr. Duffield—inclosing the return of Cloathing recieved of Mr. Sargant Agreeable to the Orders of the honble. Board of War, and Observe you request directions for the distribution of it.

The Shoes & Stockings you will deliver to the Solders where due. the Coating Baize & Shirts may be equally Divided between the Officers of the Regt. at Washington & Philadelphia—in the following Proportions—to Capts. Wylie, Jordan, Gibson & Lieut. Norris—one half of the Coating, Baize & Shirts—the Other half to be sent to me by the first safe Opportunity to be equally divided between the Officers here. Vizt. Lieuts. Dow, Stroop & Hoey—the other Share which I have a right to I intend to let Serjt. Roads of your Company have—as he is a deserving good fellow, and has long done the duty of a Commissioned Officer—and as this will take off any heart burnings there might be with Mr. Power or the Doctor who are not included in the Division, because there is not enough for us all, and they have too much generosity to desire that any of those Gentlemen who are to have it should be deprived of a Coat or a Short by their taking it, having both of them such Advantages from their professions & Business which the Others have not—many other reasons might be given why they should not be included—but this may suffice for the Present—as for Mr. Sprouls he is not an Officer of the Regt. and ought to have been dismiss'd from the works long ago—I am much mistaken if he was not dismiss'd by order of the Board of War last Winter, from a Representation that he was a Useless Officers and only having a Warrant for his Appointment—if he has obtained a Commission since it is more than I know, and as I have not the power to dismiss a Commissioned Officer please to inform Capt Wylie that his dismission much come in that case from the Board of War after full representation of Mr Sprouls conduct and unfitness for that Office which must come through the proper Channel. first from Captn. Wylie to Mr Sargant and from Mr Sargent to me, than [sic] the proper Steps will be taken—Mr. Sargant as Comy. &c. is Accountable for all deficiencies of that department—Let the Value of the Cloathing be fairly and justly Ascertained agreeable to the Resolve of the honble. Congress in that case provided—then as Congress have Allowed no depreciation beyond forty to one in Continental Money, that will be the price to be paid by each Officer on delivery of the Cloathing—Send the price fix'd with the share for the Officers here, and I will be Accountable for the Payment of the money if it is delivered to them before you come down again.—Captain Wylie must excuse my writing to him by this Opportunity, and Mr Sargant will find there are Orders for Stores neglected, if he will look over Mr Hodgdons Letters—A hint I hope will be Sufficient—

I am Yours &c

To the Board of War and Ordnance

Gentlemen November 27th 1780

The reasons that Operated at the time the Air Furnace in this City was taken possession of, being in a great Measure done away, and finding it impossible to procure the Necessary Supplies of Wood to keep the Men Employed—I am induced to think that it will be most for the publick interest immediately to dismiss the Men and deliver up the Furnace to the Owners, and thereby terminate the expence—

The Board will please to favour me with their sentiments on the Subject—Inclosed you have an Account of the Castings since the Furnace has been Occupied by the publick.—

With due respect I am Gentlemen Yours

To the Board of War and Ordnance

Gentlemen December 2nd 1780

Agreeable to your direction I have made & now present an Estimate of the quantity and Value of the Articles necessary for the ensuing Campaign—You will observe none but the most Capital Articles are Mentioned, a Multitude of Smaller will be wanting to

Compleat the Supplies.—but their value will be comparatively small and will be occasionally estimated with the Incidental expences of the dept.

If your Honble. Board should approve the estimate as it stands you will please to give me such directions as are necessary to effects its purposes.—if any Objections should arise, I should be much Obliged by early communication and shall use my best endeavours to rectify and Amend any part that may be Amiss that when made Agreeable, the proposed business may be speedily executed.—

With due Respect I am Gentlemen Your very hble servt.

Estimate of the Quantity and Value of the Articles to be purchased by Contract—and Materials necessary to employ the Men belonging to the Regt. of Artillery Artificers, for procuring Supplies for the Armies of the United States the ensuing Campaign—

10,000 Muskets Repaired	@ 30/	£15000
20,000 New Constructed Cartouch Boxes	@ 20/	20000
500 New Drums, Sticks & Carriages	@ 70/	1750
500 Swords for Light Dragoons	@ 70/	1750
500 Pairs of Pistols for Do.	@ 130/	3250
500 Caps for Do.	@ 60/	1500
1,000 Fifes & Cases	@ 5/	250
500,000 Flints	@ 60/p m.	1500
		£45,000

The above to be procured on Contract
　For the Use of the Regt. of Artificers.

10,000 Feet of Oak Plank	@ 150/	£75
3,000 do. of do. Scantling	@ 150/	22..10
25,000 of Pine Boards	@ 150/	187..10
5,000 of Cedar do.	@ 150/	37..10
80 Cords of Oak Timber Standing	@ 22/6	90
300 Axeltrees	@ 5	75
		£45487..10

(Second Page of the Estimate)
Estimate Continued

Amount brought Over		£45487..10
600 Naves	@ 4/	120
3000 Fellies	@ 3/	450
6000 Spokes	@ 16	150
30 Tons of Bar Iron	@ £40 p Ton	1200

3 Tons of Plated do.	@ £75 p do.	225
5 Tons of Nail rod do.	@ £75 p do.	375
500 lbs Weight of German Steel	@ £18..15 p do.	93..15
3000 Bushels of Charcoal	@ 1/	150
1000 Sides of Harness Leather	@ 30/	1500
500 do. of thin do.	@ 17/6	437..10
100 pounds of Harness thread	@ 7/6	37..10
200 do. of Rosin	@ /6	5
		£50231..5

For the use of the Laboratory—		
600 Reams Musket Cartridge Paper	@ 15/	450
250 do. Cannon do. do.	@ 25/	312..10
20 do. Portfire do.	@ 30/	30
50 pounds twine	@ 7/ lb	18..15
100 do. Cartridge thread	@ 7/6	37..10
5 Boxes tin plates	@ £30	150
		£51230

Discharge Certificate for John Adams

These Certify that the Bearer John Adams late a Solder in Capt Dowes Company, Colo. Flowers Regt. of Artillery & Artificers having faithfully served the full time for which he engaged—is Discharged from said Regt. & recommended to the Notice and employ of all Friends to their County, who may have Occasion for such Services as he is able to perform.—

Given under my hand at Phil 3d December 1780
Whom it may Concern—

To Ezekiel Cheever

Dear Sir   December 4th. 1780

The Moment I recd. Yours of the 17th. Ultimo informing of the Detection of Mr Collins.—the Board had recd. Yours to them, informing the same matter by the last post, & had Communicated its Contents to me[.] Never was I more Surprised: what could induce a Young Man possest of such talents as would insured him a handsome living to be guilty of such a mean peculation, I am at a loss to determine—from my Soul I pity the family which he had previously got Connected with—all the fine feelings are on the rack, while I attempt to reflect on their Unhappy situation—the part however which you have Acted was evidently your duty, and possibly may be productive of bringing to light peculations of an earlier date—on this Account as well as others that have been already enumerated, I wish you to proceed in taking an Account of the Stores—this Instance points out the necessity of its being Compleated immediately.—As to Supplies proper for the Department, must inform you the Honble. Board of War have them now under Consideration, the result will soon be known—by the next post I expect you will receive clear & full instructions relative to the post and all Concerned—

With sentiments of Esteem I am Sir—Your very humble Servt.

To W. Nancarrow

Sir Decr. 5th. 1780

The Bearer of this will Deliver you the Key of the Air Furnace, Consequently the Rent ceases.—as soon as the Gentn. Appointed determines what sum is proper to be Allowed for Rent I shall use my best endeavours to have it paid immediately.

I am Sir Yours

To Charles Hall

Sir December 6th. 1780

Mr. Ingles having resigned his imployment in the Comy. Genl. of Military Stores Department—I am under the Necessity to make a temperary Appointment, to prevent loss or damage of the Stores lately under his charge at Lancaster.—he has Mentioned you as a suitable person for the purpose, in Consequence of which if it is agreeable to you to take charge of the Stores, I shall in behalf of the publick make you such compensation as the business you may be called to transact, may deem just—if you Accept he will now deliver you the Stores, and bring me a Copy of the delivery, you will also forward me a Copy of the Articles and the quantity of each that you receipt for.—if it does not suite you to undertake you will please to inform me, by the return

of Mr. Ingles and I will forward a Conductor from this place for the purpose of taking immediate charge of the stores—
 Yours

Letters written in 1781 show that Hall accepted the charge of looking after the military stores in Lancaster, Pennsylvania.

To Mark Thompson

Sir   Decr. 6. 1780
I have wrote you several times requesting to be informed, what is the reason, that none of the Iron made by you on Contract with the United States has been forwarded, but no reply has been obtained; I once more write upon the same Subject, as the Iron is greatly wanted & Should have been delivered long ago; I have been informed, you have been in Philada. but took no notice of the request of the person who made the Contract, to call at the Comy. Genl. Mily. Stores Office to settle the matter; as an Act of duty I make this Application, shall be happy if it proves effectual. if it does not, I shall lay the whole affair before the Honble. Board of War, for their direction from whom it is probably such Orders will issue, as will convince all Concerned, that Justice is due to the publick as well as Individuals.—
 Yours—

To Henry Stroop

Sir   Decr. 8. 1780
   In consequence of Orders from the Honble. Board of War, I am to inform you that the Detachment of men Under your Command, is to be held in readiness to March for Carlisle at a moments Warning. You will therefore immediately Box up all the Tools belonging to the public under you care, and Number them in Order, taking an exact Accot. of the Contents of each—a Copy of which is to be sent to this Office and another to Carlisle—you will make a Return of such Men as wish to take their Wives with them—Noting the time such have to Continue in the service—you will also inform me upon Receiving this what time on Monday the Tools will be ready for Transportation as

the Teams are waiting to receive them
    Yours—

Stroop was a Lieutenant in the Artillery Artificer Regiment. This was marked as a circular, meaning it was sent to other officers commanding detachments.

To Ezekiel Cheever

Dear Sir   December 9th. 1780
    I received yours of the 28th. Ultimo wherein you request to be informed how to proceed with Collins: Who it seems is Apprehended and confined, the only regular Method of bringing him to speedy Justice, I think is by calling on the Authority of Massachusetts, to Aid you in a process at Civil Law; the fact for which he is confined being Confess'd secures the States from any Costs, and express resolves of Congress determines his punishment—you will therefore retain Council for the States, and prosecute to final issue by his Advice
    Having wrote upon the business of the department by the Post, and nothing particular having since Occur'd, it is needless at this time to repeat what was then Offered—the moment that any thing of importance to the post at Springfield transpires, you may depend I shall communicate it, and as it is intended by Congress to support and keep up the post, I have no doubt but that they will make provision for the immediate discharge of the debt Already Contracted—
    With Sentiments of Esteem I am Sir Yours

To Jonathan Gostelowe

Sir   Decemr. 11th. 1780
    The Honble. Board of War having directed me to collect all the Military Stores in the City, in as Narrow a compass as possible & immediately give up all buildings not absolutely necessary for their preservation,—and having further informed me that all Issues in future is to be made under my immediate Inspection, I have to request, that you in company with my Clerk Mr. Knox, would immediately by Actual Survey, take an Account of every Article belonging to the public under your direction, that I may after receiving it, determine with Certainly the Number and Situation of

Stores proper to be retains, to enable me to comply with the Boards Direction—

I am Sir Your Humbl Servant

To the Board of War and Ordnance

Gentlemen Decemr. 11th. 1780

Mr. James Byers calls on me by your Orders, for payment of the Yearly Sum Allowed him by Congress, as Superintendant of the Cannon Foundery.—the Sum of which is Eight hundred Dollars, on which he expects the depreciation agreeable to resolve of Congress expressed in the Table published by their Order. but as that was not attended to in his last Settlement, & only the Nominal sum paid—and as Mr. Byers has received considerable sums for Services performed during the period in question, the particulars of which you will see by the inclosed—

I wish the Board to give me their Sentiments on the propriety of Liquidating the Account in the manner Mr. Byers expects—for Notwithstanding I am clearly of Opinion that it is just, & the Original intention of the Board that he should realize, at all times the Sum granted, in addition to what might be paid him for other services.— yet I conceive noting Short of an Order from the Board will justify my Settling the present, and future Accounts upon the principle requested—

I am Gentn Yours

To Samuel Sarjant

Sir Decr. 12 1780

Yours of the 5th. Ultimo I have received; you begin with saying you were "Sorry I sent no Cash" surely twelve thousand Dollars is some Money, if an Order for twenty thousand on the Treasury cannot be estimated as such, as that as it may, that and the Money forwarded to pay the Regt. was two thirds of what we had on hand, and was Judged Sufficient for a temporary relief; as to the matter of Certificates it appears from what you say, that you have entirely misconceived my meaning. is it possible after Reading the paragraph in my former Letter which stands thus. "You will please to pay particular attention to such Accounts (if any there be) that have Certificates on them, altho' the delivery of the Articles have never been made" I say is it possible you should conclude, I meant to have the Accounts paid without being Certified, would it not have Appeared much more natural especially after reading the reason that was annexed, which was to prevent fraudulent practices, should any have been intended, to have concluded agreeable to express declaration, that such Accounts as were properly Certified, and the Articles charged received should have been first Paid. Indeed I know not with what propriety Accounts can be paid, untill the Articles charged in them, are regularly recd., and creditted to the public upon your Books, from thence they Issue (or should) to the Regt. or other workmen, and each branch stands accountable to you; and you to the publick.—for all articles paid for. I thought best to be thus explicit on the Subject, as the Honble. Board of Treasury have declared no expenditures of Cash shall be admitted, without a clear Account of what is become of the Articles purchased Accompanies them, 'tis therefore of importance to all concerned to have the matter explained & rightly Understood—

Inclosed I send a Resolve of Congress for removing the Men of the Regt. at this post to Carlisle—and an invoice of Tools and Articles forwarded in consequence.—the Men are under Marching Orders and will come on soon, so that the Saws formerly sent for need not now be sent,—As to the pay of the department, it is once more under the Consideration of Congress—the result shall be Communicated as soon as Officially known untill, which time all matters at your post must be continued as usual.—

In your next you will inform me what more tools will be Necessary to forward on first to get the men to work, likewise the prospect you have of obtaining Coals from Wyoming, and what Quantity of Steel will be wanted at your post during the Winter Season, & any other matters necessary to facilitate the business of the public at the Post—

Colonel Flower remains very unwell—his and Ladies Compliments attends this.—

I am Sir Your very humble Servt.

Benjamin Flower to John Hall

Dear Sir   Phila. 20th. Decr. 1780

    Yours by doctor McKroskey I received & indeed it gives me pain to know that you are not provided for equal to your merits & lament that it is not in my Power to comply with your request, relative to a Coat. the stuff you mention'd is already appropriated & I expect Capt. Jordan has comply'd with his instructions concerning it, but you are no ways connected with the Regt. of Artillery & Artificers consequently cannot be interested in its Fate whether the state adopt them or not, but you are undoubtedly entitled to a Compensation for your Services—and this you will certainly receive. there is a report now pending before Congress in which all Superintendants of Armour's, Smiths &ca is amply provided for, and you will be consider'd in that Line.

    You will soon have an additional to your Armourers—which will call for great Exertions—consequently great Pay—& you may rest assured the latter will be govern'd by the former.

    The Zeal & Integrity, you have shewn during a four years service in my departt., intitles you to every acknowledgement on my part, and a generous reward from the Public & you will always have the pleasing consolation of honestly aim'd at doing your duty, even if that compensation should not be made to you, as fully as you have a right to expect.

    I am with great regard your Friend & Humb Servt

Hall supervised the armourers at Carlisle, Pennsylvania.

Benjamin Flower to Samuel Sarjant

Sir,   Phila. 20th. Decr. 1780

    More than a year has now elaps'd since the Honble. Board of War ordered the Grinding Mill to be built on my Land & agreed to pay me the full Value for the use thereof—but as no agreement as to the Price was determin'd and as it is necessary that it shou'd now be fix'd, to prevent any disputes hereafter therefore in order to make as free from exceptions as possible you will please to get two of the disinterested and Honest men in the vicinity of Carlisle in behalf of the Public, with Capt. T. Gibson as Mine will determine what the usual rent shall be for the use of my Water—the Mill seat and other privaledges they will make use of for the benefit of the public

For my Own part I have thought that a sum not less than One Hundred pounds in specie or other current Money equivalent would be a moderate rent Per year, considering the value of the mill rent, the prejudice it must be to my Interest in the saw-mill and other improvements & that my Water may be suppos'd to be as valuable (when apply'd to public use) as Mrs. Calenders or the Patriotic Genl. Armstrongs about the utility of which waters, the latter has wrote & said so much—and as eaqual privaledge with those I have agreed to give—could not have been obtain'd of either of those People for treble the sum I ask, if it is worth more I expect to have it. as I am not a Judge of those matters & trust of their doing me impartial justice— your getting this matter done as soon as possible—and Sending the certificate of such valuation by the first oppertunity will particularly Oblidge—

Your Friend & Humble Servt.

Benjamin Flower to Samuel Sarjant

Dear Sir   Philada. 20th. Decr. 1780

I have just received your's of the 16th. with the returns for Novr. & bill for Iron by Mr. McKroskey. in future as (before requested) you will please to direct all your applications for supplies and letters in the business of your department to Major Saml. Hodgdon as far as related to the line of his duty, as he does at present superintend all those things—

I am very anxious to write you a long letter—but from my extream weak body am afraid I shall not be able to accomplish it, but as I feel much better this morning than I have been some time past will make an attempt, whether I can finish it now or not.

You say the reports tell you that all the workmen are to be removed from washington to Philadelphia. it is true there was such a motion, and I expected it would have been carried into effect. but by a strange reverse of things, it have been determin[ed] the reverse, for all the Artificers at present employed at Pennsylva. are to be removed to, and for the future to be employ'd at washington. the purchasing Comy of Provisions is order'd to lay in a Magazine of Provisions for their Support, and Genl Washington is to be requested to send on a field

Officer of Artillery to Superintend & command the whole department—Major Hodgdon has I expect enclos'd you a copy of this resolve of Congress, and inform'd you particularly of all these matters, & what is expected of you in future which I suppose you have receiv'd before this time, with the Tools &c. sent you from here last Saturday. The Men are under marching orders; and only wait to hear that a sufficiency of Provisions is laid in for them—they have had none here for near two Months, have been permitted to work for themselves on Accot about the Streets—no Pay—no Cloathes—no Provisions—no Work! alas I fear for the supplies. My whole department has had a Political purge administer'd unto it—the Physicians have wisely given the Potion without consulting the Patients, or attending to the Real cause of the disease, and I am afraid its effects will bring on a dangerous Lax, if not a total suspension of its Powers; unless timely prevented by a judicious application of remedies, which a little time will determine.

You say Genl. Irvin has inform'd you that a probability of my Regt. being taken in by the assembly as a part of the States Quota's of Troops, to be provided for accordingly. it is true I have again made application for that purpose & they are requir'd by Congress to raise a regt. of Artificers as a part of their Quota's, but the information given to the Assembly by Govr. Reed in his report relative to the Public works &c. at Carlilse, he gave them such a character as that if they had been dispos'd before to do the Artificers justice as totally (for the present at least) abolish'd every prospect. he said among other things th[at] when he visited the works all the people were Idle, no work going on nor any appearance of any having been done for some time. that there appeared to be as many Women & Children as men. that the Carriages for the 18 Pdrs were so badly made, that he was sure once firi[ng] from them would shake them to pieces, that he could put his hand in the Joints & Cracks—and that the Iron Work was most infamously done, so rough that it did not appear to have a file on any part of it, and many other matters as much to the disadvantage of the Works & your post in General. Indeed I have been inform'd that the Carriages that have arriv'd here are not fit for any service—that the Iron is very badly done, and that they must be laid up as good for nothing. with respect to the Joints & Cracks, they may be owing to the greeness of the wood, or stuff they were made of—but certainly no excuse can be given or admitted for the badness of the Iron Work. I am sorry for Capt. Wiley's reputation, which is this instance has suffered not a little great things is expected of you in future, and it is suppos'd that you are to be responsible for every thing that relates to those Works till another Officer shall be appointed to take the Charge off of you[.] but I doubt much Such an Officer being found that will be willing to go there for some time to come, altho you & Capt. Wileys last letter to Major Hodgdon would justify almost any change in the order of things, that could promise a better management. together with Capt Wileys letter of Complaint to the Bd. of War relative to his letters being suppres[sed] wherein he had inform'd them of the distress and confusion of the department. Your letter from the nature of the service you have pointed for your Clerks, Conductors Mr Glen &c—plainly leaves you nothing to do. all these things have a Weight to produce a belief that things are not Conducted as they ought to be, and to confirm the reports that have been made against the works that they are a public Nuisance &c.

You have not said one syllable about the grinding Mill or what are the prospect of its usefulness. Pray sir attend to these things, or I am afraid you will be censured

But I must conclude praying that you will take these things are friendly Hints, and believe me as ever your friend & Servt.

To John Laurens

Dear Sir   Decr. 20th. 1780

Two hundred of the Cartouch Boxes are now in the store & the others will be brought in to Morrow. I need not inform you that payment was to commence upon the delivery, nor do the Men fail to remind me of it—you will please to call at the Store—View the Boxes—and let me know where I am to obtain the Money to comply with my engagemt.

With sentiments of Esteem I am yours

Lieutenant Colonel Laurens of South Carolina was a long time advocate of arming slaves to fight for the United States. On December 9, 1780, Congress authorized a corps of 1,000 "Black Soldiers" in the South. But on December 11, Congress appointed Laurens "envoy extraordinary" to the Court of Versailles to obtain an increase in aid from the French. Laurens took the appointment and successfully gained crucial support for the year 1781, and the black troops were never recruited.

To the Board of War and Ordnance

Gentlemen   Decr. 21st. 1780

Agreeable to your directions I have forwarded the Tools of the Artillery Artificers to Carlisle—& have paid the Men up to the first Instant.—they are now ready to proceed themselves to that post.—as it will be Necessary the Quarter Master should have notice to prepare Suitable Transportation—I thought it Necessary to inform the Board the above particulars to enable them to give such further direction as they may think proper—and as they are now entirely Idle & dispersed through the City, I Concluded the sooner they were removed the Better.—

With due Respect, I am yours—

To John Laurens

Sir   Decr. 21. 1780

In consequence of the Order from the Honble. Board of War requesting me to furnish you with four hundred New Constructed Cartouch Boxes for the use of the State of South Carolina, you furnishing the Money—Necessary for the Supply.—and your own Application requesting they might be ready in ten days, at which time payment should be made—I have procured the Boxes, and they are now ready to be delivered to you, or your order for the purpose above mentioned—to comply with my engagement with the Workmen, which was to pay them twenty shillings for each Box if paid for in specie—or twenty five shillings or the exchange if paid for in Continental Money—I must beg the favor of you to furnish me immediately with four hundred pounds Pennsylvania Currency in specie, or thirty seven thousand five hundred pounds in the same Currency as an equivalent to save my Reputation which is suspended on the punctual performance of the engagement made at your particular request—founded on a declaration that payment should be made at the delivery of the Boxes.—

With Esteem I am Sir your very hbl. Servt.

NB. the 400 Muskets are also ready & wait your Order—

To Henry Stroop and Alexander Dow

Sirs   Phila. 22nd. Decr. 1780

You will have the Men of Colo. Flowers Regt. under your command ready to March to Carlisle next Monday 10 oClock in the Morning, at which time waggons will be ready to go off with the reminder of the Tools and such Small Articles of Baggage as will be allowed—You will make out a provision Return for the number to go with you, for seven days which will take them to Lancaster where they will draw—

I am Sir your Humble Servt.

_{Stroop was a Lieutenant in the Artillery Artificer Regiment.}

To John Hall

Dear Sir   Philada. 23rd. Decr. 1780

Your favor of the 14th Inst. by docr. McKrosk[ey] came safe to hand—and sorry you are so much distress'd for money and Cloathing which is at present out of my power to supply you with, hope shortly to forward a Sum sufficient to relieve the post in General—have been oblidg'd to make every possible exertion to obtain Money to pay the Men order'd to Carlisle which is now done, and they will be on their Way next week—as to the Cloathing as it was a Regimental affair I did not Interest myself in the matter—the Colo. made such distribution as he thought best and I hope it is agreeable to all concern'd however you may depend I shall take every opportunity to convince you that I am your friend, am sorry you suffer'd any illconveinance [sic] from my advice, when last down, but am perfectly indifferent about the opinion of those on my own account who took the Liberty to censure it, witht. fear, favor or Affection I ever did, and forever will, give my advice on any matter's relative to the department In great haste I conclude & subscribe myself

Your determin'd Friend

To Nathaniel Irish

Dear Sir,   Philada. 23rd. decr. 1780

    Your favor of the 13th. Inst. per Express came safe to hand was happy to hear "all was well with you."—hope by the next to be inform'd, you have receiv'd, the whole of the warrant, and that the business at your post, bids fair to answer to salutary purposes intended at its establishmen[t.] our embarassment for want of Money makes me at time[s] shudder, for the expected supplies—hope however is my support. you will See by the enclos'd resolve of Congress some new regulations are taking place in the department their Effects time must discover.

    I received a Letter from Lt. Greer a few days since dated at Carlisle, but had no opportunity to reply to its contents. suppose he may have join'd you before it comes to hand, and hope he got his business finish'd [ ] his mind, if not I will do all in my power to effect it. as to supplies during the Winter season it will be impossible to send them from here, besides if we could, the expence would be enormous. you will therefore see the Necessity of Procuring such as you find will be first wanted, either from the States Contageous [*sic*] or by purchase in the Vicinity of your Post, as it appears highly probable great demands will be made on you for which purpose when you have received & expended the Warrant you were furnish'd with, you will make out an estimate of the further Sums requisite to Carry on the Business, and enclose it with an Account of the Expenditures that were made with the last—and continue to do so by this means settlement can any time be made, & with confidence I can apply for Warrants for the Support of your Post.

    Your Family were all Well a few days since, your Sister was here & desires a kind remembrance nothing particularly new. My Compliments to all Friends with Sentiments of esteem

    I am sir your very Humble servt.

Benjamin Flower, Discharge Certificate for John Willson

These Certify that the Bearer John Willson Soldier in my Regt. of Artillery & Artificers, having a Wife & four Children, and the time for which he Enlisted expiring on the third day of April next—falls under the description of those which the Honble. Board of War have directed me to discharge—& he is discharged accordingly.

Given under my hand in Philadelphia Decr. 26th 1780—
Whom it may concern—

To Alexander Dow

Sir   Philada: Decr: 27th 1780

You will immediately proceed with the Men under your command to Carlisle by the following rout and observe the following directions Vizt: the Men being paraded you will call the Roll to See & know who are present. these you will move off with & the Waggons that carries their Baggage & proceed with them by the most direct & convenient road to Lancaster when there arrived, you will halt the Men and make a Return for such further supplies of food & forage as will take you on to the next Magazine. you will be very carefull to keep the Men from plundering or ill treating the Inhabitants on the Way; when arrived at Carlisle you will again call the Roll & know who (if any) are missing and make a return thereof to the commanding Officer of the Post, who will give Such directions as are necessary for the comfort of the men, and their getting immediately to work—

You will consider the whole party as under your immediate command and provide for them, and give orders accordingly. you will leave a list of the Names of the Men left behind with me. I wish you a pleasant Journey and a safe arrival with your command to the place of your destination—

Yours

To Mr. Rush

Sir   Philada: Decr: 28th 1780

The air Furnace being now given up to the proprietors, and having it in my power to make payment for its use while in the hand[s] of the public, to the owners satisfaction, it only remains to be inform'd what Sum the Gentn: appointed by the Parties have set to be paid pr month as rent. you will please to let me know as soon as convenient that I may finish the Business—

With Sentiments of esteem—

To George Ross Jr.

Sir   Philada. Decr. 29. 1780

I expected long since to have had the Bar Iron—Supposing you had received the Pig metal agreeable to Contract—by the settlement of Mr. Moses Youman's Account, Seven Tons one hundred of Metal is acknoledged to be in his Possession belonging to the Public—on these I grounded the Order I gave you—and this quantity he must produce together with damages Occasioned by disappointment—I have heard that he converted it to his own use, this in Addition to the horrid work he made with the Metal which he drew, will be the subject of a future enquiry

If you can obtain the within mentioned seven tons I have no Objection to your drawing it on the Conditions mentioned in the Contract—by at present it is not convenient to enlarge that Order or make a new Contract—the Honble. Board of War have it in Contemplation either to sell the Remainder of the pigs or make Contracts for drawing them at the Furnace to which they are most Contiguous, if this last mode should be Adopted it is probable you may come in for a share—of this I shall inform you in some future Letter—

I am sir your huml servt.

To Jacob Weiss

Dear Sir   Philada: Decr. 29, 1780

I am informed by Colonel Thompson that he has a Considerable quantity of barr Iron belonging to the Continent at his Forge at Change Water, ready for transportation this sir is wanted at this place—must beg the favor of you to forward it as quick as possible by such Conveyance as you think best—by the Contract there is about five tons & half—which is intended to be Converted into steel—

Weiss served as a Deputy Quartermaster General at various locations.

To Henry Knox

Dear Genl.   Philada. Decr. 29, 1780

Yours by Mr. Pierce came safe to hand, am sorry to find you are so much in want of the Sword Blade, as it is yet out of my power to procure a Blade—not one to be purchased in the City or it should have been done long since,—for two months our Men have been unemployed for want of Provisions—one of the Officers has repeatedly promised to furnish a Blade, But no rations, no work, has been the cry—they will shortly (I hope) be supplied—and I will use by best endeavours to Comply with your wishes—I have made enquiry relative to the Swords Ordered by Congress to a number of Gallant Officers, as a gratuity or Acknowledgement for Special Services—among which was Colonel Meigs named—I am informed that three were made by the best Workmen that could be found—but were not tho't equal to the intention of Congress and therefore not presented—after this the Board of War wrote to France requesting their Agent to procure and forward such as should be compatible with the honor of Congress to give, and ornamental as well as useful to the Gentlemen, who were to receive them, but by some Fatality they never Arrived—they however assure me, methods shall be taken to procure them soon—of which I will give you the most early Information—in the mean time shall endeavour to keep it in remembrance of the Board untill performed—

With Sentiments of Esteem I am Sir Your very Hble. Servt.

To Samuel Sarjant

Sir, Philada. Decr. 30. 1780

The wool lately forwarded to you is intended for the use of the Regt. you will consult the Paymaster, & know which will be best to be made for the Mens Comfort, Blankets or Stockings, and have it converted to one or other of these uses immediately—as the season must be far spent before Blankets can be made of it—I am inclined to think it had better be spun Suitably & made into Stockings—By the Bearer I send you Seven hundred weight of blistered Steel—shall send more as Opportunities presents—no money on hand at present, shall sent [sic] you a portion of the first we receive—

the debts due from the Soldiers lately marched for your post to the Inhabitants of the City Obliged me to pay them up to the first instant—without this they could not have got away—Shall as soon as possible make provision for the payment of the rest of the Regt. to the

same time—
    I am Sir Yours

To John Wilcox

Sir   Philada: Decr. 30th 1780

I have made enquiry and Find the four half Bbls of powder you mentioned, were left in the Magazine at the time the enemy were approaching towards this City, and to prevent its falling into their hands was taken away by the publick. I have also ascertained their weight, find it be be 200 lb neet of this I have received 120 lb neet the other 80 lb to compleat the whole is ready & waits your orders—
    I am Sir Your very huml. Servt.

To John Lamb

Dear Sir   Philada: Jany. 1st. 1781—

Yours of 17th Novr. Inclosing your account of expences in a journey to Springfield came Safe to hand, the charges are very moderate, regularly inserted, and sufficiently Vouched by the declaration at the Bottom. I have forwarded the acct. by Megr. Story for final Settlement, you will please to sign the receipts and pay him the Ballance—

I shall be happy to execute any commands you may have in this City, nothing new—
    With Sentiments of Esteem I am Sir

Lamb was Colonel of the Second Continental Artillery Regiment.

To Mr. Keran

Sir   Philada. January 3d 1781—

As you have quitted the Laboratory-it becomes an Act of duty to Account with me in behalf of the public, for the materials with which you was furnished for carrying on the business—and the more necessary as by my books there appears a very great deficiencty—your Books shall be delivered you for this purpose on

your Application to this Office,—I expect you will attend to this matter immediately
            I am Yours

This may be Isaac Coren who had been a Captain in Flower's Regiment of Artillery Artificers. He had been working in the "laboratory" since early 1777 and was cashiered on June 30, 1780.

To Mr. Evans

Dear Sir   Philada. January 3d. 1781.
    This is to inform you that the public having no further use for your Stores No. 1: 7: & the Loft—they are this day to cease to draw rent; the Bearer will deliver you the keys.—as soon as possible I will pay the Rent due
            With Esteem—I am Yours—

To The Board of War and Ordnance

Gentn: Jany 7th. 1781
    Agreeable to your direction I send you an estimate of the quantity & value of materials necessary for making 1,000,000 M Cartridges, to which is added an acct. of such part of the materials as we have on hand. a further Sum will be necessary to procure some other articles for the use of the Laboratory, in the preparation of Cann. Ammunn: and the purchase of Flints, of which last article we are almost destitute. perhaps some part of the warrants, already granted may be obtained to answer these purposes, if not it seems needless to apply for others. I thought however, it might be proper to mention, such additional supplies are were likely soon to be wanted that the means to obtain them might be unde[r] consideration in time to prevent disappointments when the Stores shall be called for—
    If it be necessary a state of the warrants that remain unpaid shall be laid before you. the Sum necessary for the Genl. estimate of supplies laid before your honble. Board some time Since will naturally be abridg'd in proportion to those now obtained—
    With due respect I am Gentn. Yours

Estimate of Sums Needed to Make One Million Cartridges

Estimate of the Sums necessary for procuring materials & making one Million of Musket Cartridges.

	Continental Dolls.
200 Reams of M Cartridge Paper will make & Pack One Million at 15/ Specie amots. to	30.000
834 Boxes for packing the above, allowing them to Contain 100 Dozen each @ 7/6 p ps. amounts to	62550
167 lbs thread for making & Packing the above @ 7/6	12.525
20 Men will be employed 125 Days making the above @ 30 Dollars each p^r day	75.000

Extract From Meeting Minutes of the Board of Ordnance

At a Board of Ordnance Monday 8th. Jany 1781
    Present Mr. Peters
        Genl. Cornell
Agreed

    That John Glenn Contractor for stuff at Carlisle in the Dept. of Comy. Genl. Mily. Stores be dischargd. from further employment, there being in opinion of the Board no necessity under the present Circumstances for such an Officer & that Mr Gleen [*sic*] deliver up to Saml Sergant Esqr. Comy. of Mily. Stores at Carlisle all public property in his possession

    That the Comy of Mily. Stores at Carlisle be & is hereby directed to procure all the Stuff & materials for the Workmen at that place & that the Officer at the head of each Branch of business assist the Commissary On So doing when thereto requested by him
        Extract from the Minutes
           Joseph Carleton Secy

To The Board of War and Ordnance

Gentn. Philada. Jany. 8th 1781
    The following Facts relative to the powder imported in Vessells belonging to Mr: Blair Mc.Clenaghan on acct. of the United States,

together will the inclosed Bills of Lading I beg leave to lay before your honble Board for perusal previous to the intended enquiry Vizt:

On the 28th April last the Brig Fame arrived from St Eustatia having on board 50 half Barrells powder, which without notice given was put into the State Magazine, and there remain'd untill the Same Vessell return'd from Statia a Second time, and brought 60 ½ Barrells, & 28 ¼ Barrells powder ship'd as before the Invoice of which came safe to hand, some days after her arrival upon enquiry I found it was Sent to the Magazine, without being regularly receiv'd or examined. I immediately applied to the State Comy who is in charge of the Magazine to know how the matter was managed, at which time he informed me of the first importation, a considerable quantity of which he Said had been drawn out by Mr: Mc:Clenaghan's order, and the remainder lay in a ruinous condition; I immediately wrote to Mr: Mc:Clenaghan and requested him to make a delivery of both parcells in order that I might insert them in my books and cancel the Bills of Lading to this he made no reply, after waiting Some Days and hearing that he was drawing upon his last parcel I applied to him personally upon the Subject, when he Said he would order a delivery of the whole to be made. nothing further was ever done about the delivery. after laying the affair before you honble Board & the commercial Committee I rested—

On the 1st Septr. the Ship Governor DeGraaf arrived having powder belonging to the States. the Bill of Lading came immediately to hand, and I applied for delivery of the contents which was 66 ½ Bbls & 58 ¼ Barrells of which 10 pr Cent was agreed to be received for freight or its real value in Cash. but of this only 30 half Bbls & 58 ¼ Bbls have been received, the rest amounting to one third part was retained for freight, thus the matter rests at present, notwithstanding I have done all in my power to bring it to an equitable & peaceable settlement. to your honble Board I now again refer it, and doubt not, that you will take such measures as are necessary for this desireable end

With due respect I am Gentlemen Yours—

To the Board of War
Gentn.   Philada: Jany. 8 1781
With this you will receive the return of stores forwarded to the Southward, all of which except those delivered Coll: Carrington, and

those delivered the Maryland Division, being detain'd on the road by accident, did not arrive untill after the action of the 16 August, and consequently are on hand. whether the two first mentioned deliveries, arrived before tha[t] period, I am not able to say, but believe if they did a considerable part of them was saved. this is forw[ar]ded on a Letter, I received from Coll. Carrington dat[ed] ye: 24th August wherein he mentions our having suffer'd a considerable loss of Stores, had the whole been lost he would naturally have said so—

With respect I am Gentlemen Yours—

To Isaac Caristin

Sir   Jany. 8th 1781

You will immediately proceed with the waggon you have in charge to the vicinity of trenton, and when there arrived halt the waggon, and proceed with the Lett[er] you have to Governor Livingston, who will furnish y[ou] with Such further orders, as are necessary for the deliv[ery] of the Stores you have under charge, which having effec[ted] you will take a receipt agreeable with the Invoice and return with all possible dispatch to this City

Yours

Caristin or Caristen, was a Conductor of Military Stores.

To William Livingston

Jany: 8th 1781

The Bearer Mr. Isaac Caristin Condr. M Stores waits on you in charge of 1000 lb Lead & 552 lbs powder both neet [*sic*] for the use of the State of New Jersey forwarded by order of the Honble. Board of War. I have ordered him to halt in the Vicinity of Trenton, and wait on you for direction where to deposit it, and to whom to deliver it you will please to give him such orders as the complexion of things may render necessary—

With due respect I am Your Excellencys Most Obedt. huml Servt.—

Livingston, a native of New York, moved to New Jersey in 1772, and was elected to the Continental Congress. He served as governor of the state from August 31, 1776 until he died in 1790.

To Lewis Nicola

Sir Jany: 8th 1781

Yours of this day I have receiv'd must inform you that no men answering the description you give have returned in any Arms, and therefore conclude with you that those you mention are a part of the mutineers and as Such ought to be apprehended; shall accordingly be very particular in examining them should they make their appearance, and offer their Arms—

With Sentims of esteem, I am Sir Yours

Nicola was a Philadelphia businessman who was made Colonel of the Invalid Regiment in 1777, and a brevet Brigadier General in the Continental Army in 1783.

To Thomas Jones

Sir Philada. Jany. 10th. 1781

I have enclosed a receipt for 500 Dollars Advanced Mr Parvin which if in Cash, you will please to remit me, and charge to his Accot. as his necessity has Obliged me to lend it out of my own Stock—he informs me he has received no pay since he Commenced Conductor, if this is the case, he certainly has been injured, you will please to attend to his case, and if in your power do him equal justice—

I have been at a loss for your long silence, pray inform me the Occation, and at the same time, whether if you could Obtain a Lieutenancy of Artillery, you would have any Objection to going to the Southern Army, and Acting as a field Comy. provided a handsome provision is made for it,—your Answer will determine me how to Act, should I again be Advised on such an Appointment—my Compliments & kind regards to all friends.—

I am with esteem Yours

To Jacob Weiss

Dear Sir   Philada. January 10th. 1780 [sic]

Yours of the 4th: Inst. p Mr. Parvin, came safe to hand, together with the Ordnance and Stores that Accompanied it, should be exceeding glad if the means in your power would permit getting on the remainder & the Iron. some portion of Cash has been furnished the Boatmen, perhaps sufficient to induce them to make another trip, should this be the case, your Attention I am sure will not be wanting to compleat my wishes in this respect—

The Pig metal I can now make use of to great Advantage, hope it will be possible to get it on, or a part—pray inform me what quantity of Pigs you suppose are at and near Easton—

With Sentiments of esteem I am Yours

Weiss was Assistant Deputy Quartermaster General at Easton, Pennsylvania. Hodgdon addressed him with the rank of "Colonel."

To Jonathan Gostelowe

Sir   January 11th. 1781

The Honble. Board of War having directed me to give up all Stores not absolutely necessary for the use of the public, I am under the necessity of giving up that Occupied by you as a Drum Factory—as that branch of Business is at a Stand at present—and should it revive we have other buildings which may answer the purpose quite as well at a great deal less expence—

By Contract with Colonel Proctor in behalf of the States I have one quarter in the House from the 25th. Instant at £50. p Ann[um] he paying all the Taxes, this if you are disposed to keep the hou[se] you may avail yourself of, and agree in future as you think proper

I am Sir your Humble Servant

To Daniel Joy

Sir   Jany. 12th. 1780

The Honble. Board of War have directed me to forward you with all Convenient Speed to the Several Furnaces that have been lately in Blast on Account of the United States to the Southward of this City, in Order to have the Shott & shells by them Cast, proved, properly piled, or prevent damage or Embezzlement, & an Accurate return made of such as stand proof—

You will please to make immediate preparations for setting out on this business & inform me when you think you can go.
                    Yours

To Nathaniel Irish

Dear Sir   Jany. 15. 1781

I embrace this Opportunity by the post to inform you that I recd: yours of the 30th. Ultimo, will do all in my power to forward the Bayts. requested, & will wright immediately to Carlisle, to be informed whether enough may now be made at that post, now the Regt. is all together, to furnish both their own Armoury & yours. I think there may, if so, it shall without loss of time be set about, the Glue shall also be Sent,—as to your carrying on the works upon a larger Scale as Col Grayson Recommends, I wish it was possible to be done, but the Old proverb hold good in this Case, you must creep before you run,—the deranged situation of our finances destroys every attempt to enlarge our works, perhaps circumstances may shortly make his ideas elligible, when this is the case, it shall cheerfully be attended to, As to forwarding the Men you mention, at present it cannot be done, without the Board will consent to detach some from Carlisle, or direct me to engage some for the particular purpose, however I will lay the matter before them, and inform you the result, by the next Opportunity. I am sorry Mr. Clarke turns out so poorly, his Character was good, when he was engaged, but if he continues to behave ill, he must be displaced—Colo Grayson was mistaken relative to the Laboratory's being removed to Carlisle, that is not the case, the Company is Annexed to Colonel Proctors Regt., & is now Commanded by Capt. Porter & established at the Laboratory in this City, I am sorry Lieut. Greer absented himself so much is now Commanded by Capt. Porter & established at the Laboratory in this City, I am sorry Lieut. Greer absented himself so much beyond the time granted him for bringing his Family to your Post, as every moments time in the Laboratory at this time must be important I have seen nothing of him, hope he has since returned,—the bar Iron Nail Roads, & Steel shall be forwarded if circumstances will possibly permit, thus much for business,—the inclosed resolve will inform you what pay is fixed for the Department in future,—on this I shall make no comment,—Yesterday I had a Letter from Captain Jordan all was well when he wrote at Carlisle

 my Compliments to all friends—I am Sir Your Humble Servt.

That the Commanding Officer of Artillery for his extra services in the Affairs of the Ordnance Department, receive forty Dollars per Month in Addition to his pay as an Officer in the Line, in Bills of the new emissions, from and After the first day August last.—

That the Surveyor of Ordnance for Defraying his expences in the exercise of his Office, be Allowed from & after the first day of August last forty dollars p Month in Bills of the new emissions besides his Appointments as a Field Officer of Artillery.

 Extract from the Minutes
  Geo: Bond Dept. Secy.

         In Congress January 12th. 1781.—

Congress took into consideration the Report of the Board of War of December 8th. Whereupon.—
Resolved.

That from and after the first day of August last, the pay and Appointments of the Officers, in the department of Commissary Genl. of Mily. Stores, be as follows.—the Sums hereafter mentioned to be paid in Bills of the new Emissions, & all monies received in Bills of the Old emissions since the first day of August, to be Accounted for according to the Table of depreciation as fixed by the treasury board.—

	Pay pr Month	Rations pr day
Commissary General of military stores	100 Dolls	3—
Deputy Comy. General	80 do.	2—
Commissaries	70 do.	2—
Deputy Commissaries	55 do.	2—

Conductors	45 do.	1—
Clerks	40 do.	1—

no rations in addition to the above mentioned are to be allowed for servants

That the Officers and Men of the Regiment of Artillery Artificers have the same pay from and after the said first day of August, in the Bills of the new emissions, as was Originally fined in Bills of the then emissions by the regulation of the Department made by Congress on the 11th. day of February 1778 and that they draw the number of Rations then directed—

That the Appointments of the Field Commissary of military Stores and his Subordinate Officers be as follows—

From and after the first day of August last, the pay be received in the Bills of the new emissions.

	Per Month	Rations pr day	Servt included
Field Commissary	90 Dolls	2	
Deputy Field Comy.	70	2	
Conductor	45	1	
Clerk	40	1	

That the Commanding Officer of Artillery for his extra services in the Affairs of the Ordnance Department, receive forty dollars per Month in Addition to his pay as an Officer in the Line, in Bills of the new emissions, from and After the first day of August last.—

That the Surveyor of Ordnance for defraying his expences in the exercise of his Officer, be Allowed from & after the first day of August last forty dollars pr Month in Bills of the new emissions beside his Appointments of a Field Officer of Artillery.

Extract from the Minutes Geo: Bond Dep: Secy.

Captain Nathaniel Irish had served in the Regiment of Artillery Artificers since February 7, 1777. In November 1780, he wrote to Hodgdon that he had found a barn at Westham, five and a half miles from Richmond, Virginia. The barn was used as a workshop and armory, and a laboratory was set up in a stable to produce fixed ammunition, portfires and tubes. In 1781 he was appointed Deputy Commissary of Military Stores in the Southern Department and continued in the service until 1783.

To the Board of War and Ordnance

Gentn.   Jany. 19th. 1781

Inclosed you have an estimate of the cost of an 8 Inch Howitzer which I believe is pretty exact, to which is added the value of the Same article at the furnaces in Europe, what they would cost at Second hand am not able to Say; I have also subjoin'd the Expence of building a furnace supposing the house or shed to which it is to be annexed already built. shall just add by way of information, that there is a suitable house already provided for the purpose at Carlisle, and plenty of Bricks & Lime on hand, belonging to the publick for Building the furnace, the only objection that Seem[s] to arise to fixing it at that post, (should it be determined to set up any where) is the expence of transporting the metal which is principally at Springfield in the State of Massachusetts where also is plenty of building [sic] Suitable to annex a Furnace & probably materials on hand. if so the expence of transportation would be Saved. would further remark that as the metal for present purpose is on hand, the furnace might be built & the Howitzer cast in less time than a Single passage is usually accomplished to Europe which in addition to the risque perhaps may be proper to attend to. if any further information is necessary shall with pleasure attend & give it—

I am Gentlemen With respect Yours &c.

Estimate of the expence of an 8 Inch Howitzer Cast at Phila. 10th. Jany. 1781 Wt. 11 Cwt. allowing the Metal to be on the Spot, where the Casting is made, and the Furnace in Order

Mr. Byers' pay as undertaker	@ 3/.p lb	£ 110. 0. 0
35 days work one Assistant	@ 10/.	17. 10. 0
1 Cord Oakwood		1. 10. 0
Clay Hair & Hay		1. 0. 0
300 Wt. of Iron		4. 0 .0
4 Files for Cleaning	@ 7/6	1. 10. .0
Engraving U.S.		1. 10. .0
1050 Wt Copper	@ 3/6	131. 5 .0
150 Wt. Tin	@ 3/9	28. 2. 6
	793 dollar s	£ 296. 7. 6

Estimate to Cost of the above Howitz at the Furnaces at Europe—
8 Inch Howtizer Wt. 1100 at 3/1. Sterg.   £ 169. 11. 8
  753 38/54 dollars

Expence of Building a Furnace		
5000 Bricks	@ 45/.	£ 11. 5. 0
2 Mens Pay for 40 days in buildg. Furnace	@ 40/.	40. 0 0
40 Bushels Lime	@ 3/.	6. 0.0
20 Loads Stones for the Foundation	@ 10/.	10. 0 0
10 Loads Sand	@ 10/.	5. 0.0
	dollars 192 60/90	£ 72. 5.0

Certificate of Discharge for Jacob Server

These Certify that the Bearer Jacob Server a Soldier in my Regt: of Arty. Artificers being unwell & unfit for Service, and likely to remain so for a long time from the nature of his complaints, at his own request is discharged from said Regt. and at full Liberty to dispose of himself as he thinks proper—

Given under my hand at Philadelphia this 20th day of Jany. 1781
    B. Flower Col. A&A
Whom It May Concern

To Samuel Sarjant

Sir   Philada: 20th Jany. 1781

In consequence of an application made to Congress, on the Settlement of your acct. for Cartouch Boxes, with your attorney Captn. Stevens, I am now in possession of a warrant for the Ballance, drawn agreeable to Captn: Stevens request on Nathl. Appleton Esqr: Commissioner of Loans in the State of Massachusetts. this upon your impowering some person here to have you attend to all these matters, and doubt not you will answer all their Expectations. for fear it may not yet come to hand, I enclose you another Copy, of the Boards Order, to prevent unnecessary loss of time in Carrying them into Execution

I am Sir Your very Humbl Servt

To Ezekiel Cheever

Dear Sir   Philadelphia 23rd. 1781

By this days Post, I receiv'd your favor of the 13th. Inst. am sensibly affected for the loss of your Son. think it must be a heavy tryal for you at this time of Life, May God support you under it and in the Multitude of distracting thoughts, which may naturally be Suppos'd to Arise, on Such an Occasion. may his comfort abundantly abound, to delight & cheer your meditations, that so this dispensation may redound to his glory, & your unspeakable advantage

I am fully sensible of the difficulties you labour under, in making up your Accounts, & have a disposition to remove them, but fate seems to determine against my exertions[.] I have frequently urged to the Honble. Board of War the necessity of forwarding Money to support the post at Springfield—they too have seen the propriety of the measure, but the deranged situation of our finances have baffled all attempts for this purpose however this days post carries a Commission & instructions to Mr. Joseph Hiller to repair as Comy. of Mily. Stores immediately to springfield & use his endeavours to get things once more in order there—these are forwarded by the Honble. Bd. of war, but whether any methods are fallen upon, to supply him with Money, am unable to Say. Should Mr Minets kindiness bring him to your Assistance, I think it will be best to get your Cash Accounts ready for settlement, first as it will perhaps be difficult to get another grant for the post, under present Circumstances, untill all former ones are accounted for. the return of stores on order to account for all that have pass'd though your hands, will next command your attention. Surely Colo. Mason will not retard this so necessary a business—if he shou'd I think you are properly furnish'd, to demand a return of every article, he may have under his care, and as to his drawing Stores for the Laboratory, while another is appointed for that service, it is manifestly wrong let his pretensions be what they will—the fact is Congress have dismiss'd him, & the Honble. Board of War have ordered Capt. Bryant to take charge off [sic] and carry on the business formerly under his directions. whether either of these Body's have done wrong is not now the Question. Certain it is that Capt. Bryant will receive pay as director of the Laboratory & common Sence determines that he alone is accountable for all Stores delivered for its use. however I would have you Consult, the Orders you receiv'd from the Honble. Board of War on the Subject, &

endeavour to act accordingly if after all you meet with Opposition you will apply to them for further direction

As to obtaining your depreciation can only say that I think there can be no difficulty in procuring it from the State upon producing proper documents. however if there should, Congress have Resolved that when Circumstances will admit, they will have this piece of Justice done all their Officers, shall be happy to have it in my power to afford you any assistance on this matter

With Esteem I am Sir Your Humble. Servt

Certificate of Discharge for Richard Thomas

These Certify that the Bearer Richard Thomas late Soldier in Colo. Flower['s] Regt. of Artillery & Artificers having servd. the full time of his engagement in Said Regt: is dischargd. & at Liberty to employ himself as he thinks Proper

Given under my hand in Philadelphia this 23rd. day of January 1781.

To William Alexander

Sir Philadelphia 23d. Jany 1781.

I am unhappy to inform you that it is out of my power to comply with your request in finishing the draft you have upon me, I never undertook to be responsible to Mr. Faesh for the debt due him from the public—faster than I received it—I have done all in my power to procure a further sum on his account but as yet have been unable—shall continue to apply—and the moment it comes to hand, shall feel happy in gratifying his and your wishes,

With great respect I am Sir Your Most Obt.

Source: Peter Force Collection, Mss 19,061, Series 7E, Roll 1, Item 1, Library of Congress. Usually called Lord Stirling, William Alexander was a Major General in the Continental Army.

To Jonathan Gostelowe

Sir   Jany. 24th. 1781

You will immediately get all the Stores under your care into the Brick Store, which you now occupy, in order to give up all others. should Mr: Cox still insist upon having his given up, I have a prospect of getting others at a less Rent, that will answer very well. at any rate 'tis best to have all the Stores collected in one place, whether they are finally removed or not, and you will proceed accordingly—

I am Sir Yours—

To Jonathan Gostelowe

Sir   Philada. Jany. 27th 1781

You will pack up every species of Leather left with you by Captn. Dow, and any other you may have on hand, either in old Casks or Boxes, as may be most convenient, as I intend shortly to forward it to Mr: Sargent to be wrought by the men at Carlisle—

I am Yours

To The Board of War and Ordnance

                                                      Philadelphia 30 Jany 1781

Return of Iron Cannon suitable for Shipping & the place where deposited being the property of the United States

At Messrs. Danl. & Samuel Hughes	52 Pieces	12 pdrs.
works in Maryland	8 do.	4 pdrs.
On Board the Galley Indepandency at Annopolis in Maryland	2 do.	12 pdrs.
At Hopewell Furnace belonging to Mark Bird Esqr.	24 do.	12 pdrs.
At the Ordnance Yard Philadela	4 do.	12 pdrs.
2 do.	4 pdrs.	
On Mr Willing Wharf	2 do.	12 pdrs.
At Mr Hughes works in Maryland made	12 do.	12 pdrs.
for the United States & which	11 do.	18 pdrs.
have not as yet been paid for not bored nor proved		

In the Qr. Mr store Philadelphia 44 Howitzers
                                  6 Swivels

The size of the above Howitzers are Suppos'd to be 5 ½ Inches and Under.—

To The Board of War and Ordnance

Philadelphia Jany. 30th. 1781

Return of Stores wanted for the Southern Army together with those that can be supplied, with the Cost of those that are to be Purchased.

Total Articles Wanted	Can be Supplied	To be Purchass'd	Price pr. ps. in Specie	Total Amount
4 Tons Cannon Powder	4			
5 do. Musket do.	5			
12 6 pd. Ladles	12			
24 Gunner Belts Compleat with implements		24	20/.	£ 24
50 lb Block Tin	50			
2,000 Flints		2000	60/. Pm	60
20 Reams M Car Paper		20	15/.	15
12 lb Cartridge Thread	12			
1 Box Tin		1		30
				£ 129

Extract of Minutes of the Continental Congress

In Congress Jany. 31st 1781

The Committee to whom was referred the Memorial of Samuel Hodgdon delivered in a report whereupon **Resolved** That the Commissary of Military Stores or first Officer in that Department, be and hereby is allowed from and after the first day of August last, one hundred & fifteen Dollars pr month in Bills emitted pursuant to the

act of the 18th March last, And that the Depy. Comy Genl. or Second Officer in that Department be and hereby is allowed from the Said first day of August the Sum of ninety Dollars pr month in Bills aforesaid in lieu of the Sums allowed them respectively by the Resolution of the 12th. Instant—
Extract from the minutes
Geo. Bond Depy Secy

To Jonathan Gostelowe

Sir   January 31. 1781

Upon the Arrival of the Continantal Schooner at the wharf Commanded by Captain Montgomery, you will immediately proceed to put on Board, all such Arms as are in Boxes, none must go on Board loose. when the Schooner is loaded Capt. Montgomery will receive further instructions.—
Yours

Certificate of Discharge for Peter Stoy

These Certify that the Bearer Peter Stoy soldier in Colo. Flowers Regt: inlisted Septr. 8th 1777 for three Years or during the War having produced a Certificate from Mr. George Glenthworth Surgeon that he is unfit for further Service, and as his own request is discharged from Said Regt: and is at full Liberty to employ himself in any way he thinks best for the maintenance of himself, his wife & five Children, and is recommended to the well disposed, as an honest & deserving Man—

Given under my hand at Philada. this 1st day of January [sic] 1781 Whom it may Concern

This appears in the letterbook after a letter of February 6, and before the Extract of Minutes of Congress, dated January 31, 1781.

Certificate of Discharge for Thomas Huggins

These Certify that the bearer Thomas Huggins Soldier in Colo. Flowers Regiment of Artillery & Artificers being unable by weakness to join his Compy. & the time to which he engaged to serve being nearly arrived. Vizt. 10th. Aprill 1781.—is at his own request dischargd. from Said Regt. and at Liberty to dispose of himself as he thinks proper.
        Given under my Hand at Philadelphia this 1st day of February 1781
Whom it may Concern

To George Ross Jr.

Sir   Philada. Feby. 2d. 1781
    Your Favor of 21st ulto. I received in answer to which must inform you that I have not had opportunity to consult the Board sufficiently to determine whether the Pig Metal will be Sold or worked up. however to prevent loss of time and in compliance with my own Judgement I have enclosed an order on Coll. Weiss DQMr. for 12 Ton 10 hund. which added to that you have received of Mr. Yamans will neet us 4 Tons Barr Iron agreeable to Contract this as fast as ready you will please to deliver to Coll. Weiss who I have requested by this conveyance to forward as fast at it comes to hand. I have wrote to him to be informed what quantity of Pigs are at Easton, upon receipt of this intelligence I will inform both him & you how it is to be disposed of
    As to Mr. Yamans shall take Such steps as his conduct merits—
I am Sir Your very huml. Serv.

To Jacob Weiss

Sir   Feby. 3 1781
    Please to deliver Mr: George Ross on order twelve Tons ten hundred weight of Pig metal the property of the United States, to be by him converted into Barr Iron agreeable to Contract—
    I am Sir Your huml Servt.

To Jacob Weiss

Sir   Feby. 3d. 1781

This day I forwarded an Order on you in favour of Mr. George Ross for twelve tons ten hundred Pig Metal; to be by him converted into Barr Iron Agreeable to a Contract made with him, this Quantity with what he has Already received will neat for Tons Bar Iron, a part of which he informs me is ready to be delivered—which with what he will make by virtue of this Contract, I have requested may be delivered to you.—by which I expect it will come to hand here in reasonable time, & prevent the mischievious consequences that have been experienced by former delays.—I wrote you some time since respecting a quantity of Bar Iron, in the hands of a Mr. Thompson, since which have received a curious Letter, in which he informs, that five Tons & a half have been ready this two months, but even that is not to be Delivered untill payment is Obtained for hawling Eight Tons five hundred & ten pounds of Pig metal—as this matter comes immediately before you, I trust enquiry will be made, & the difficulties removed—that after two years waiting, the publick may receive this small portion after which there will be due Agreeable to Contract one ton & one eighth of a ton more, lacking a few Pounds of Pig Metal, as he Acknowledges the receipt of 21 T 7 C 3 qrs 18 lbs & he was to receive 3 ½ Tons of Pigs for every ton of Bar Iron. this small quantity of two hundred & ten pounds of metal you will please to supply him with, after which I shall insist upon an immediate compliance with the Contract agreeable to my Orders—

Please to inform me as soon as possible of the quantity of Pigs at Easton & its Vicinity & any Other Stores belonging to the C G. M Stores Department which you may have under Charge—

Yours

To Mark Thompson

Sir,   Philada. Febry 3d. 1781

Yours of the 5th Ultimo enclosing you [sic] Account I have received by which I perceive you have received 21 t 7 C 3 qrs 10 lb of Pig Metal. this with the Addition of two hundred & ten pounds which I have requested Colonel Weiss to Supply, makes you Debtor to the United States, Six Tons two hundred & fifty Weight of Bar Iron Agreeable to Contract which must request you would deliver to Colo.

Weiss to be transported to this place without further delay.—as to the matter of Carting the Pigs as it is expressly in the Quarter Masters Department, we have Nothing to do with it, upon Application to Colonel Weiss I doubt not will settle it—and as to your expecting a further Allowance of Pigs because circumstances makes it proper to give it at this time—you may give up the Idea, as nothing of this kind will be attended to, a Litteral and immediate fulfillment of the Contract is what I am Ordered to insist on, as the publick has suffered Sufficiently by it already
    Yours

Thompson operated Changewater Furnace at what is now Changewater, Warren County, New Jersey. This was addressed to him at "Change Water."

William MacDonald, Enlistment Agreement

These Certify that I William Macdonald a native of Scotland but living Since a resident at a placed called the Yellow Springs in Penna. by trade a Shoemaker Do voluntarily inlist myself in Colo. Benja: Flowers Regt. of Artillery Artificers to Serve therein in the room & stead of Daniel Berkmire the full time of which he was engaged, hereby acknowledging that I have received from him full & ample Satisfaction to comply with his engagement, and that I have no claims on the United States except a Soldiers dues, as monthly Pay, and allowance of Cloathing common to others. and I further declare that I am free to undertake this service, and that I do not belong to any Corps in the American Army. that I have no rupture nor was ever troubled with Fits and that I will Serve my time of engagement faithfully and obey the orders of my particular Officers and all others who have a right to command me—
Sworn before P. Fleeson
Feby. 3 1781—

Michael Broadbeck, Enlistment Agreement

    These Certify that I Michael Broadbeck a native of Germany but lately discharg'd from the German Regiment, by trade a Shoemaker, Do voluntarily inlist myself in Colo. Benja: Flower's Regt: of Arty: Artificers to Serve therein in the room & stead of

William Brown the full time of which he was engaged, hereby acknowledging that I have received from him full & ample Satisfaction to comply with his engagement & that I have no Claims on the United States, except a Soldiers dues as monthly pay, and allowances of Cloathing common to others. and I further declare that I am free to undertake this Service & that I do not belong to any Corps in the American Army. that I have no rupture nor was ever troubled with fits & that I will Serve my time of engagement faithfully & obey the orders of my particular Officers and all others who have a right to command me—

Return of Arms and Accoutrements Wanted

Return of Arms & Accoutrems: wanted to compleat Coll. Moyland & Sheldens Legionary Corps with the probable cost of each article in Specie— Philada. Feby. 3 1781

243 Muskets to be repair'd	@ 30/.	£ 364..10.
417 pair pistols	@ 130/.	2719..10.
262 Bayonets	@ 12/6.	163..15.
243 new Constructd: C Boxes	@ 20/.	243..
465 horsemens Carte: Boxes	@ 15/.	348..15.
408 Swords	@ 70/.	1428..
388 Sword Belts	@ 10/.	194..
140 Bayt: Belts	@ 7/6.	52..10
		£ 5505..

To the Board of War and Ordnance

Gentn.   Feby. 3d. 1781

The foregoing articles selected from the two Returns received from your honble. Board this day are usually procured by the Comy. Genl. M Stores to all which the present prices in specie are fix'd; agreeable to order—

I am Gentn. Your very huml Servt.

To Ezekiel Cheever

Dear Sir   Philadelphia 5th. Feby. 1781

This days Post, brought me your favor of the 27th Ultimo was glad to hear you was getting better.—hope shortly to receive your Accounts & Returns—your Situation from the want of Money and Harness leather I have laid before the Honble. Board of War, they as far as in their power are disposed to afford relief—but the truth is the deranged State of our finances gives but little to expect in the Money way—however a particular application will be made immediately to Congress, from which I hope your post will experience every reasonable Wish; the necessary supply of Leather will be ordered by this post—the Board having agreed to direct Mr. Lamb to furnish such quantities & kinds as the Comy. of Mily. Stores shall from time to time find Occasion for—the supply of Coals I was in hopes would have been obtained, thro' the Qr. Master as it usual but conclude, from his not doing of it, the malady is general. perhaps Stone or sea Coals may be had from the Quarter-masters Stores at Hartford or Boston, if not you must remain in want untill the sluices are again Opened & money flows to your relief

With regard to Major Tallmages application, it was forwared [sic] (or a Copy of it) sign'd by Colo. Sheldon, and had been acted upon before yours arrived. this instance points out the necessity of such applications being made to The Honble. Board of War his Excellency the Commander in Chief or Genl. Knox agreeable to express order of Congress, previous to their being prefer'd for if Countersign'd by either of these, a double supply will be prevented, and in future, for any capital Article, you will insist on the signature of one of these, or the Commanding Officer of a separate detachment where these from circumstances cannot be obtain'd. extraordinary cases indeed, may make it necessary to vary but of these you will judge how far it is proper to comply. relative to the Barracks, can only say that as they will be a temporary receptacle and under present Circumstances not greatly interfere, with our Workman—I think if others cannot readily be obtain'd they may be occupied—the more care will be necessary to prevent embesselment, and shou'd we obtain money to set the men at work, they must turn out but in and every other Occurence, merely transient—were particular instructions, would be impossible to give—you must depend upon your own judgment, and after obtaining the best information, the nature of the case admits, act accordingly always keeping in mind that it is the duty of every Public Officer to give every possible assistance, to such as may find it necessary whether they expressly belong to their own, or any other department, under Congress

I am Sir with Sentiments of Respect Your Very humble servt.

To the Board of War and Ordnance

Gentn.   Feby. 6 1781

When I received your order to Send for Mr. Hoey to take charge of the Laberatory in this City, I was directed to inform him that he should have a Lieut. of Artilleries Commission to give him the necessary command of the men to be employed under him and a certain Sum pr day as director. these terms I offer'd him and to these he acceded, and a Commission was made out accordingly, but the unsettled Situation of the Company prevented its being presented. that now difficulty is now done away, the company is annexed to Coll. Procters Regiment, and he now applies for his Commission. I have mentioned the matter to the President of this State who is disposed to comply with his request, but previous to its being done, wishes that a Line on the Subject from your honble. Board may be address'd to him in Council upon which the Commission, after the proper Ceremonies will be given. as the arrangement of the Line will shortly be made, and the appointment requested injures no one, the Sooner this matter is done the better. from these circumstances I take the Liberty to request that your honble. Board would prefer what is Suitable to his Excellency & the Council to obtain the Commission, agreeable to my promise & your direction—

With due respect I am Gentn Yours—

To the Board of War and Ordnance

Gentn.   Philada: Feby. 6 1781

I am of opinion that 100 Sides harness Leather & Sixty of thin Leather will be Sufficient for the present to employ the men in that Branch at Springfield. the Comy. by forwarding the estimates of the quantity and kind Suitable for the Business on hand, may in time receive Such further Supplies as under circumstances, the Board may think proper to order on being informed to what use it is intended to be appropriated— With due respect I am Gentn. Yours

To Samuel Sarjant

Sir Feby. 7th. 1781

By virtue of an order from the Honble. Board of War I have contracted with the Bearer for an exchange of Sulphur for an equivalent of powder Vizt: for every eight pounds Sulphur he is to return one pound of best warranted powder. in consequence of which you will without further advice deliver four Tons of the Sulphur you have on hand, for which agreeable to Contract you will receive three hundred & seventy five pounds of Rifle powder and one hundred & twenty five pounds of Cannon powder both to be of the best quality upon the receipt of which & your Certificate, that the Contract is punctually complied with I will give directions for continuing it (if requested) untill the whole is exchanged—

I am Sir Your very huml Servt:
Mr. Jno. M'Conkey
Mr: Sarjant CMS

M'Conkey is assumed to be the bearer of the letter.

To William Moore

Sir Feby. 8 1781

Hearing that you was the owner of the building now occupied by the publick as a Laboratory in Fifth Street I have judged it proper to apply to know what is to be rent. if the house in the yard is free for letting I should be disposed to hire both for the use of the publick, provided, the Rents were moderate. you will much oblidge me, by informing me, the value you have Set on them—

I am Sir Your very huml Servt

Moore was on the Pennsylvania Committee of Safety and Board of War during the early part of the Revolution. He served as Vice-President of the Pennsylvania Supreme Executive Council from October 1779 until November 1781, and then as President until October 8, 1782.

To Mr. Knight

Sir— February 9th. 1781

Mr. Andrew Doz being engaged I have got Capt Danl. Joy on the part of the public to determine the rent of the Stores if conveninant to the Gentlemen on your part. Capt. Joy will meet him at the Store to morrow Afternoon at 4 oClock precisely—of this you will please to inform me

With esteem I am Sir, Your very humble Servant

Certificate of Discharge for William Brown

These Certify that the Bearer Willm. Brown Soldier in Colo. Flowers Regt: Arty Artificers having engag'd an able bodied man by the name of Michael Broadbeck to Serve in his room & stead the full time for which he was inlisted is discharg'd from said Regt: and at liberty to employ himself as he thinks properr, for the maintenance of his Family—

Given under my hand at Phila. da. this 10th day Feby. 1781— Whom it may Concern

To Thomas Wylie

Sir Philada. Feby 10th 1781—

The bearer who comes in charge of a certain Michael Broadbeck, who has engaged to Serve the time for which Brown was inlisted. the man it Seems is a shoemaker by trade, consequently likely to be more usefull to the United States, than Brown who is a Barber. he is indeed advanced in Years, but as it is generally expected that all that were inlisted during the War or for three Years will be discharged at that Period that first arrives. he may answer the present engagement as well as anyone but other circumstances, which it is not necessary at present to mention, makes the exchange eligible upon his return with your Certificate that the man has join'd his Company, I shall proceed as directed to give him a discharge—

The two inlistments shall be forwarded by the first Safe conveyance, my compliments to Captn Jordan

I am Sir Your very huml Servt.
PS. I had a Letter from Captn. Irish last Post he was well & had got his men to work upon the old Shot and Suffered but very little loss by the enemies excursion

Certificate of Discharge for Daniel Berkmire

These Certify that the Bearer Daniel Berkmire Soldier in Colo. Flower's Regt: of Arty & Artificers having engaged an able bodied man by the name of Wm. Mc:Donald to Serve in his room & stead the full time for which he was enlisted, is discharged from Said Regt: and at liberty to employ himself as he thinks proper for the maintenance of his Family—
Given under my hand at Philada: 17th Feby. 1781—
Whom it May Concern

Return of Arms and Accoutrements Received from the Pennsylvania Line

Return of Arms & Accoutrements Received from the Pennsylvania Line Since January 1st 1781, the most of them unfit for Service—

1658 Muskets	3 Drum Shells
68 Rifles	21 Serjeants Swords
1516 Bayonets	10 Sword Belts
55 do Belts	4 Fifes
14 do Scabbards	26 Gun Worms
1698 Cartouch Boxes	97 Screw drivers
53 Pouches	1100 Flints
34 Powder Horns	20 Bullet moulds
1 Serjeants Sash	19 Espontoons
20 Drums	
9 Pairs drum Sticks	

Estimate of Sum Needed for the Repair of Arms

Philada. Febry. 17th 1781

Estimate of the Sum necessary for the repair of the Arms & Cartouch Boxes received from the Pennsylvania Line previous to their being redelivered—

1726 Muskets	@ 7/6 each	£ 647..5..
1698 Cartouch Boxes	@ 2/6 each	212..5..
	£ 859..10..	

To the Board of War and Ordnance

Gentlemen   Philada. Febry. 19th. 1781

Inclosed you have an exact return of Stores received from the Pennsa. Line since the 1st Jany. last, and an Estimate of the Sum necessary to put the Muskets & Carte Boxes into repair,—Shall immediately proceed to get the Arms from Mud Island, in Order to prevent the loss of time, should Congress think proper to grant a warrant for the above purpose

With due respect I am Gentlemen Yours—

To Jonathan Gostelowe

Sir   Philada. Febry. 19th. 1781

You will please to call on Captain Boise for the redelivery of the Arms & Stores lately sent to Mud Island, if he has not the means of conveyance within himself, you will apply to Colo. Miles who will furnish a Vessel for the purpose. as the Muskets & some other Articles are wanting for the Brigade but must have the necessary repairs first; no time should be lost in getting them up,—to prevent which I will call on Col Miles myself this morning for the most expeditious Transportation—

Yours

To Benjamin Harrison

Sir,   February 19th. 1781 Philadelphia

The five waggons that you directed the Quarter Master to send to the Magazine to be loaded with powder for the State of Virginia, having taken in three tons and eighty four pounds neet, being as much, it seems as they can carry, they, the waggoners inform me, you have no particular directions for its delivery at Carlisle. We have a Commissary there and a Magazine, who may receive and deposit the

powder safely until further orders. but he is by no means furnished to get it on and without a special order from the Quarter Master here accompanies it, it may lay there this six months. from this you will see the necessity of procuring an order on the Qr Master at Carlisle, to have it forwarded immediately on its arrival. if this is not done, it might as well lie here, for any service it will be to the State
You will please to call and give me a receipt for what is forwarded.
    I am Sir, your very humble servt

Harrison was Signer of the Declaration of Independence, Colonel in the Virginia Militia and elected Governor of Virginia in 1782.
Source: William P. Palmer, ed. *Calendar of Virginia State Papers and Other Manuscripts, 1652-1781, Preserved in the Capitol at Richmond* vol 1 1652-1781 (Richmond, 1875), 528.

To Samuel Sarjant

Sir   Philada. 19th Feby. 1781

    The five waggons that comes with this are loaded with 135 Casks powder weighing 6084 pounds neet, the property of the State of Virginia, and under the direction of Colo. Benja: Harrison, untill it arrives to prevent dissappointment or delay it is to be got on by the way of Carlisle. you will please to receiv[e] this & Store it in the magazine, untill other waggon[s] are prepared to take it to the next stage, at which time you will deliver him as much more Muskt. Powder as will make in the whole 4 Tons neet, and charge the Same to the State of Virginia, deliver[ed] Colo. Harrison, taking a receipt of the person you deliver the additional quantity too, and forwardg an Invoice to Colo. Harrison, that he may know that the whole order from the Honble. Board of War in favor the State of Virginia which was for four Tons neet has been forwarded—upon casting over the Invoice Sent from hence we find it to be 6104 neet, consequently you will have to Supply 1896 neet pounds M. Powder to compleat the order—
    I am Sir Your very huml Servt.

To the Board of War and Ordnance

Gentlemen					Philada. Febry. 20th. 1781

The Situation of the Men employed at Springfield for want of money, and the total Stagnation of business for want of materials, has determined me once more to try whether it were possible by laying their circumstances & the consequent detriment to the public before your Honble. Board to give them any Relief—

By a Letter from Mr. Comy. Cheever, which I do myself the Honor to enclose you, it appears that about two hundred thousand Dollars is due for pay of the men at the post,—and it is probable as much more for Supplies of materials, in the Vicinity, timber, & Other Articles, have been furnished upon promises that the money would be paid in a reasonable time. this not having been the Case all confidence in public Officers is at an end, & having no money, all is at a Stand, & the department thus circumstanced is become a public nuisance.—

Mr. Joseph Hiller being lately appointed to Superintend that Department, & being about to enter on the duties of it,—is the reason of my laying its true State before you,—that the post is capable of yielding considerable Supplies and that it is the expectation of Congress they will be drawn forth is past all doubt; from these considerations duty Obliges me to request, that a Sum at least Sufficient to discharge the present demands on the post may be granted,—a person from hence (if Judged best) may be forwarded to make the Settlements & pay all the Balances that may be found due, bring on the former Accounts of expenditures & make a General return of every species of stores found at the post—this I supposed absolutely necessary to be done previous to the present Officers quitting, especially as the Comy Genl is made Accountable for all monies heretofore forwarded for the use of that part of his department, & his General Account is expected to come shortly under consideration.—perhaps three hundred thousand dollars, old emission may be sufficient to set the business forward but I am certain that a less sum will answer no valuable purpose—

I am Gentlemen your very huml Servt.

Estimate of the Sum Necessary for Arms and Stores for the Southern Army

For the Infantry

5000 Stand of Arms to be repaired	@ 30/.	£7500..
5000 New Constructed Cartouch Boxes	@ 25/.	6250..
100,000 Flints	@ 60/.pm	300..
20 Tons Lead	@ £100..	2000..
100 Drums, Sticks, & Carriages	@ 60/.	300
100 Fifes & Cases	@ 5/.	25
		£16375

For the Cavalry

200 Pairs Pistols	@ £6..10	£1300..
200 Cartouch Boxes	@ 15/..	150..
200 Swords	@ £ 3..10	700..
200 Sword Belts	@ 10/..	100..
		2250

For the Artillery
Materials for making the following Ammunition

2000 Rounds of 6 pds.	Strap'd Shott	
500 do. 3 pds.	Case do.	
2000 do. 3 pds.	Strap'd do.	
500 do. 3 pds.	Case do.	
750 Yards Flannel	@ 7/6.	£281..5..
6 Reams Cannon Cartridge paper	@ 30/.	9..
10 Pounds Twine	@ 7/6.	3..15
5 Boxes Tin plates	@ £30.	150..
380 Boxes for packing Ammunition	@ 7/6.	142..10
2500 Tubes 6 pds.	@ 50/p 6	62..10
1500 do. 3 do.	@ 50/p 6	62.10
50 Tube Boxes	@ 10/.	25..
50 Leather Haversacks	@ 40/.	100..
50 Priming Horns	@ 3/9.	9..7..6
20 Horn Lanthorns	@ 55/.	55..
50 Gunners Belts Compleat	@ 20/.	50..
100 Pounds Slow Match	@ 1/.	5.. 955..17..6
		£19580..17..6

Materials for making 500,000 Musket Cartridges to be forwarded with the foregoing   Viz.

	Amot. brought up	£19580..17..6	
13 Tons Lead	@ £100	£1300	
80 Reams M. Cartridge paper	@ 18/.	72..	
70 Pounds thread	@ 7/6	26..5	
410 Boxes for Packing	@ 7/6	153..5	
Mens Labour in making & Packing		187..10	1739
		£21319..17..6	

The following Articles are on hand
    50 Tons Powder
     9 do. Lead
   857 Powder horns too small for the Use
   115 pounds twine
   465 do. portfire paper
   153 do. Cartridge thread
   565 Sheets tin
   494 Yards Flannel
  42210 Flints
   211 Fl [sic]
  1001 Cartouch Boxes
    95 Repaired Muskets
   145 Drums
    37 Pairs Drum Sticks
    13 Pistols
    35 L. Horsemens Swords
    34 do. C. Boxes
    10 Sword Belts
    83 3 pd. Tubes
    19 Tube Boxes
    33 tin Lanthorns
     9 Gunners Belts
  177 Slow Match
   64 Reams M. Cartridge paper
 153 lbs thread

To Samuel Sarjant

Sir   Philada. Febry. 23d 1781

By the Bearer you will receive some Articles of Cloathing & a quantity of Steel, agreeable to the Inclosed Invoice.—next monday I expect to forward two Waggons more, these will be principally loaded with materials for the Leather branch, & shall as quick as possible after send on two Tons more Steel for the purpose of making Bayonets as these will be much wanted Shortly.—

Captain Wylie informs that he has long since given in Returns of materials necessary to employ the Men for some time perhaps Six Months,—which he Supposes have been sent to Philada., you will please to inform him that his Supposition is groundless, to take off any force from his intentional oblique charge.—I should indeed be glad to be favoured with estimates, both of Supplies for the work, & the Sums of money necessary to procure them, as least such part as are attainable at or near Carlisle,—the Others I will do all in my power to procure & forward as usual,—must request you, as soon as possible after the Steel Arrives to have made & forwarded five hundred Bayonets with short Sockets suitable for the French Charleville Muskets for compleating a number of those kind which we have on hand, which are wanted for the Penna. Line[.] You will please to direct them to be made eighteen Inches in the blade and of the usual Fashion.—the following is the work that I could wish to have in hand, at Carlisle, and Seems at present the most likely to be useful to the public the ensuing Season Vizt.

   20 Ammunition Waggons—with Harness Compleat—
   12 Travelling Forges   with   ditto—
   12 6 pds.   Travelling   Carriages with ditto—
   12 3 pds.   do. do. with ditto—
   10 Setts Spare wheels for 6 pd. Carriages—
   10 do. do.   3 pds.   ditto—
   12 Garrison Carriages for 18 pds. with Beds & Quoins Compleat
   12 do. do.   12 pds. with ditto—
    2 Travelling Carriages for 8 Inch Howitzers—
    2 do. do.   5 ½ ditto—

I am Sensible it will be difficult to obtain the necessary dimetions to Compleat the Carriages, to get rid of this, if the books are not sufficient, I would propose that a Suitable person be sent where these Sized Ordnance are deposited, & take proper drafts or measurements.—of this you will inform yourself & me.—Should be glad to have an Account of the debts due at your post both for Labour & Materials, up to the first Instant, that I may have an Opportunity of laying it before the Honble. Board of War, & if practicable obtain a Sum equal for payment; & to procure materials Suitable for the work you are about to take in hand—

Nothing new,—Col. Flower remains as Usual,—Mrs. Ashton is dead & buried from Mrs Youngs.—

I am Sir Your very Hble Servt.

P.S. You will please to mention to Captain Jordan the propriety of making trial with the New Breeches & Hatts, upon such men that are likely to be soon discharged, whose Services are the most valuable at the Works, & make report what Additional encouragement he thinks necessary to induce them to reinlist.—

To Thomas Wylie

Sir Philada. Febry. 24 1781

In answer to your last Letter to Col. Flower; I am requested to inform you, that it is the expectation of those, who alone have Authority to take Cogniance, & determine upon, the Inlistments of the Artificers, that they will & must be dealt with upon the same principles as those of the Line, to prevent the "disagreeable consequences" which you Seem to apprehend & to make that an Act of favour, which Appears an Act of Justice, you will immediately upon the receipt of this, examine the whole of their Inlistments, & make Return of the whole State of the Regt., particularly noting those engaged for the War—those (if any) for three Years and those for three years or during the War, with the dates of each Inlistment—after which, if the men require Certificates, you will proceed to give them, at the same time assure them that the matter will be immediately taken into consideration, & their cases treated in the same manner as similar ones have been in the line, and ample Justice be Administered to the whole.—the decision will be transmitted for your Instruction without a moments unnecessary delay—

It will be necessary to forward with the return your Apprehensions of the mode & terms most proper to be fallen upon to induce the men to reinlist, especially such as are the best workmen in the Several Branches, & are Single Men, or have Small families with any other remarks, you may think useful.—I have forwarded by this conveyance, to Mr. Sargent, a Return of Work, most likely to be wanted, consequently will first demand your Attention for the Completion of which, every Assistance in my power shall be given upon Applications, shall add a number of other Articles, as soon as I know what Strength you may have to perform those already Mentioned.—perhaps in the unsettled state of the Regt. it may be as well to employ some of the Smiths in making turnscrews, & Gun Worms a great number of which will shortly be wanted, & we have none of either on hand—

I am Sir Yours

To Benjamin Hoey

Sir, Philadelphia 26th. Feby 1781

immediately upon the receipt of this you will employ the Men in making the following stores—the whole to be ready in three days for transportation—to induce the men to work I promise to give them; a gallon of Rum, as soon as the work is finished—and a quart a day while in hand, provided they are done in the time mention'd—

300 Rounds strap Shot for 12 Pounders
 77 8 Inch Fuze's prim'd fit for use
 95 5 ½ Inch   do. do. do.
 54 24 Pdr paper Cars. Empty
823 18 Pdr. do . do. do.
  6 24 Pdr. Spunges to be covered
  1 8 Inch Howitzer Spunge
  5 lbs Quick match
  3 do. Kitt
 18 Fuse setts 8 & 5 ½ Inch an equal number of Each
 18 Malletts for the above
 24 Rocketts for signals of a large size

You will call on me for every requisite to compleat the above—not a moments time must be lost—

To Andrew Porter

Sir,   26th Feby. 1781

When the fatigue party under your command is ready—you will please to march them to the Ordnance yard, Capt. Joy will be their, [sic] & direct which pieces of the Cannon, are to be mounted, to prevent any mistake, it is proper to inform you the Calibres that is first to command your attention they are as follows

Vizt.—3—24 pounders
        4—18   do.
        4—6   do.
        3—5 ½ Inch Howitzers

To induce the men to work I shall apply to the Board of War, for an allowance of Liquor—

I am sir Your most Obedt.

Porter was a Captain in the Fourth Continental Artillery Regiment.

To Nathaniel Triplett

Sir   March 1st. 1781

Immediately upon the receipt of this you will prepare yourself to proceed with the stores under your charge of which you have an Invoice annex'd with the detachment of Artillery commanded by Lieut. Colo. Stevens to the place of their destination. you will first take charge (upon your arrival at Christiana) of the stores at present in charge of Mr. Shaw & if you want his Services you may take him on to the head of Elk, where after your embarkation if any Stores should be left, or any others arrive he may forward them on before he returns to this City. you will consider yourself as subject to the command of the Officer, that commands the Division and Colo. Stevens consequently will issue stores to their orders, and if in the course of the execution of the Service, which the troops are ordered on, any stores should be taken from the enemy, or in other way come to hand, you will be carefull to take a particular account of them, and make me a return thereof as quick as possible, after you receive them. should the expedition not prove fortunate, you will do all in your power to

Save the stores, or if lost, keep an account of the number, and by what means for further instructions as it is probable circumstances may vary, I must refer you to the order of Colo. Stevens and your own judgement, and shall expect that you will be able to acct. for all the Stores committed to your charge—

I heartily wish you a prosperous Campaign a joy full sight of your friends, and speedy return—

and am with esteem Your friend

Triplett was a Conductor of Military Stores.

To Samuel Miles

Sir   March 3d. 1781

I have this day received an order from the Honble. Board of War, to forward five Tons of powder to Virginia immediately. you will please to inform me when the waggons necessary for transporting it may be necessary—

I am Sir Yours

To Benjamin Hoey

Sir,   Philadela. 5th. March 1781

You will immediately, proceed to finishing all the tubes, of every size, you have on hand, and all the fuzes, at the same time, let the Men pack up all the fixd Ammunition you have on hand, for which purpose you will pick out all the boxes that want repairs and let the Men up stairs Perfect them

I want as quick as possible to following Articles, to replace those totally delivered

    1000 8 Inch fuzes   Primd. and Packed
    1000 5 ½ do. do.   do.   do.
    300   Rounds 6 pdr. strap shot
    100   do.   do. Case do.
    20   pounds Kitt
    1000 6 pound Tubes   Primd and packd
    1000 3 do. do.   do.   do.
    1000 tubes for 8 Inch Howitzs. do.   do.
    1000 5 ½ Inch do   do.   do.

You will please to send me a return of what is necessary, in addition to what you have on hand to compleat the above and it shall be sent you immediatly

am sir Your humble Servt.

To the Board of War

Gentlemen 10th March 1781

Inclosed you have the several Estimates requested which I hope will answer the purpose, and meet the approbation of your Honble. Board

With due respect I am Gentleman Yours

To Nathaniel Barber

Dear Sir Phila. 12 March 1781

Your favor of the 11th. Ultimo came Safe to hand—its contents made me in degree unhappy for the following reasons Vizt. your determination to quit the department—the inconveinances you have experianced from not having regularly receivd. your salary, or rather pittance & finally it being out of my power, to obtain ample justice for you even at this late hour. the Enclosed will inform you how Congress have determin'd, upon your last application to the Honble. Board of War. on this I shall leave you to comment, and shall proceed to inform that the post, by your resignation is disolved, and all that may arrive in future, shall be received by the D. Q. M Genl. and by him forwarded with all possible dispatch to Springfield, which Post is to be supported, & Augmented, that the benefits formerly experianced, from its happy situation, may flow as Usual.

As it is probable you may not have seen the last resolution, relative to the department, from which your three months Pay is valued I thought it best to inclose it—and as it is expected that you will receive depreciation upon the previous establishments—agreeable to the table approved by Congress the 28th. of last June the mode of final Settlement of your pay is very easy. that of the stores had best be done & forwarded in a return—specifiying the whole receiv'd in one Line, and after having delivered those at present on hand, agreeable to the enclosed, inserting the deliveries under it the ballance (if any) remains to be accountd. for—I mention this as a partial settlement, proper to be lodged in this Office until a final adjustment tales place.

I have nothing further to add at present but my best wishes for your Happiness

I am yours

Resolved— In Congress March 5th. 1781

That the resignation of Nathl. Barber Comy. of Military Stores at, Boston in the State of Massachusetts be accepted

That Nathl. Barber be intitled to receive a Similar allowance for past services with other Officers of the like stations in the department of Military stores.

That it be & hereby is recommended to the Executive of the state of Massachusetts, to advance to Nathl. Barber on Acct. Two Hundred & Ten dollars in Bills of the New Emissions being 3 Months pay & charge the same to the united States of America

Extract from the minutes
George Bond Depy. Secy.

To Samuel Lord

Dear Sir, Phila. 12th. March 1781

Your favor of the 12th. Feby, came safe to hand, its contents have been fully noticed but as the post is to be discontinued—am unable to serve you by recommending you to succeed to the appointment which from the knowledge I have of you I should chearfully have done.

I have Enclosed Mr. Barber, the resolve of Congress, accepting his resignation in this he is empowered to draw Three Months pay at the Value of the last establishment—which as the idea exists in the minds of Congress, that depreciation will be made up, to all who have been employed in the Service as well Staff as Line can only be considered as on Account)—Justice demanded that I shou'd make a demand, for a like grant, for all such as would necessarily be displaced, at breaking up the post. this I have done, & have receivd for answer from the Honble. Board of War, that equal justice shall be administer'd to all concern'd, can only at present hope that it will be done. You will find by the Act for discontinuing the Post that the reformation has taken place meerly from necessity, not any blameable cause—in those concern'd—this I think must aford consolation, to the faithful servants of the Public. the deranged Situation of our finances call loudly for every possible retrenchment and every department is experiancing its effects, a little longer struggle, & I hope the conflict will be over—have nothing further to add, but a tender of my services, when you may find Occasion for them, & to assure you I am your friend

A Samuel Lord was a merchant at Boston.

To William Finnie

To Wm. Finnie
Dr.
To pay & Subsistance due me as a Comy. M. Stores
at Richmond from Octor. 1st. 1779 to August 1st. 1780
is 10 months   Dolls
        at 8 88/90 Dolls. pr   Month   89 70/90
To pay due me as above from August 1st to October 1st.
       1780, is 2 Months @ 70 Dolls. p mo.   140.
To 1 Ration Retain'd pr day for 2 Months @
      5 Dolls. pr. mo.   <u>10.</u>
                 Specie Dolls   239 70/90

Dear Sir   Philada. 15th. March 1781
    Agreeable to your request signified in your favor of the 17th. Ult:—I have Attended to what I think a just Liquidation of your Account for Services performed in the Com: Genl of Military Stores Departmt the above is the State which equity will warrant.—You will Observe the One hundred & eighty Dollars is reduced to what the table of depreciation says was its Value in Specie on the 1st. Octor. 1779. This charge is continued att that Sum, untill the 1st. August following, at which time Congress Determined by a Retrospective Resolve pass'd the 12th January last, that the sum of Seventy Dollars, & 2 Rations valued at five dollars each in the New Emitted Bills, be paid the Commissaries pr Month for their Services the only difficulty that Arises, is to determine the Value of the New Bills Congress say they are worth forty for one, Some States echo that Value—Other States say they are worth Seventy five for one, & Receive and pay

them Accordingly,—to Remedy the whole, Congress have it now in contemplation to declare that Salaries formerly granted—be settled according to their Specie Value at the time of granting—to be Ascertained by the table—& those lately granted to be paid in Specie or its Real Value—thus the matter stands at present and as I have made no Other Settlements yet with any Officers in the department except such as have been made agreeable to the Strict Letter of the former Resolves—can do no more than lay the facts before you for own information, & you will Act Accordingly—

Am much obliged by the kind tender of your services Should I have occation for them in the part where you dwell—

With esteem I am Sir Your Humble Servt.

Finnie was a Deputy Quartermaster General in Virginia.

To the Board of War

Gentn   20th. March 1781

The Order, of your honble. Board for discontinuing the Post, under the Direction of the Commissary General of Military Stores at Fishkill & dismissing the Officers station'd there, has been handed me, to be forwarded. previous to which Duty oblidges me to request, to be informd. whether any provision, has been made for obtaining a Settlement of the Accounts of the Officer before he quits the post—as large Sums of Money have formerly been furnish'd Mr. Ruddock for which the Comy. Genl. is made accountable, and from recent intelligence it seems that large Sums are due from him, for supplies long since furnish'd, both in the vicinity of the post, and in the state of Connecticut. if the Contractor is gone, how are these Accounts to be settled, & by whom. by an order from the Board of Treasury which I do myself the Honor to enclose, we are informed that it is indispensibly necessary to account, for the Articles purchased, before the Cash accounts of Purchases can be admitted. nothing of this kind has accompanied, any of Mr. Ruddock's and unless he is now called upon, never will, nor shall we know whether the Articles yet to be paid for, were ever received. nor can Such Accounts be paid until certify'd by him, the Act of which is an acknowledgement of his having receiv'd the Articles charged, at the prices stated and consequently makes him accountable for their appropriation

I cannot while writing on this Subject, avoid mentioning the present Situation of the post at Springfd. the principal Officers of which have been long since dismiss'd, but until this Hour, have not accounted for either Money, or Stores. it is peculiarly hard Gentn. that the Head of a departt. shou'd be made accountable for his under Officers conduct, without having it in his power to call them to any Account. in the present Case dismission is ordered, & some of the Officers inform'd, not from any blamable cause, yet no person Authoriz'd or directed to Settle their Accounts, for want of which the post at Springfield will very shortly be abandoned and the Stores exposed to the mercy or plunder of the Inhabitants[.] from these considerations and others too tedious to enumerate I am led to conclude that, I can no ways more effectually serve my Country, and the department, than by being permitted to visit these posts, properly impowered and instructd to make the necessary settlements, and arrangements for employing the Men in future, and bringing the Accounts to amicable adjustments. the time necessary for this the Board will determine, in the mean time I shall endeavour to make Such dispositions, as are necessary, to prevent the business from suffering at this post

with due respect I am Gentn. Yours

To Charles Hall

Sir   Philada. March 23d. 1781
Colonel Miles has informed me, that Empty Waggons returning to Philada. often pass thro' Lancaster, & would often be glad to take with them, any Loads that might be wanted here. should this soon happen you will please to forward the following Stores.—
VIZ—400 12 pds. fixed Shott—27 6 pds. ditto, 114 6 pds. Case—225 3 pds. fixed, 226 pounds slow match,—24 powder horns if they are large—30 Reams Musket Cartridge paper,—the whole of the damaged Ammunition, and the two brass bullet moulds if of a good quality, if no Opportunity for forwarding should present, Colo. Miles promises to procure other means for getting them down—you will send a proportion of each, as you forward them, the bullet moulds if good are greatly wanted—

I am Sir Yours—

To Samuel Sarjant

Dear Sir   Phila. 27th. March 1781

This moment I receiv'd your favor acknowledging the receipt of three Letters from me, and requesting information relative to Mr. Mc.Conkeys, chusing the sulphur.—in answer must inform you that, it was rational to conclude that he would make a choice of such as would best answer his purpose, but it was never agreed, nor expected, that he should select out the Quantity & Quality he wanted, by opening every Cask and taking part from one, & part from another—the choice of Casks intire he may have, but nothing further was talked of or ever intended—suppose long before this, the Powder I mention'd belonging to the State of Virginia has arrived, and with the additional quantity been forwarded—the memorandum for supplies wanted in each branch, I have received and if circumstances permit shall procure them—am glad to hear things go on "well" but am very sorry the article of Cash, cannot yet be obtain'd. sure I am the want will be severly experianced, of this very necessary Article—at present the prospect is by no means promising—but should we be agreeably disappointed, the post at Carlisle shall not be neglected. Colo. Flowers remains very low his and Ladies compliments attends this to you & daughters, in return for your's Capt. Jordan is here waiting for the moving of the waters, how he will fare, when they are troubled cannot say but fear a number will Step in before him, the paymaster being closely watched—the subject of the post at Carlisle is once more brought before Congress—and from appearances I fear will undergo, a change nearly equal to a dissolution of this shall give you notice

I am Sir Your Humble Servant

To Nathaniel Irish

Dear Sir   Philadelphia 27th. March 1781

Your esteemd favor of the 16th. instant came safe to hand, was glad to be inform'd your party was busily employ'd, for the destruction of the Arch Traitor Arnold—am sorry to find, by some recent accounts, that he is like to escape once more—as to the request you make, to have Capt. Gibson sent to your assistance, can only say, that by appearances it is likely he will soon be at Liberty to dispose of himself as he thinks best—On Account of the times, of a number of the men being nearly expired, and the determination to discharge, all such as were inlisted during the War, or for three years, at the period that first arrives—a Motion has been made in Congress to discharge all the Officers, and men of the Regt. except fifty nine Men which are confessedly enlisted during the War and two Officers (Wylie & Jourdan) and the motion I believe will obtain—how or where they will be employed time must discover.—

I am exceedingly surpriz'd to hear that Colonel Harrison has undertaken to appoint field Commissaries, but a Moments reflection, oblidges me to think, that he has done it as a temporary expedient, dictated by the state & that the Gentn. appointed, is to be considered as a state Officer, for by the system at the establishment of the department the Board of War, alone, are allowed to make appointments this they have done, for the southern Army, and the Gentlemen appointed will shortly come on to his Command. what use there can be for a Field Commissary in Virginia I know not, but as the establishment knows but one, whose residue is always to be with the Main Army, any other necessary, can be but deputies and as I mention'd before one deputy for the southard is already made. as to your subordination to such orders, you need only consult your instructions, to know to whom you are amenable, and you will act accordingly. should the dissolution of the post at Carlisle be determin'd on, I will endeavour to procure one of the Clerks now there, & send him to your Assistance. as to a Warrant for more money, must consult the Board before I can say a thing to purpose on the subject. this shall be done immediately, & the information communicated by next post. to set you and Lt. Greer right in the matter of his & parties pay, I have enclosed a pay roll made on the firm basis of Resolves of Congress, this cannot be controverted the additional pay as Laboritarians is subjoined which determines his expectations, and makes your duty plain. the post going cannot enlarge, nor have I time to enclose the pay roll mentioned, both shall be done & forwarded by the next post, interruption often prevents my doing as I could wish, but every thing must be attended to

    Your with regard

Dubouy, Receipt for Stores

Providence [R.I.] Jany. 31st: 1781

Received of Samuel Nightingale Junr. as he is claiment of the Arms, Cloathing, Medicines &c. late imported in the Schooner Le Committee, Brison late Master, the following Chests, Casks, Boxes, & Bales of Goods, belonging to the state or Virginia[.] By Virtue of an order, drawn on him, dated december 30th. 1780 by Messrs. Medison & Bland, Delegates at Congress, from the state of Virginia, and by Monsr. De Toriche, commander in chief to his most Christian Majesty, now at Rhode Island. Vizt. forty five Chests of Arms No. 2, 3, 4, 6, 7, 9, 10, 13, 14, 16, 18, 19, 24, 25, 28, 29, 30, 32, 35, 36, 38, 40, 41, 43, 44, 46, 47, 49, 50, 51, 54, 55, 56, 61, 64, 71, 73, 74, 75, 83, 84, 86, 87, 88, 90, Markd. SV. six Casks Merchandize No. 20, 34, 37, 38, 41, 43, Markd. SV five boxes Merchandize No. 14, 15, 16, 18, 25, 26, 29, 32 Marked SV. Three Casks Medicines No. 23, 24, 30, Markd. SV/M. Three Boxes medicines No. 22, 27, 28, Markd. SV/M. one Bale of Medicines No. 31 markd. SV/M I have signed three receipts of this Tenor & Date

Test John Foster   Dubouy

To William Knox

Sir,   Philadelphia 27th. March 1781

You will proceed, with the above Invoice, down the River, to where the French Frigate Hermione lies, & under the direction of Colo. Febiger (who will be there present) receive such Boxes, Bales, & Casks, as are to be brought up carefully taking the Marks & Numbers of each, & comparing them with the above, & noting deficience's (if any should happen) having taken them of on board, you will proceed with all possible dispatch, to this City & immediately upon your arrival, you will direct the Captain to haul his vessel too at [sic] the Armory wharf & inform me

Knox was a Clerk in the Department of Military Stores.

Extract of a Resolve of Congress

IN CONGRESS March 29th. 1781
RESOLVED that all the non Commissioned Officers and Men of the Regiment of Artillery Artificers at Carlisle, whose times of Service are unexpired be formed into one or more Company or Companies, and the Officers at that place, except Captains Wylie & Jordan be no longer considered in the Service of the United States.
Extract from the Minutes
Geo: Bond Depy Secy

To John Compty

Sir   Philada. March 30th 1781

You will immediately proceed with the waggons loaded with Military Stores by the safest & best rout, to the commanding Officer of the Southern Army, and deliver them agreeable to Invoice to him or his order. you will be very careful of the Stores while on the road & by every possible exertion prevent there being exposed to damage by the weather, to accident for want of attention, or peculation by neglect. for this purpose you will halt them in the most convenient places & examine their state every night & morning &c, as often in the day as you may find occasion. as a great deal depends on their timely arrival & safe delivery, I doubt not you will endeavour that both these ends may be answered—
Yours &c

Compty was a wagon conductor who was taking ten wagons of ammunition, and fourteen of clothing, to Nathanael Greene's army in the Carolinas.

To John Ruddock

Sir,   Philadela. March 31st 1781

I am directed by the Honorable Board of War to inclose a copy of an order of theirs for discontinuing the Post and dismissing the Officers in the Military stores department at Fish Kill. I feel a reluctance to the communication of orders, of this nature, but as duty oblidges me to do it, I rely on the generosity of those affected to consider me, in these instances, only in my Official Character

whether the alterations that have taken place, in the department I have the honor to Superintend, be beneficial or not is not for me to determine—altho in our present circumstances, I am free to declare, that I think every possible retrenchment, in any department, not only prudent, but indespensibly necessary. the stores you perceive are to be delivered to the Quarter Master at the post, after which you will make out a general Return, of all the Stores that have passed thro' your hands, and of all debts due either on Contract, or for payment of wages at the post while under your direction and transmit them immediately to this Office, that proper settlements may be made, and the means of payment procured.—

I am Sir Your very humble Servt.

DOCUMENT CHRONOLOGY

All letters are by Samuel Hodgdon, unless otherwise noted.

To John Ruddock, July 19, 1778.
To William Butler, July 19, 1778.
To Ezekiel Cheever, July 27, 1778.
To John Ruddock, (two letters), August 4, 1778.
To John Ruddock, August 5, 1778.
To John Ruddock, August 7, 1778.
To John Ruddock, August 9, 1778.
To Benjamin Flower, August 17, 1778.
To John Ruddock, August 19, 1778.
To John Ruddock, August 29, 1778.
To Jasper Maduit Gidley, August 29, 1778.
To Captain Langdon, August 31, 1778.
To the Director of Hibernia Furnace, August 31, 1778.
To Philip Van Rensselaer, August 31, 1778.
To John Ruddock, August 31, 1778.
To John Ruddock, September 3, 1778.
To Jasper Maduit Gidley, September 3, 1778.
To Ezekiel Cheever, September 3, 1778.
To Anthony Post, September 5, 1778.
To Stephen Buckland, September 5, 1778.
To Timothy Pickering Jr., September 14, 1778.
To Jonathan Gostelowe, October 5, 1778.
To James Pearson, October 5, 1778.
To Henry Knox, October 7, 1778.
To James? Gilliland, October 8, 1778.
To Thomas Gray, October 8, 1778.
To John Ruddock, October 8, 1778.
To Jasper Maduit Gidley, October 8, 1778.
To Timothy Pickering Jr., October 10, 1778.
To Benjamin Flower, October 10, 1778.
To William Maxwell, October 12, 1778.
To Benjamin Freeman, October 12, 1778.
To Henry Knox, October 26, 1778.
To John Ruddock, October 26, 1778.
To Giles and Alexander Thompson, October 26, 1778.
To Captain Langdon, October 28, 1778.
To Benjamin Flower, November 8, 1778.
To James Pearson, November 8, 1778.
To Jonathan Gostelowe, November 8, 1778.
To Udny Hay, November 13, 1778.
To Benjamin Flower, November 13, 1778.
To Jonathan Gostelowe, November 13, 1778.
To James Pearson, November 13, 1778.

To John Ruddock, November 13, 1778.
To Nathanael Greene, November 23, 1778.
To Richard Frothingham, November 24, 1778.
To Samuel French, November 25, 1778.
To John Lamb, November 29, 1778.
To Mr. Giles, November 29, 1778.
To Alexander Thompson, November 29, 1778.
Richard Frothingham to Benjamin Flower, December 1, 1778.
To Benjamin Flower, December 8, 1778.
To Henry Knox, December 8, 1778.
To Richard Frothingham, December 8, 1778.
To John Lamb, (two letters), December 15, 1778.
Richard Frothingham to Samuel Hodgdon, December 16, 1778.
To Henry Knox, December 20, 1778.
To Jasper Maduit Gidley, December 20, 1778.
Richard Frothingham to Benjamin Flower, December 20, 1778.
To Richard Frothingham, December 21, 1778.
To Thomas Jones, December 22, 1778.
To Mr. Lefabure, December 23, 1778.
Richard Frothingham to Benjamin Flower, January 10, 1779.
Richard Frothingham to Samuel Hodgdon, January 11, 1779.
Richard Frothingham to Alexander Scammell, January 13, 1779.
Richard Frothingham to James Pearson, January 15, 1779.
Richard Frothingham to James Pearson, January 23, 1779.
Richard Frothingham to Jonathan Gostelowe, January 24, 1779.
Richard Frothingham to Samuel Hodgdon, January 24, 1779.
Richard Frothingham to Alexander McDougall, February 3, 1779.
Richard Frothingham to Samuel Hodgdon, February 6, 1779.
Richard Frothingham to James Pearson, February 10, 1779.
Richard Frothingham to Benjamin Flower, February 19, 1779.
Richard Frothingham to William Stevens, February 26, 1779.
To William Richards, April 12, 1779.
To Benjamin Flower, April 14, 1779.
To James Lovell, April 14, 1779.
To James Pearson, April 20, 1779.
To George Washington, April 28, 1779.
To James Lovell, May 7, 1779.
To Benjamin Flower, May 7, 1779.
To Jonathan Gostelowe, May 13, 1779.
To Udny Hay, May 14, 1779.
To Thornton Taylor, Undated.
To James Pearson, May 14, 1779.
To Thomas Jones, May 15, 1779.
To Benjamin Flower, May 28, 1779.
To Henry Brower, June 3, 1779.
To Major Lindley, June 3, 1779.
To James Abeel, June 3, 1779.
To Benjamin Flower, June 3, 1779.

To Thomas Jones, June 3, 1779.
To Cain and Blair, June 8, 1779.
To James Thompson, June 9, 1779.
To Thomas Jones, June 12, 1779.
To Henry Knox, June 12, 1779.
To James Thompson, June 13, 1779.
To James Thompson, June 15, 1779.
To Cornelius Austin, June 15, 1779.
To James Abeel, June 21, 1779.
To Henry Brower, June 21, 1779.
To Nicholas Ricketts, June 21, 1779.
To Christian Holmes, June 21, 1779.
To William Davies, June 23, 1779.
To Henry Knox, June 29, 1779.
To Nathanael Greene, June 29, 1779.
To James Pearson, June 30, 1779.
To Jonathan Gostelowe, June 30, 1779.
To Samuel French, June 30, 1779.
To Nathanael Greene, July 1, 1779.
To Thomas Jones, July 1, 1779.
To William Richards, July 1, 1779.
To Cornelius Austin, July 6, 1779.
To Christian Henry Schenemann/Sheineman, July 6, 1779.
To William Brower, July 6, 1779.
To John Ruddock, July 6, 1779.
To James Pearson, July 6, 1779.
To Jonathan Gostelowe, July 6, 1779.
To Christian Henry Schenemann/Sheineman, July 6, 1779.
To James Thompson, July 7, 1779.
To James Pearson, July 7, 1779.
To Nathanael Greene, July 10, 1779.
To Thomas Jones, July 16, 1779.
To John Ruddock, July 16, 1779.
To William Cook, July 17, 1779.
To John Glover, July 19, 1779.
To Henry Knox, July 21, 1779.
To Christian Henry Schenemann/Sheineman, July 22, 1779.
To Mr. Quaily, July 22, 1779.
To William Cook, July 22, 1779.
To Thomas Jones, July 23, 1779.
To John Banks, July 23, 1779.
To Mr. Pennington, July 24, 1779.
To William Cook, July 29, 1779.
To Edward Carrington, July 29, 1779.
To Mr. Pennington, July 30, 1779.
To Timothy Pickering Jr., August 1, 1779.
To James Pearson, August 2, 1779.
To the Board of War and Ordnance, August 2, 1779.

To Henry Knox, August 4, 1779.
To James Boyer, August 6, 1779.
To John Jacob Faesh, August 6, 1779.
To Henry Knox, August 7, 1779.
To Charles Harrison, August 11, 1779.
To William Stephenson, August 12, 1779.
To Henry Knox, August 12, 1779.
To Friedrich Wilhelm Augustus, Baron de Steuben, August 16, 1779.
To Henry Knox, August 16, 1779.
To Daniel Kemper, August 16, 1779.
To William Stephenson, August 16, 1779.
To James Pearson, August 17, 1779.
To Daniel Kemper, August 19, 1779.
To Philip Van Rensselaer, August 19, 1779.
To Henry Knox, August 28, 1779.
To John Ruddock, August 28, 1779.
To Henry Knox, September 2, 1779.
To Thomas Jones, September 3, 1779.
To James Pearson, September 3, 1779.
To William Stephenson, September 9, 1779.
To Henry Knox, September 9, 1779.
To James Pearson, September 10, 1779.
To Philip Van Rensselaer, September 20, 1779.
To Henry Knox, September 23, 1779.
To William Stephenson, Undated.
To John Eayres or Asa Copeland, September 23, 1779.
To Timothy Pickering Jr., September 25, 1779.
To Jonathan Gostelowe, September 25, 1779.
To the Clothier General With the Army, September 27, 1779.
To Henry Knox, September 27, 1779.
To John Ruddock, September 27, 1779.
To William Richards, September 28, 1779.
To Henry Knox, October 1, 1779.
To William Stephenson, October 1, 1779.
To James Pearson, October 5, 1779.
To the Board of War and Ordnance, October 6, 1779.
To Henry Knox, October 11, 1779.
To Henry Weisner, October 19, 1779.
To John Ruddock, Undated.
To Robert Erskine, November 10, 1779
To James Pearson, November 11, 1779.
To James Pearson, Undated.
To Robert Erskine, November 14, 1779.
To John Jacob Faesh, November 16, 1779.
To Ebenezer Branham, December 10, 1779.
To Whom it May Concern, December 10, 1779.
To John Jacob Faesh, January 1, 1780
To William Brower, January 9, 1780.

To Henry Knox, January 9, 1780.
To John Lillie, January 9, 1780.
To Mr. Cooper, January 10, 1780.
To Henry Knox, January 10, 1780.
To Henry Knox, January 11, 1780.
To Unidentified, January 12, 1780.
To Henry Knox, January 14, 1780.
To Henry Knox, January 15, 1780.
To John Stark, January 16, 1780.
To John Ruddock, February 20, 1780.
To William Richards, February 20, 1780.
To Thomas Frothingham, February 20, 1780.
To Henry Knox, March 3, 1780.
To William Thorne, March 22, 1780.
Benjamin Flower to the Board of War and Ordnance, March 28, 1780.
To the Board of War and Ordnance, April 1, 1780.
To Robert McFee, April 1, 1780.
To John Denton, April 1, 1780.
Benjamin Flower to John Denton, Undated.
Benjamin Flower to the Continental Congress, April 3, 1780.
To William Egerton Godfrey, April 4, 1780.
To Isaac Coren, April 4, 1780.
To the Several Officers Commanding Companies in Colonel Flower's Regiment in Philadelphia, April 5, 1780.
To Isaac Cox, April 17, 1780.
To Gustavus Risberg, April 17, 1780.
To John Mitchell, April 18, 1780.
To Samuel Sarjant, April 19, 1780.
Deserter Notice, April 22, 1780.
Discharge Certificate for George Marshal, April 25, 1780.
Thomas Procter, Rental Agreement With Hodgdon, April 25, 1780.
To Gabriel Ogden, April 28, 1780.
To Daniel Burrell, April 28, 1780.
To Isaac Coren, April 28, 1780.
To George Perkins, April 28, 1780.
To The Board of War and Ordnance, April 29, 1780.
To William Egerton Godfrey, April 29, 1780.
To John Jacob Faesh, April 30, 1780.
To Joseph Eayres, May 2, 1780.
To Samuel Sarjant, May 2, 1780.
To Daniel Burrell, May 3, 1780.
To the Board of War and Ordnance, May 3, 1780
To the Board of War and Ordnance, May 4, 1780.
To Mark Thompson, May 5, 1780.
To George Ingells, May 6, 1780.
To George Ross Jr., May 6, 1780.
To Samuel Sarjant, May 6, 1780.
To James Pearson, May 8, 1780.

To Samuel Sarjant, May 8, 1780.
To the Board of War and Ordnance, May 10, 1780.
To Seth Harding, May 10, 1780.
To Seth Harding, May 11, 1780.
To Jonathan Gostelowe, May 12, 1780.
To John Mitchell, May 12, 1780.
To Jonathan Gostelowe, (two letters), May 13, 1780.
To Philip Van Rensselaer, May 13, 1780.
To Isaac Warner, May 13, 1780.
To Richard Frothingham, May 13, 1780.
To John Lamb, May 13, 1780.
To Peter Gordon, May 13, 1780.
To Thomas Potts, May 16, 1780.
To Isaac Coren, May 17, 1780.
Discharge Certificate for Christoper Lane, May 17, 1780.
Benjamin Flower to the Board of War and Ordnance, Undated.
Benjamin Flower to the Board of War and Ordnance, May 17, 1780.
Benjamin Flower to the Board of War and Ordnance, Undated.
Benjamin Flower to Robert Patton, May 22, 1780
To the Board of War and Ordnance, May 24, 1780.
Benjamin Flower to the Board of War and Ordnance, May 1780.
To William Egerton Godfrey, May 25, 1780.
To Isaac Coren, May 25, 1780.
Benjamin Flower to Unidentified, May 25, 1780.
To Joseph Watkins, May 25, 1780.
Benjamin Flower to William Thorne, May 29, 1780.
To George Perkins, May 30, 1780.
To George Parks, May 30, 1780.
To Thomas Wylie, May 30, 1780.
To Two Wagoners Going to Carlisle, May 30, 1780.
To Samuel Sarjant, May 30, 1780.
To Jonathan Gostelowe, May 31, 1780.
To George Perkins, May 31, 1780.
To William Thorne, May 31, 1780.
To Robert Lettis Hooper Jr., May 31, 1780.
To Moses Yamans, May 31, 1780.
To Alexander Dow, June 1, 1780.
To the Board of War and Ordnance, June 1, 1780.
To the Board of War and Ordnance, With Answer by Richard Peters, June 1, 1780.
To Simon Murray, June 1, 1780.
To Robert Lettis Hooper Jr., June 1, 1780.
To Mark Thompson, June 2, 1780.
To William Egerton Godfrey, June 4, 1780.
To Alexander Turner, June 5, 1780.
To John Patton, June 5, 1780.
To William Egerton Godfrey, June 5, 1780.
To Walter Stewart, June 9, 1780.

To Jonathan Gostelowe, June 9, 1780.
To Daniel Joy, June 9, 1780.
To William Egerton Godfrey, June 9, 1780.
To Jonathan Gostelowe, June 10, 1780.
To the Board of War and Ordnance, June 10, 1780.
Directions for establishing a standing Laboratory given in to the Board of War and Ordnance June 7
To Moore Furman, June 13, 1780.
To David Mason, June 15, 1780.
To Benjamin Hoey, June 15, 1780.
To John Denton, June 15, 1780.
Discharge Certificate for George Smith, June 16, 1780.
Estimate of Necessaries Requisite for an Army of 40,000 Men
To the Board of War and Ordnance, June 17, 1780.
To George Perkins, June 17, 1780.
To Isaac Warner, June 17, 1780.
To William Thorne, June 20, 1780.
To the Board of War and Ordnance, June 20, 1780.
To Archibald Shaw, June 22, 1780.
To the Board of War and Ordnance, June 22, 1780.
To George Ingells, June 23, 1780.
To Henry Knox, June 24, 1780.
To Thomas Jones, June 26, 1780.
To the Board of War and Ordnance, June 26, 1780.
To the Navy Board, June 27, 1780.
To Nathaniel Chapman, June 30, 1780.
To Ezekiel Cheever, June 30, 1780.
To the Board of War and Ordnance, June 30, 1780.
To William Chambers, July 3, 1780.
To Lewis Nicola, July 4, 1780.
To John Mitchell, July 4, 1780.
To the Board of War and Ordnance, July 6, 1780.
To William Smith, July 6, 1780.
Agreement With Simon Murray, July 6, 1780.
To Charles Lukens, July 7, 1780.
To Samuel Sarjant, July 7, 1780.
To John Jordan, July 7, 1780.
To the Board of War and Ordnance, July 10, 1780.
Discharge Cerificate for John Spelerback, July 10, 1780.
To Philip Van Rensselaer, July 14, 1780.
To the Board of War and Ordnance, July 15, 1780.
To the Board of War and Ordnance, July 18, 1780.
To Archibald Shaw, July 20, 1780.
To Moore Furman, July 20, 1780.
To Richard Frothingham, July 20, 1780.
To Mr. Donaldson, July 20, 1780.
To Blair McClenachan, July 20, 1780.
To James Clark, July 20, 1780.

311

To the Board of War and Ordnance, July 24, 1780.
To the Board of War and Ordnance, July 25, 1780.
To the Board of War and Ordnance, (two letters), July 28, 1780.
To William Egerton Godfrey, July 29, 1780.
Discharge Certificate for John Treacy, July 31, 1780.
Agreement With Walter McFarland, August 1, 1780.
Agreement With William Clark, August 2, 1780.
To William Egerton Godfrey, August 4, 1780.
To Benjamin Hoey, August 4, 1780.
To the Board of War and Ordnance, August 5, 1780.
To the Board of War and Ordnance, August 7, 1780.
To W. Nancarrow, August 8, 1780.
To Henry Valentine, August 8, 1780.
To John Mitchell, August 8, 1780.
To James Byers, August 8, 1780.
To Samuel Sarjant, August 8, 1780.
To William Thorne, August 8, 1780.
To John Jordan, August 8, 1780.
To the Board of War and Ordnance, August 9, 1780.
Extract From the Minutes of Continental Congress, August 12, 1780.
To William Egerton Godfrey, August 19, 1780.
Certificate Regarding Services of John Rugan, August 20, 1780.
To the Board of War and Ordnance, August 21, 1780.
To William Egerton Godfrey, August 21, 1780.
To Thomas Wylie, August 22, 1780.
To Richard Backhouse, August 22, 1780.
To Nathaniel Irish, August 23, 1780.
To Ezekiel Cornell, August 24, 1780.
To Unidentified, partial letter August 24, 1780.
To Samuel Miles, partial letter.
To Timothy Pickering Jr., August 28, 1780.
To the Board of War and Ordnance, September 1, 1780.
To Archibald Shaw, September 1, 1780.
To Richard Frothingham, September 1, 1780.
To David Mason, September 6, 1780.
To Joseph Eayres, September 6, 1780.
To Nathaniel Chapman, September 6, 1780.
To William Hawes, September 6, 1780.
To Ezekiel Cheever, September 6, 1780, With Extracts from July 26
    and August 30 Resolves of Congress.
To Henry Knox, September 6, 1780.
Timothy Pickering Jr. to Joseph Hiller, September 7, 1780.
Discharge Certificate for Philip Clumburg, September 7, 1780.
To John Bryant, September 7, 1780.
To the Board of War and Ordnance, September 8, 1780.
To John Stith, September 8, 1780.
To the Acting Quartermaster at the Head of Elk, September 8, 1780.
To the Commercial Committee of Congress, September 9, 1780.

To Philip Van Rensselaer, September 12, 1780.
To Charles Lukens, September 13, 1780, With Extract From August
    30 Resolve of Congress.
To Samuel Sarjant, September 13, 1780.
To Henry Knox, September 14, 1780.
To John Jordan, September 15, 1780.
To Timothy Matlack, September 16, 1780.
To Benjamin McCowen, September 21, 1780.
To Thomas Rutter and Thomas Potts, September 21, 1780.
Thomas Potts, Agreement to Exchange Steel for Pig Iron, September 21, 1780.
To John Jacob Faesh, September 23, 1780.
To Nathaniel Triplett, September 24, 1780.
To the Board of Treasury, September 27, 1780.
To Mr. Frothingham, October 3, 1780.
To Mr. Hughes, October 7, 1780.
To James Johnson and Company, October 10, 1780.
To the Board of War and Ordnance, October 19, 1780.
To Ezekiel Cornell, October 23, 1780.
To Joseph Hiller, October 24, 1780.
To Isaac Craig, October 25, 1780.
To James Boyer, October 25, 1780.
To the Board of War and Ordnance, October 26, 1780.
To Samuel Sarjant, October 27, 1780.
To Benjamin Hoey, October 27, 1780.
To the Board of War and Ordnance, November 1, 1780.
Statement Concerning James Meck, November 2, 1780.
To the Board of Treasury, November 4, 1780.
To Samuel Sarjant, November 6, 1780.
Benjamin Flower to John Jordan, November 13, 1780.
To the Board of War and Ordnance, November 27, 1780.
To the Board of War and Ordnance, With an Estimate of Articles
    Needed by the Artillery Artificers, December 2, 1780.
Discharge Certificate for John Adams, December 3, 1780.
To Ezekiel Cheever, December 4, 1780.
To W. Nancarrow, December 5, 1780.
To Charles Hall, December 6, 1780.
To Mark Thompson, December 6, 1780.
To Henry Stroop, December 8, 1780. Circular
To Ezekiel Cheever, December 9, 1780.
To Jonathan Gostelowe, December 11, 1780.
To the Board of War and Ordnance, December 11, 1780.
To Samuel Sarjant, December 12, 1780.
Benjamin Flower to John Hall, December 20, 1780.
Benjamin Flower to Samuel Sarjant, (two letters), December
    20, 1780.
To John Laurens, December 20, 1780.
To the Board of War and Ordnance, December 21, 1780.
To John Laurens, December 21, 1780.

To Henry Stroop and Alexander Dow, December 22, 1780.
To John Hall, December 23, 1780.
To Nathaniel Irish, December 23, 1780.
Benjamin Flower, Discharge Certificate for John Willson, December 26, 1780.
To Alexander Dow, December 27, 1780.
To Mr. Rush, December 28, 1780.
To George Ross Jr., December 29, 1780.
To Jacob Weiss, December 29, 1780.
To Henry Knox, December 29, 1780.
To Samuel Sarjant, December 30, 1780.
To John Wilcox, December 30, 1780.
To John Lamb, January 1, 1781.
To Mr. Keran, January 3, 1781.
To Mr. Evans, January 3, 1781.
To The Board of War and Ordnance, January 7, 1781.
Estimate of Sums Needed to Make One Million Cartridges, Undated.
Joseph Carleton, Extract From Meeting Minutes of the Board of Ordnance, January 8, 1781.
To The Board of War and Ordnance, (two letters) January 8, 1781
To Isaac Caristin, January 8, 1781.
To William Livingston, January 8, 1781.
To Lewis Nicola, January 8, 1781.
To Thomas Jones, January 10, 1781.
To Jacob Weiss, January 10, 1781.
To Jonathan Gostelowe, January 11, 1781.
To Daniel Joy, January 12, 1781.
To Nathaniel Irish, January 15, 1781, Undated Resolve Attached.
To The Board of War and Ordnance, January 19, 1781, With Estimate of Expense of an Eight Inch Howitzer, and Expense of Building a Furnace
Benjamin Flower, Certificate of Discharge for Jacob Server, January 20, 1781.
To Samuel Sarjant, January 20, 1781.
To Ezekiel Cheever, January 23, 1781.
Certificate of Discharge for Richard Thomas, January 23, 1781.
To William Alexander, January 23, 1781.
To Jonathan Gostelowe, January 24, 1781.
To Jonathan Gostelowe, January 27, 1781.
To The Board of War and Ordnance, Return of Iron Cannon Suitable for Shipping, January 30, 1781.
To The Board of War, Return of Stores Wanted for the Southern Army, January 30, 1781.
Extract from Congress, January 31, 1781.
To Jonathan Gostelowe, January 31, 1781.
Certificate of Discharge for Peter Stoy, January 1, 1781.
Certificate of Discharge for Thomas Huggins, February 1, 1781.
To George Ross Jr., February 2, 1781.

To Jacob Weiss, (two letters), February 3, 1781.
To Mark Thompson, February 3, 1781.
William MacDonald, Enlistment Agreement, February 3, 1781.
Michael Broadbeck, Enlistment Agreement, Undated.
Return of Arms and Accoutrements Wanted, February 3, 1781.
To the Board of War and Ordnance, February 3, 1781.
To Ezekiel Cheever, February 5, 1781.
To the Board of War and Ordnance, (two letters), February 6, 1781.
To Samuel Sarjant, February 7, 1781.
To William Moore, February 8, 1781.
To Mr. Knight, February 9, 1781.
Certificate of Discharge for William Brown, February 10, 1781.
To Thomas Wylie, February 10, 1781.
Certificate of Discharge for Daniel Berkmire, February 17, 1781.
Return of Arms and Accoutrements Received from the Pennsylvania Line, February 17, 1781.
Estimate of Sum Needed for the Repair of Arms, February 17, 1781.
To the Board of War and Ordnance, February 19, 1781.
To Jonathan Gostelowe, February 19, 1781.
To Benjamin Harrison, February 19, 1781.
To Samuel Sarjant, February 19, 1781.
To the Board of War and Ordnance, February 20, 1781.
Estimate of the Sum Necessary for Arms and Stores for the Southern Army, Undated.
To Samuel Sarjant, February 23, 1781.
To Thomas Wylie, February 24, 1781.
To Benjamin Hoey, February 26, 1781.
To Andrew Porter, February 26, 1781.
To Nathaniel Triplett, March 1, 1781.
To Samuel Miles, March 3, 1781.
To Benjamin Hoey, March 5, 1781.
To the Board of War and Ordnance, March 10, 1781.
To Nathaniel Barber Jr., March 12, 1781, With Resolve of Congress, March 5, 1781.
To Samuel Lord, March 12, 1781.
To William Finnie, with an Account, March 15, 1781.
To the Board of War and Ordnance, March 20, 1781.
To Charles Hall, March 23, 1781.
To Samuel Sarjant, March 27, 1781.
To Nathaniel Irish, March 27, 1781.
To William Knox, March 27, 1781, with Dubouy, Receipt for Stores, January 31, 1781.
Extract of a Resolve of Congress, March 29, 1781.
To John Compty, March 30, 1781.
To John Ruddock, March 31, 1781.

INDEX

Abeel, James, 51, 58, 228, 229
   letters to, 52, 58
Adams, John
   discharge notice, 242
Adams, Mr., 43
Albany, N.Y., 6, 18, 86, 87, 189
   armorers at, 22, 85
Alexander, William
   letter to, 271
Ambrister, Mathias, 155
Ammunition
   cannon, 1, 5, 6, 7, 8, 9, 13, 52, 53,
      58, 68, 70, 72, 74, 75, 79, 80,
      81, 83, 89, 90, 92, 93, 100,
      104, 105, 107, 108, 109, 112,
      118, 123, 124, 159, 164, 176,
      187, 196, 199, 202, 221, 227,
      228, 230, 234
   cannon, patterns for, 206, 230
   shell casting problems, 91
Anthony, Mr., 49
Appleton, Nathaniel, 269
Arms
   cartridge boxes, 17
   muskets, 30, 36, 65, 80, 82, 137,
      138, 145, 161, 171, 210, 236,
      252
   muskets, cost of repairs, 241
   muskets, damaged, 2, 40, 48, 62,
      64, 67, 90
   muskets, French, 66
   muskets, price of, 132
   muskets, price of repairs, 221
   muskets, repair of, 57
   muskets, repairable, 171, 187
   muskets, sappers, 53
   pistols, 12, 21, 23, 24, 29, 36, 40,
      133, 154, 156, 162, 206
      for horsemen, 154, 210
   pistols, for horsemen, 82
   pistols, price of, 241
   rifles, 200, 224, 283
   swords, 152, 154, 156, 175, 217,
      257
   swords for cavalry, 162, 210, 241

Arms and Accoutrements
   return of, 278
Arms, manufacture of ammunition
   for, 288
Armstrong, John, 144, 249
Army, British
   depredations by, 29
Army, Continental
   movements of, 186
   recruits for, 1
Arnold, Benedict, 299
Arnold, Jonathan
   description of, 125
Artillery
   at Philadelphia, 173
   cannon, 45, 85, 89, 100, 101, 136,
      179, 187, 199, 202, 229, 272,
      292
   cannon, cost of, 191
   cannon, mounting of, 146, 218
   howitzers, 106, 118, 124, 173,
      268, 273, 289, 292
   howitzers, cost of manufacture,
      268
   mortars, 106
   swivels, 229, 273
Artillery, carriages, 5, 9, 84, 85, 146,
   289, 290
   poor quality of, 250
Artillery, materials for ammunition,
   287
Ashton, Mrs., 290
Austin, Cornelius, 64, 65, 78, 79, 80,
   90, 101
   letters to, 57, 64
Austin, John, 2, 64, 85
Backhouse, Richard
   letter to, 206
Baggs, Mr., 204
Baker, Henry, 10, 11, 16, 106
Baker, Mr., 42, 85, 100, 101
Baldwin, Mr., 99
Banks, John, 74, 116
   letter to, 75
Barber, Nathaniel, 133

Barber, Nathaniel, Jr., 295
  letter to, 294
Barr, Thomas, 41, 93
Barry, John, 189
Bayonet belts, 3, 11, 21, 30, 64, 69, 70, 73, 80, 81, 137, 147, 161
Bayonet belts, price of, 188
Bayonet makers, 163
Bayonet scabbards, 11, 64, 65, 161, 210, 221
Bayonets, 2, 7, 21, 30, 65, 132, 145, 161, 210, 221
  price of, 131, 132
Belden, Ezekiel Porter, 76
Berkmire, Daniel, 277
  certificate of discharge for, 283
Berry, Sidney, 56, 64, 81
  shot at, 187
Bird, Mark
  iron furnace of, 272
Blair, Mr.
  letter to, 53
Bland, Theodorick, 301
Board of Treasury
  letters to, 229, 238
Board of War and Ordnance, 20, 29, 40, 43, 46, 52, 77, 80, 84, 88, 90, 92, 95, 98, 109, 112, 116, 120, 124, 130, 134, 135, 136, 138, 141, 147, 154, 157, 160, 165, 175, 177, 179, 189, 193, 197, 199, 203, 204, 208, 213, 215, 216, 218, 220, 221, 223, 225, 229, 230, 239, 243, 244, 245, 248, 252, 254, 256, 257, 262, 264, 265, 270, 279, 285, 290, 292, 295, 300
  extract of meeting minutes of the, 260
  letters to, 79, 102, 118, 128, 132, 133, 136, 143, 144, 145, 148, 156, 162, 163, 171, 173, 174, 176, 178, 180, 183, 187, 191, 192, 193, 196, 197, 202, 205, 210, 221, 231, 235, 237, 240, 246, 252, 259, 260, 261, 268, 272, 273, 278, 280, 284, 286, 294, 297

Boiling Springs, Pa., 143
Boise, Captain, 284
Bolton, John, 185, 215, 218
Bond, George, 217, 266, 267, 274, 295, 302
Boston, Mass., 133
  Clothier General at, 103
  magazine at, 185
  ship from, 129
  stores at, 128, 279, 295
Bostonian
  the character of, 45
Box, hat, 34, 36
Boxes
  cartridge, 76
Boxes, ammunition, 12, 39
Boxes, cartridge, 3, 8, 9, 10, 12, 15, 17, 20, 21, 24, 30, 36, 44, 64, 65, 66, 67, 69, 71, 72, 73, 76, 77, 80, 82, 88, 137, 147, 161, 162, 171, 182, 188, 251, 252
  price of, 241
Boxes, cutting
  price of, 167
Boxes, Tub, 5
Boyer, James, 25, 26, 34, 35, 36, 37, 38, 41, 68, 80, 81, 97, 114, 115, 116, 181, 195, 198, 199, 201, 202, 233
  letters to, 80, 234
Boylston, Edward, 185, 215, 218
Bradford, Jonathan, 65
Branham, Ebenezer, 110, 113
  letter to, 108
Brass foundry, 145
Brison, Captain, 301
Broadbeck, Michael, 282
  enlistment agreement, 277
Broderick, Anthony?, 68
Brower, Henry, 51, 52, 58, 59, 64
  instructions for, 51, 58
Brower, Mr., 71
Brower, William, 59, 110
  instructions for, 65
  letter to, 109
Brown, Mr., 132
Brown, William, 278
  certificate of discharge for, 282

Browner, Mr., 68
Bryant, John, 212, 216, 218, 233, 270
   letter to, 220
Buckland, Stephen
   letter to, 9
Buell, Mr., 116
Burgoyne, John, 45
Burrell, Daniel
   letters to, 127, 132
Butler, Richard, 59
Butler, William, 32
   letter to, 1
Byers, James, 145, 146, 196, 199, 202, 246, 268
   letter to, 199
Cain, Mr.
   letter to, 53
Calender, Mrs., 249
Call, Nathaniel, 3
Callender, Mrs., 143
Camden, Battle of, 211
Canteens
   price of, 171
Caristin, Isaac, 262
   letters to, 262
Carleton, Joseph, 260
Carlisle, Pa., 135, 145, 146, 156, 201, 203, 223, 224, 225, 244, 254, 265, 266, 289
   arms at, 200
   artificers at, 209
   artificers to be sent to, 252, 253, 255
   boring and grinding mill at, 144
   Congressional resolve on, 247, 302
   estimate on, 235
   ideal for leather factory, 147
   leather work at, 272
   magazine at, 134, 260, 284, 285, 299, 300
   possible furnace at, 268
   property evaluation at, 248
   stores at, 124, 136, 153
   stores from, 93
   treasurer at, 226
   wagons and forges built at, 289

Carrington, Edward, 70, 76, 207, 261, 262
   letter to, 76
Cartridges
   forty rounds per man ordered, 38
   musket, 66, 78
Caulaux & Co., 156
Cavalry
   equipment for, 82, 147, 154, 156, 162, 168, 170, 210, 221, 241, 278, 287, 288
Cavalry, British, 9
Chalk, 35
   price of, 167
Chambers, William, 178, 180
Change Water Ironworks, N.J., 141, 256
Chapman, Nathaniel, 216, 217
   letters to, 177, 213
Charcoal, 163, 210
   manufacture of, 127, 132
   price of, 168
Charcoal for gunpowder, 86
Charleston, S.C.
   siege of, 130, 141, 159
Cheever, Ezekiel, 184, 185, 212, 213, 214, 216, 217, 218, 235, 286
   letters to, 1, 8, 177, 215, 242, 245, 270, 279
Chester, N.Y., 78
Chevalier des Touches, Charles-Rene-Dominique Sochet, 301
Christiana, Del.
   shot at, 187
Church, Mr., 111
Clark, James
   discharge notice, 190
Clark, John, 89
Clark, William
   agreement with, 195
Clarke, Mr., 265
Cloth, 228
Cloth, duck, 63
Clothier General
   letter to, 97
Clothing, 70, 94, 98, 99, 103, 177, 239, 253, 257
   prices of, 112

shortages of, 34, 182, 192, 193, 232
Cluggage, Robert, 136
Clumberg, Philip, 49, 60, 61, 62, 66, 104
  recommendation for, 220
Colles, Christopher, 56
Collins, John, 9, 103, 218, 242, 245
Collins, Mr., 80
Commercial Committee of Congress
  letter to, 222
Compty, John
  letter to, 302
Continental Congress
  extract of a resolve of the, 302
  extracts from the minutes of the, 202, 216, 217, 273
  letter to, 120
Cook, William, 61, 66, 71, 72, 83, 84, 86, 97
  instructions for, 74, 76
  letters to, 70
Cooper, Mr.
  letter to, 111
Copeland, Asa, 76, 77, 85, 91
  letter to, 94
Copeland, Asa?, 98, 140
Coren, Isaac, 121, 128, 148, 149, 150, 193
  letters to, 122, 127, 142, 150
Cornell, Ezekiel, 260
  letters to, 208, 232
Cotton
  instead of slow match, 39
Coventry Forge, Pa., 227, 228
Cowell, Ebenezer, 123
Cox, Isaac
  letter to, 123
Cox, Mr., 272
Craig, Isaac, 112, 124
  letter to, 233
Cuningham, Mr., 39
Cunningham, Mr., 5, 8, 13, 18, 60
Cups
  custom, 102
Currey, James, 68
Davies, William
  letter to, 59

Day, Aaron, 164
Dayley, Mr., 136
Denton, John, 119
  letters to, 120, 166
Deserter Notice, 125
Dickinson, Thomas, 237, 238
Donaldson, Mr.
  letter to, 189
Doughty, John, 82
Douglass, John, 9, 75, 77, 89
Dow, Alexander, 125, 205, 239, 272
  letters to, 155, 253, 255
Downes, Mr., 31, 36
Doz, Andrew, 282
Drake, Samuel?, 140
Drum Factory, 126
Drummers, 194, 203
Drums, 3, 9, 35, 44, 47, 64, 65, 77, 80, 93, 101, 137, 160
  price of, 241
Duff, Mr., 21
Duffield, Mr., 239
Duncan, Stephen, 226, 236
Duportail, Louis Lebigue, 53
Easton, Pa., 44, 157, 158
Eayres, John, 76, 77, 85, 91, 98, 140
  letter to, 94
Eayres, Joseph, 214, 216, 217
  letters to, 129, 212
Edison, Thomas, 224
Edmonds, Mr., 38
Edmunds, Mr., 35
Elizabeth Furnace, Pa., 123
Elizabeth, N.J., 10
Equipment
  list of camp, 170
Erskine, Robert
  letters to, 105, 107
Estaing, Charles Hector, Count d'
  reported naval engagement of, 93
Evans, Mr., 119
  letter to, 259
Faesh, John Jacob, 80, 83, 126, 229, 234, 271
  letters to, 81, 108, 109, 129, 228
Farrall, Mr., 202
Farrell, Thomas, 176
Faxon, Richard, 185, 215, 218

Febiger, Christian, 301
Fifers, 203
Fifes, 3, 49, 64, 65
  price of, 241
File cutters, 231
Finley, Mr., 107
Finnie, William
  letter to, 296
Fireworks, 178, 179
Fisher, Mr., 111
Fishkill, N.Y., 3, 7, 9, 12, 36, 39, 48, 49, 58, 70, 106, 117
  arms at, 22, 69
  magazine at, 20
  post to be closed, 302
  powder at, 105
  stores at, 13, 14, 18, 19, 26, 28, 29, 30, 31, 32, 33, 34, 36, 49, 59, 63, 103, 111, 175, 297
Fleeson, Plunkett, 277
Flints, musket, 65, 76, 133, 137, 161
Flints, pistol, 162
Flints, price of, 241, 287
Flower, Benjamin, 17, 20, 23, 36, 41, 44, 46, 48, 49, 66, 79, 90, 95, 101, 106, 107, 112, 115, 129, 130, 135, 139, 150, 153, 160, 176, 177, 200, 201, 225, 228, 236, 238, 247, 290
  discharge signed by, 269
  health of, 299
  letters from, 118, 120, 143, 144, 145, 147, 148, 150, 151, 239, 248, 249
  letters to, 4, 16, 19, 23, 28, 29, 35, 37, 42, 47, 50, 52
Food
  shortages of, 33, 56
Ford, Mr., 108
Forges, traveling, 49, 65, 84
  price of, 168
Forges, travelling, 289
Fort Pitt, Pa., 176, 200
Fort Roberdeau, Pa., 136
Foster, John, 301
Fredericksburg, N.Y.
  stores at, 18, 25, 26, 27, 28, 29, 30, 31, 33, 34, 36

Freeman, Benjamin, 10, 11, 17, 19, 38, 39
  letter to, 17
French Alliance
  celebration of, 40, 41
French, Samuel, 2, 4, 7, 8, 11, 16, 19, 22, 24, 25, 29, 31, 33, 34, 35, 36, 37, 38, 39, 46, 47, 48, 50, 53, 67, 96, 151, 173
  letters to, 26, 62
Frothingham, Mr.
  letter to, 229
Frothingham, Richard, 34, 43, 44, 60, 70, 115, 116, 139, 141, 152, 188, 211, 228
  letters from, 28, 32, 35, 37, 38, 39, 40, 41, 42
  letters to, 25, 30, 35, 140, 189, 211
  to act as a principal in the department, 35
Frothingham, Thomas, 72, 94, 211
  letter to, 116
Furman, Moore
  letters to, 164, 188
Furnaces
  air, 196, 197, 199
  iron, 80, 123, 159
Gates, Horatio, 16, 20, 22, 43, 45, 46, 176
Gibbons, Colonel
  shot at, 187
Gibson, Captain T., 248
Gibson, James, 131, 135, 239, 299
Gidley, Jasper Maduit, 4, 5, 13, 14, 24, 34, 36, 38, 42
  letters to, 5, 8, 15, 34
Giles, Mr., 1, 13, 18, 28, 31, 34
  letters to, 18, 27
Giliand/Gililand/Gilliland, James, 4, 14, 15, 18
  letter to, 13
Glenn, John, 251, 260
Glenworth, George, 274
Glover, John
  brigade of, 83, 84, 88, 89
  letter to, 71

Godfrey, William Egerton, 122, 148, 179, 191, 196, 205, 208
   letters to, 121, 128, 149, 159, 160, 162, 193, 195, 204, 205
Gordon, Captain, 131
Gordon, Peter, 93, 139
   letter to, 141
Gorton, Benjamin, 114
Gostelowe, Jonathan, 17, 39, 126, 152
   letters to, 10, 21, 23, 40, 47, 62, 67, 96, 137, 138, 154, 161, 162, 245, 264, 272, 274, 284
Gray, Thomas, 13, 14
   letter to, 14
Grayson, William, 152, 235, 265
Greene, Mr., 103
Greene, Nathanael, 48, 49, 54, 111
   letters to, 25, 60, 62, 69
Greer, Henry, 204, 205, 207, 209, 254, 266, 300
Grenades, hand, 133
Guilliam, John
   description of, 125
Guinup, Mr., 34
Gun worms, 137, 153, 161, 182
Halifax, N.C., 173
   arms sent to, 171, 173
Hall, Charles, 238, 239
   letters to, 243, 298
Hall, John
   letters to, 248, 253
Hall, Mr., 206
Hamilton, Alexander, 8
Hammond, Mr., 204
Harding, Seth
   letters to, 137
Harrison, Benjamin, 285, 300
   letter to, 284
Harrison, Charles
   letter to, 82
Haversacks, 61
Hawes, William, 185, 215, 218
   letter to, 214
Hay, Mrs., 48
Hay, Udny, 5, 6, 32, 48, 49
   letters to, 22, 48
Head of Elk, Md., 173
   letter to Quartermaster there, 222
   shipping point, 172, 292
Henry, Mr., 44
Hiller, Joseph, 270, 286
   letters to, 218, 233
Hodgdon, Samuel, 28, 120, 149, 150, 151, 152, 219, 240, 249, 250, 251
   letters to, 32, 38, 40, 41
Hoey, Benjamin, 165, 191, 192, 196, 239, 280
   letters to, 165, 196, 237, 291, 293
Hoffman, Valentine, 160, 161
Hollingsworth, Henry, 173
Holmes, Christian
   letter to, 59
Hooper, Robert Lettis, Jr., 158
   letters to, 155, 157
Hornkeith, Mr., 204
Horses, 25, 27, 28, 56, 58, 82, 111, 179, 219
   poor condition of, 83, 84, 107
   shortages of, 55, 104
   unfit, 68, 104
Howe, Baxter, 43, 45, 56, 60
Hubener, George, 227
Huggins, Thomas
   certificate of discharge for, 275
Hughes, Colonel, 147
Hughes, Daniel
   iron furnace of, 272
Hughes, Mr.
   letter to, 230
Humphreys, Mr., 133
Humphreys, Whitehead, 133, 157, 158
Huntington, Pa., 136
Independence Day
   celebration of, 178, 179
Indians
   attacked by British cavalry, 9
Ingells, George, 134, 243
   letters to, 134, 174
Irish, Nathaniel, 180, 181, 193, 194, 195, 200, 201, 204, 205, 283
   letters to, 206, 254, 265, 299
Iron
   bar, 133, 141, 158, 159, 163, 256, 266, 276

bar, price of, 167, 241
  pig, 155, 157, 158
Irvin, Mr., 204
Irvine, William, 250
Jacob, John
  shot at, 187
Johnson, James and Company
  letter to, 230
Johnston, Francis, 109
Jones, Mr.
  letter to, 263
Jones, old, 6
Jones, Peregrine, 136, 195, 204
Jones, Sergeant, 127
  recommendation for, 127
Jones, Thomas, 1, 25, 26, 31, 33, 34, 37, 42, 52, 54, 55, 56, 70, 72, 75, 76, 77, 78, 83, 85, 91, 94, 99, 115, 140, 189
  instructions for, 53, 63, 69
  letters to, 36, 50, 55, 74, 89, 175
Jordan, John, 127, 135, 143, 146, 153, 187, 195, 200, 201, 202, 204, 224, 236, 248, 266, 282, 290, 299, 300, 302
  letters to, 182, 226, 239
Joy, Daniel, 131, 202, 230, 282, 292
  letters to, 161, 265
Judah, Mr., 223
Kemper, Daniel, 70, 84, 85
  letters to, 84, 86
Keran, Mr.
  letter to, 258
Kerker, Mr., 73
Kettles
  price of, 170
Kiman, Mr., 105
King, Mr., 94
Kings Ferry, N.Y., 66
Kingwood, N.J.
  stores at, 104
Kinnan, Peter, 107
Kircher, Mr., 13
Knapsacks
  price of, 171
Knight, Mr.
  letter to, 282

Knox, Henry, 4, 5, 6, 7, 8, 9, 10, 15, 16, 17, 19, 20, 25, 26, 29, 36, 38, 40, 41, 43, 45, 46, 49, 53, 55, 57, 60, 65, 69, 70, 74, 75, 78, 79, 81, 82, 83, 93, 95, 100, 102, 103, 105, 108, 109, 140, 234, 279
  letter from, 19
  letters to, 12, 18, 30, 33, 55, 60, 71, 80, 82, 83, 84, 87, 88, 92, 98, 99, 104, 110, 111, 112, 113, 117, 175, 217, 225, 256
Knox, Lucy, 175
Knox, William, 181, 245
  letter to, 301
Lamb, John, 28, 34, 55, 80, 140
  letters to, 27, 31, 32, 141, 258
  regiment of, 159
Lamb, Mr., 279
Lamb, Richard, 87, 186, 223
Lancaster, Pa., 123, 253, 255
  stores at, 134, 243, 298
Lane, Christopher
  discharge notice, 142
Langdon, Captain, 18
  letters to, 6, 19
Langdon, Mr., 22
Lansing, Mr., 87, 139, 186
Lansingh, Mr., 7
Latimore, William
  description of, 125
Laurens, John
  letters to, 251, 252
Lead, 18, 66, 106, 128, 133, 166, 185, 262, 288
  price of, 287, 288
Lead Furnace, 231
Lead, red, 39, 40
Lead, white, 2, 5, 6, 9, 10, 44
Lear, John, 166
Leather, 66, 138, 168, 272, 279, 280, 289
  price of, 242
Leather factory, 146, 147
Leaver, Mr., 47, 49
Lebanon, Conn.
  ammunition from, 69
Leddell, Doctor, 129
Lee, Henry, Jr., 82

Lefabure, Mr.
  letter to, 37
Lefebure, Mr., 31, 36
Lillie, John, 76
  letter to, 110
Lindsley, Matthew?, 50, 51, 55
  letter to, 51
Litchfield, Conn., 113
  stores at, 72, 92, 111, 175
Livingston, William, 262
  letter to, 262
Long, Nicholas, 172, 173, 222
Lord, Samuel
  letter to, 295
Lovell, James
  letters to, 43, 45
Lucas, Mr., 96, 100
Lukens, Charles, 151, 201, 224, 225
  letters to, 181, 223
Lyle, Captain, 222
MacDonald, William
  enlistment agreement, 277
Madison, James, 301
Malcom, William, 10
Marshal, George
  discharge of, 125
Mason, David, 166, 184, 185, 214, 215, 216, 218, 220, 270
  letters to, 165, 211
Match, quick, 41, 291
Match, slow, 39, 124, 288, 298
  price of, 287
Matlack, Timothy
  letter to, 227
Maxwell, William, 10, 17
  brigade of, 113
  letter to, 17
McClenachan, Blair, 222, 260, 261
  letter to, 190
McClenachan, John, 190, 222
McConkey, John, 281, 299
McCowen, Benjamin, 227
  letter to, 227
McDonald, William, 283
McDonnald, Colonel, 53, 54
McDougall, Alexander, 30, 36
  letter to, 40
McFarland, Walter

  agreement with, 194
McFee, Robert, 90, 120
  letter to, 119
McGlaughlin, Francis, 205
McKnight, Mr., 34
McKroskey/McCroskey, A., 248, 249, 253
Meck, James
  statement on health, 238
Meigs, Return Jonathan, 257
Mendham, N.J., 58, 59, 65, 67
Mifflin, Thomas, 217
Miles, Samuel, 284, 298
  letters to, 209, 293
Militia, 147
Minet, Mr., 270
Mitchell, John, 90, 174, 188, 209
  letters to, 123, 138, 179, 198
Money
  depreciation of, 97
  shortages of, 130, 186, 197, 223, 246
Monmouth, Battle of, 1
Montgomery, Captain, 274
Moore, William
  letter to, 281
Morriss, Mr., 40
Morristown, N.J.
  powder mill at, 50, 51, 52
  stores to, 152
Mount Hope Furnace, N.J., 80, 83, 234
Moylan, Stephen
  Corps of, 278
Muhlenberg, John Peter Gabriel
  brigade of, 108
Murray, Simon, 156
  agreement with, 180
  letter to, 157
Musical instruments, 3, 49, 91, 100, 288
  price of, 287
Nancarrow, W., 199
  letters to, 197, 243
Navy Board
  letter to, 176
New Milford, Conn., 37

stores at, 12, 26, 29, 31, 34, 36, 42, 63
    stores removed from, 72
    temporary magazine at, 15, 20
New Windsor, N.Y., 74, 75, 77, 83, 85
New York City
    expected evacuation of, 23
Newburgh, N.Y., 86, 94
Nichols, Noah, 88, 89, 110
Nicola, Lewis, 155, 205
    letters to, 179, 263
Nightingale, Samuel, Jr., 301
Noble, John, 200
Norris, George, 239
Noyce, Mr., 24
Obrian, Richard, 142
Ogden, Gabriel, 129
    letter to, 126
Oil, 9, 132, 147, 200
    linseed, 93, 182
    sweet, 35, 124
Padlocks, 3
Paint, 2, 9, 44, 73, 76, 110
    shortages of, 9
Paper, 22, 23, 47, 110, 132
    cannon cartridge, 76, 124, 191
    list and price of, 170
    musket cartridge, 55, 242
    price of, 242
Parks, George, 41
    letter to, 152
Parson, Major, 40
Parvin, Matthew, 263, 264
Patten, Mr., 9
Patton, John, 153, 159
    letter to, 160
Patton, Robert
    letter to, 147
Paul, John Christopher, 186
Pay, 203, 204
    increase of, 178
Pearson, James, 23, 29, 43, 123, 166
    letters to, 11, 20, 24, 39, 41, 44, 49, 61, 66, 68, 78, 85, 89, 92, 100, 106, 135
Pearson, Mr., 177
Peekskill, N.Y.
    stores at, 13, 18
Peirce, Mr., 129
Pennington, Mr., 76
    instructions for, 75, 77
Perkins, George, 127, 132, 133, 143, 145, 146, 162
    letters to, 127, 152, 154, 171
Peters, Richard, 260
Pettit, Charles, 11
Philadelphia, Pa.
    labratory in, 196
Pickering, Timothy, Jr., 217, 226, 233, 234
    letter from, 218
    letters to, 10, 15, 77, 95, 209
Pierce, Mr., 256
Pistols
    holsters for, 50
Pittsburgh, Pa., 118, 124
Pluckemin, N.J., 65, 67, 78, 80
    magazine at, 61
    stores at, 112
Poor, Thomas?, 40
Porter, Andrew, 266
    letters to, 292
Portfires, 85, 164
    price of, 242
Post, Anthony, 25, 27
    letter to, 9
Potts, Thomas, 227
    letter to, 142
Powder, 18, 50, 51, 52, 56, 58, 59, 63, 72, 85, 86, 88, 89, 90, 92, 94, 100, 104, 105, 124, 134, 137, 174, 176, 190, 209, 210, 211, 222, 227, 258
    cannon, 55, 93
    manufacture of, 210
    musket, 55, 93
Powder Measures, 49
Powder, Ink, 47
    cost of, 170
Power, Alexander, 239
Prisoners
    from Burgoynes's surrender, 27
Prisoners, Hessian, 135
Procter, Thomas, 129, 264
    regiment of, 225

rental agreement with Hodgdon, 126
Putnam, Israel, 36
Qualiey/Quailly/Quaily, Mr.
    instructions for, 73
Randolph, Mr., 140
Reed, Joseph, 250
Rensselaer, Philip Van
    letters to, 7, 93
Richards, William, 31, 34, 63
    letters to, 42, 63, 99, 115
Ricketts, Nicholas, 65, 73
    letter to, 59
Ringwood, N.J., 106
Risberg, Gustavus
    letter to, 123
Rittenhouse, David, 117, 121, 156
Roads
    poor condition of, 12, 28, 33, 83, 143
Roads, Sergeant, 239
Robinson, Mr., 110
Ross, George, 275, 276
    letter to, 275
Ross, George, Jr., 134, 155, 158
    letters to, 134, 256
Ruddock, John, 3, 6, 13, 14, 18, 19, 22, 28, 29, 59, 63, 69, 72, 87, 89, 92, 297
    letters to, 1, 2, 3, 4, 7, 14, 18, 24, 65, 70, 88, 98, 105, 114, 302
Rugan, John
    certificate of services of, 204
Rush, Mr.
    letter to, 255
Rutledge, Mr., 204
Saltpeter, 104, 209, 210
Saratoga, Battle of, 21, 45
Sarjant, Samuel, 134, 144, 153, 201, 226, 235, 240, 257, 260, 272
    letters to, 124, 131, 135, 136, 153, 182, 200, 224, 236, 238, 246, 248, 249, 269, 281, 285, 289, 299
Scammell, Alexander
    letter to, 39
Schenemann/Sheineman, Christian Henry, 64, 73, 81, 90

    letters to, 64, 67, 73
Schultz, Mr., 66, 67, 69
Schutz, Mr., 101
Scott, Sergeant, 112
Screwdrivers, 161, 162, 182
Server, Jacob
    certificate of discharge for, 269
Shannons, Dr.
    shot at, 187
Shaw, Archibald, 188, 211, 292
    letters to, 173, 188, 210
Shaw, Major, 87
Shaw, Samuel, 113
Sheineman, Mr., 65
Sheldon, Elisha, 279
    Corps of, 278
    regiment of, 76
Ships
    Batchelor, *132*
    Confederacy, *137, 152*
    Fame, *222*, 261
    Governor De Graff, *222*
    Governor DeGraaf, 261
    Hermione, 301
    Le Committee, 301
Shot guage, 90
Smith, George
    discharge notice, 166
Smith, William, 190
    letter to, 180
Smiths Clove, N.Y., 55
Southern Army, 176, 207, 221, 232, 263, 300
Southern Army, arms and stores
    needed for, 287
    destroyed at Camden, 211
    stores for, 302
    stores needed for, 273
Spear, Mr., 6, 7
Spelerback, John
    discharge notice, 186
Spirits, 122
    price of wine, 191
    rations of, 119
Springfield, Mass., 3, 8, 141, 191, 203, 216, 245
    artificers at, 44
    large and important post, 130

magazine at, 20, 103, 148, 177,
   235, 270, 280, 294
 problems at, 183, 212, 214, 218,
   220, 286, 298
 stores at, 66, 128, 268
Springfield, Pa., 153
Sproul, John, 239
Stark, John
 brigade of, 113
 letter to, 114
Starr, Ezra, 27, 31, 32
Steel, 24, 44, 49, 52, 141, 142, 153,
   228, 236, 247, 256, 266, 289
 blistered, 228, 257
 German, 21, 41, 48, 49, 53
 German, price of, 242
 poor quality of, 153
 price of, 167
 shortages of, 11
Stephens, Captain, 269
Stephenson, William, 83, 84
 letters to, 83, 85, 91
Stephenson, William, 84
Stephenson, William, 92.
Stephenson, William, 93
Stephenson, William
 letters to, 94
Stephenson, William, 99
Stephenson, William
 letters to, 100
Steuben, Friedrich Wilhelm
   Augustus, Baron de, 85
 letter to, 84
Stevens, Ebenezer, 3, 5, 40, 105, 140,
   141, 292
Stevens, Mr., 237
Stevens, William
 letter to, 42
Stewart, Francis, 159
Stewart, Walter
 letter to, 160
Stiles, Captain, 152
Stiles, Mr., 190
Stith, John, 222
 letter to, 221
Story, Megr., 258
Stoy, Peter
 certificate of discharge for, 274

Strach[in], Mr., 53
Stroop, Henry, 239
 letters to, 244, 253
Succasunna, N.J., 152
Suffolk, Va., 172
Sugar, 4, 129
Sullivan, John
 division of, 105
Sulphur, 104, 210
 high price of, 210
Sussex, N.J., 44
Swedes Ford, Pa.
 artillery at, 187
Sweers, Cornelius, 150, 151, 152,
   181
Talmadge, Benjamin, 279
Tarry Town, N.Y., 6
Taylor, Thornton, 48, 49, 50, 108,
   109
 Instructions to, 48
Tea, 4
Teeple, Mr., 65, 81
Tents, 32, 170
 horsemen's, 170
Thomas, Richard
 certificate of discharge for, 271
Thompson, Alexander, 27, 28, 34, 36
 letters to, 18, 28
Thompson, James, 25, 58, 83, 104
 letters to, 54, 56, 57, 68
Thompson, Mark, 141, 157, 256, 276
 letters to, 133, 158, 244, 276
Thompson, Mr., 31, 229
Thorne, William, 149
 letters to, 117, 151, 154, 172, 201
Tin, 39, 200, 273
 price of, 242
Tin, much wanted, 124
Tin, price of, 268
Tinkfield, Mr., 204
Tinman, 73, 81
Tinmen, 156, 162, 164, 180
Tinmen, superintendent of, 157
Tinmen, tools for, 163
Tools, 5, 65, 79, 132, 153, 161, 200
 carpenters, list and price of, 169,
   170
 intrenching, list and price of, 169

list and prices of, 167
Saddlers, list and price of, 167, 168
ships carpenters, list and price of, 169
shortages of, 61, 66
Tools, blacksmith, 6
Tools, smiths, list and price of, 168
Transportation
  problems, 59, 174
Treacy, John
  discharge notice, 194
Trenton, N.J., 55, 81, 90, 93, 138, 139, 140, 188, 262
Trested, Sergeant, 148
Triplett, Nathaniel, 222
  letter to, 228, 292
Trusdall, James
  description of, 125
Tubes, Tin, 2
Turner, Alexander, 2, 61, 68, 160
  letter to, 159
Turpentine, 41
Valentine, Henry
  letter to, 198
Valley Forge, Pa.
  shot at, 187
Van Rensselaer, Mrs., 87
Van Rensselaer, Philip, 22, 85, 86, 140, 189, 223
  letters to, 87, 106, 107, 138, 186
Virginia, 203
  labratory in, 195, 204, 205, 206
Wagons, 164, 188
  ammunition, 58
  marked and numbered, 3
  shortages of, 56, 64, 89, 209
Warner, Isaac, 89, 90, 106, 107, 138, 140, 173
  letters to, 139, 171
Warwick Furnace, Pa., 227
Washington, George, 15, 17, 38, 95, 98, 103, 225, 249, 279
  letter to, 44
Watkins, Joseph
  letter to, 150
Weisner, Henry
  letter to, 104
Weiss, Jacob, 54, 275, 276
  letters to, 256, 264, 275, 276
West Point, N.Y., 9, 61, 65, 70, 72, 74, 75, 76, 80, 85, 91, 113, 117
  cannon sent to, 100
  fortifications at, 45
  stores at, 78, 92, 111
  stores sent to, 76, 77, 104
  stores to be sent to, 80, 83, 91, 94, 211
West, Jacob?, 206
Whittlesey, Charles?, 114
Wilcox, John
  letter to, 258
Wiley, Thomas, 250, 251
Wilkinson, James, 97
Willhelmn, Adam, 229
Willing, Thomas, 272
Willson, John
  discharge certificate, 254
Wilty, John, 39, 40
Winder, Levin, 44, 45
Winslow, Captain, 19
Wire, 41
  price of, 167
Women, 159, 180, 244, 250, 254, 274, rations for, 204
  the Brat, 116
Wood, 196, 198, 199, 231, 236, 240, 268
  for cartridge boxes, 147
  for gunpowder, 86
  price of, 241
  quality of, 250
Wood, Doctor, 32
Wood, Ezra?, 40
Woodford, Dr., 34
Woodruff, Mr., 166
Wylie, Thomas, 131, 182, 239, 240, 289, 300, 302
  letters to, 152, 205, 282, 290
Yamans, Moses, 155, 275
  letter to, 155
Yamans, Mr., 275
Yellow Springs, Pa., 277
Youman, Moses, 256
Young, Mrs., 290

Other Heritage Books by Joseph Lee Boyle

"My Last Shift Betwixt Us & Death": The Ephraim Blaine Letterbook, 1777–1778

"Their Distress is Almost Intolerable": The Elias Boudinot Letterbook, 1777–1778

From Redcoat to Rebel: The Thomas Sullivan Journal

"this grand supply": The Samuel Hodgdon Letterbooks, 1778–1784
Volume 1: July 19, 1778–March 31, 1781
Volume 2: April 3, 1781–May 24, 1784

Writings from the Valley Forge Encampment of the Continental Army:
December 19, 1777–June 19, 1778
Volume 1

Writings from the Valley Forge Encampment of the Continental Army:
December 19, 1777–June 19, 1778
Volume 2, "Winter in this starved Country"

Writings from the Valley Forge Encampment of the Continental Army:
December 19, 1777–June 19, 1778
Volume 3, "it is a general Calamity"

Writings from the Valley Forge Encampment of the Continental Army:
December 19, 1777–June 19, 1778
Volume 4, "The Hardships of the Camp"

Writings from the Valley Forge Encampment of the Continental Army:
December 19, 1777–June 19, 1778
Volume 5, "a very Different Spirit in the Army"

Writings from the Valley Forge Encampment of the Continental Army:
December 19, 1777–June 19, 1778
Volume 6, "my Constitution got quite shatter'd"

www.ingramcontent.com/pod-product-compliance
Lightning Source LLC
Chambersburg PA
CBHW060941230426
43665CB00015B/2022